THE ABORTION CONTROVERSY

Other Books in the Current Controversies Series:

THE ABORTION CONTROVERSY

David Bender, *Publisher*
Bruno Leone, *Executive Editor*

Katie de Koster, *Managing Editor*
Scott Barbour, *Senior Editor*

Charles P. Cozic, *Book Editor*
Jonathan Petrikin, *Book Editor*

CURRENT CONTROVERSIES

Cover photo: © Magnum/Meiselas

Library of Congress Cataloging-in-Publication Data

The abortion controversy / book editors, Charles Cozic & Jonathan Petrikin.
    p   cm. — (Current controversies)
    Includes bibliographical references and index.
    ISBN 1-56510-229-0 (lib.) — ISBN 1-56510-228-2 (pbk.)
    1. Abortion—Juvenile literature. [1. Abortion.] I. Cozic, Charles P.,
1957-   . II. Petrikin, Jonathan S., 1963-   . III. Series.
HQ767.A173   1995
363.4'6—dc20   94-28196
                                                            CIP
                                                            AC

© 1995 by Greenhaven Press, Inc., PO Box 289009, San Diego, CA 92198-9009
Printed in the U.S.A.

Contents

hood. But abortion rights should also recognize men's desires not to become responsible for unwanted children. Abortion is not murder, but emancipation from unwanted pregnancy and parenthood.

Chapter 2: Should Abortion Rights Be Protected or Restricted?

Abortion Rights Should Be Protected

Abortion Rights Should Be Restricted

Chapter 3: Should Women Have Greater Access to Abortion?

The risks of menstrual extraction—including incomplete abortions, uterine perforation, hemorrhage, and infection—far outweigh any of its advantages. Trained professionals can provide safer environments and services for pregnant women than less qualified "self-help" menstrual extraction groups.

Chapter 4: Should Protesters Target Abortion Clinics?

Yes: Protesters Should Target Abortion Clinics

No: Protesters Should Not Target Abortion Clinics

ful protests of earlier anti-abortionists have escalated on a continuum of violence to outright terrorism that must be stopped.

Chapter 5: Should Aborted Fetuses Be Used for Medical Research?

Yes: Aborted Fetuses Should Be Used for Research

This British study of the attitudes of 694 women toward fetal tissue research found that the overwhelming majority (94 percent) supported fetal tissue research and less than 8 percent of those about to have an abortion felt the need for their doctors to be separate from fetal tissue researchers.

No: Aborted Fetuses Should Not Be Used for Research

Although the popular press has uncritically accepted the use of fetal tissue transplants in the treatment of Parkinson's disease (PD), this course of treatment is ethically wrong. It is also medically unproven; studies backing such treatment were not conducted scientifically. Other treatments hold more hope for PD sufferers.

The use of tissue from aborted fetuses for medical research and transplantation has been urged by both pro-life and pro-choice advocates as a way to save lives. Although such appeals are hard to resist, using tissue from aborted fetuses goes against both moral and legal codes, and it would institutionalize and possibly increase the number of abortions by making society dependent on this source of fetal tissue.

Fetal tissue research is likely to lead to more deliberately terminated pregnancies because the medical benefits of aborted fetal material will help persuade women to choose abortion. Nor will the medical community be inclined to prevent the rise in abortions, since many of its jobs and research grants will be dependent on the steady supply of fetal tissue.

Women are routinely asked to be altruistic with their reproductive systems in the fields of surrogacy and in vitro fertilization. But fetal tissue research will go even further by subjecting women to risky abortion techniques—designed to procure the fetus whole—and the psychological pressures to "donate" their fetuses. It is likely that women will be exploited as mere fetal tissue containers.

Foreword

By definition, controversies are "discussions of questions in which opposing opinions clash" (Webster's Twentieth Century Dictionary Unabridged). Few would deny that controversies are a pervasive part of the human condition and exist on virtually every level of human enterprise. Controversies transpire between individuals and among groups, within nations and between nations. Controversies supply the grist necessary for progress by providing challenges and challengers to the status quo. They also create atmospheres where strife and warfare can flourish. A world without controversies would be a peaceful world; but it also would be, by and large, static and prosaic.

The Series' Purpose

The purpose of the Current Controversies series is to explore many of the social, political, and economic controversies dominating the national and international scenes today. Titles selected for inclusion in the series are highly focused and specific. For example, from the larger category of criminal justice, Current Controversies deals with specific topics such as police brutality, gun control, white collar crime, and others. The debates in Current Controversies also are presented in a useful, timeless fashion. Articles and book excerpts included in each title are selected if they contribute valuable, long-range ideas to the overall debate. And wherever possible, current information is enhanced with historical documents and other relevant materials. Thus, while individual titles are current in focus, every effort is made to ensure that they will not become quickly outdated. Books in the Current Controversies series will remain important resources for librarians, teachers, and students for many years.

In addition to keeping the titles focused and specific, great care is taken in the editorial format of each book in the series. Book introductions and chapter prefaces are offered to provide background material for readers. Chapters are organized around several key questions that are answered with diverse opinions representing all points on the political spectrum. Materials in each chapter include opinions in which authors clearly disagree as well as alternative opinions in which authors may agree on a broader issue but disagree on the possible solutions. In this way, the content of each volume in Current Controversies mirrors the mosaic of opinions encountered in society. Readers will quickly realize that there are many viable answers to these complex issues. By questioning each author's conclusions, students and casual readers can begin to develop the critical thinking skills so important to evaluating opinionated material.

Current Controversies is also ideal for controlled research. Each anthology in the series is composed of primary sources taken from a wide gamut of informational categories including periodicals, newspapers, books, United States and foreign government documents, and the publications of private and public organizations. Readers will find factual support for reports, debates, and research papers covering all areas of important issues. In addition, an annotated table of contents, an index, a book and periodical bibliography, and a list of organizations to contact are included in each book to expedite further research.

Perhaps more than ever before in history, people are confronted with diverse and contradictory information. During the Persian Gulf War, for example, the public was not only treated to minute-to-minute coverage of the war, it was also inundated with critiques of the coverage and countless analyses of the factors motivating U.S. involvement. Being able to sort through the plethora of opinions accompanying today's major issues, and to draw one's own conclusions, can be a complicated and frustrating struggle. It is the editors' hope that Current Controversies will help readers with this struggle.

Introduction

Observers describe the abortion debate in America as bitter and intractable, marked by passionate adherence to extreme and irreconcilable positions. Many of those who define themselves as pro-choice contend that a woman's right to abortion is absolute and should never be restricted. They are resolutely set against those who call themselves pro-life, many of whom maintain that a fetus has an unequivocal right to life that is violated by abortion at any stage of its development. Some pro-lifers insist that since abortion offends the sanctity of life, it should not be permitted in any circumstances. Rhetoric, often inflammatory, from extremists on both sides seems to drown out attempts at meaningful dialogue.

Yet a 1991 Gallup poll identified 55 percent of Americans as either neutral or only moderately pro-choice or pro-life; and even many of the most extreme adversaries, perhaps weary of tedious debate, are seeking grounds for compromise. According to Loretto Wagner, a pro-life activist who was once jailed after a demonstration and who participates in pro-choice/pro-life forums, "How can anyone hear if we refuse to acknowledge the other side except to shout at them? I learned that you have to work with people who don't agree with you."

Since the landmark 1973 *Roe v. Wade* decision legalizing abortion, proposed compromises on limiting or allowing abortion have taken two forms: those based on the reasons for abortion and those based on fetal development at different stages of pregnancy. Compromises of the first type would allow abortion for "hard" cases (rape, incest, or risk to the life or health of the pregnant woman) but not for "soft" cases (financial hardship, inconvenience, or failure of birth control). The second type of compromise would allow nontherapeutic abortions but only until a given stage of pregnancy, often much earlier than the medically accepted definition of viability (when the fetus can survive outside the womb).

Although compromises based on the reasons for abortion have been incorporated into law (the Hyde Amendment, for example, restricts Medicaid funding for abortion to the so-called hard cases), many people now focus on time-based restrictions. According to writer Maria McFadden, this is "the new idea for compromise, one used more by politicians and others who see it as more realistic and practical." Drawing an early line, it is argued, could protect older fetuses and still safeguard the rights of the vast majority of women seeking abortions, thus serving as an attractive alternative to current law for most Americans.

Efforts to find a compromise received a boost from the 1992 Supreme Court decision in the case of *Planned Parenthood v. Casey*. In *Casey*, the Court upheld *Roe v. Wade*'s ruling that a state could not forbid a woman to have an abortion prior to fetal viability. However, the Court rejected *Roe*'s "rigid trimester framework"—which generally allowed elective abortion without any interference from the state until the beginning of the second trimester of pregnancy—in favor of a right of states to attempt to dissuade a woman from abortion at any time during pregnancy, so long as they did not impose an "undue burden" on her right to an abortion. This switch in judicial emphasis—from highlighting the woman's unrestricted right to abortion during early pregnancy to focusing on the state's continuing interest in the fetus—has intensified attempts to find a moral compromise with which a majority of Americans could be comfortable.

The majority opinion in *Casey* noted that while nonviability remained the criterion for elevating the woman's right to self-determination over the state's interest in the fetus, the stage at which the fetus can now be considered viable has changed. Medical science has advanced the ability of the fetus to survive outside the womb from about 28 weeks at the time of *Roe* to 23 to 24 weeks in 1992, with possible further progress to come. Noting these changes, many suggestions for compromise propose a cutoff date for discretionary abortions well before viability, at eight to sixteen weeks.

One of the more stringent proposals calls for proscribing abortions after approximately the eighth week, when fetal brain waves are readily detectable. Biomedical ethicist Baruch Brody argues that the criterion of brain-wave activity to establish the beginning of human life is appropriate because it is the same standard used by doctors to determine the end of life. Besides being ethically acceptable, according to Brody, an eight-week cutoff could also prove successful politically. "This position serves as the basis for a middle ground that might attract a substantial following," he contends. This opinion appeared to be confirmed by Republican George Allen, who supported an eight-week cutoff during his successful bid to become governor of Virginia in 1993.

In proposing instead that restricting abortion after a less-stringent sixteen weeks is feasible, University of Colorado philosophy professor Nancy Davis contends that this "would acknowledge that women have the right to make reproductive decisions and that they may need a reasonable period of time in which to acquire and assess relevant information." Davis argues that this restriction would be less objectionable to pro-choice adherents, since 90 percent of all abortions are performed by the twelfth week of pregnancy.

But despite the optimism of Davis, Brody, and others, such proposals have not come without criticism. In fact, millions of pro-choicers and pro-lifers alike believe that any such compromise would be not only impossible, but unconscionable. From different ends of the argument they denounce any proposal of time limits that would, according to one side, violate the rights of women or, according to the other, violate the rights of fetuses. They agree with pro-choice Harvard law professor Laurence Tribe, who argues that compromises "denying some fetuses life and some women liberty hardly offer a solution." The flaw, critics maintain, is that the protection of some fetuses or some women, and not others, simply because of a difference of days or weeks is unjustifiable.

Disagreement and rejection of compromise among abortion adversaries illustrate how polarized the debate is. *The Abortion Controversy: Current Controversies* explores the many contentious issues surrounding abortion, including controversial activists' tactics and new abortion procedures, while examining the broader legal and moral aspects of the conflicting rights of all involved in this emotional and increasingly violent debate.

Chapter 1

Is Abortion Immoral?

Abortion and Morality: An Overview

by Jeffery L. Sheler

About the author: *Jeffery L. Sheler is a senior writer for* U.S. News & World Report.

Not since slavery has an issue so polarized American society—and perhaps never has an issue posed a greater moral dilemma. The modern debate over abortion, as it is played out in the nation's courts and legislative halls, is a conflict of competing moral visions and of fundamental human rights: to life, to privacy, to control over one's own body. Yet when stripped of the political rhetoric and the entangling legal arguments, it is an issue that rests on basic theological questions. What is human life? When does it begin? What is its value and source?

With such strong religious overtones, it is little wonder that church and religious groups have been on the front lines of the abortion battle. . . . But the churches are far from united on the subject. While the Roman Catholic Church and evangelical Protestants have been highly visible in opposing abortion, scores of religious groups are fervent defenders of abortion rights. Some 35 Christian and Jewish organizations, for example, are members of the Religious Coalition for Abortion Rights, a grass-roots lobbying group formed two decades ago to counter Catholic and evangelical antiabortion efforts.

More and more, churches are finding their flocks divided over the issue. The Presbyterian Church (U.S.A.), the United Methodist Church and other mainline denominations that stand officially in favor of abortion rights face a growing tide of dissent within their ranks. And among those officially opposed to abortion, such as Catholic, Southern Baptist and Mormon churches, leaders are hearing more internal arguments these days from members who are uncomfortable with rigid antiabortionism. On both sides of the debate, church leaders are feeling pressure to explain and justify their positions.

Yet in making their cases, both sides appeal to the same Judeo-Christian ideals. Ultimately, both base their stands on biblical tenets and religious tradition. Their polarization underscores the complexity and the historical ambiguities of religious teaching on abortion.

The issue has plagued the church almost from the beginning. The Bible itself is virtually silent on abortion. The Ten Commandments state "Thou shalt not kill," but neither the Old nor the New Testament contains explicit sanctions against intentionally destroying a fetus. Some modern theologians find that remarkable, given the harsh penalties for abortion evident among other Middle Eastern cultures in biblical times. The fact that the Apostle Paul failed to mention abortion, though he wrote plenty on sexual morality, says Paul D. Simmons, professor of Christian ethics at the Southern Baptist Theological Seminary in Louisville, suggests that "he regarded abortion as a matter to be dealt with on the basis of faith, grace and Christian freedom." Others interpret the silence as suggesting that abortion was not a problem among early Christians. "Abortion was a dangerous option for women," says James L. Nash, assistant professor of moral theology at the Catholic University of America in Washington, D.C. "Among Christians, it simply wasn't practiced."

> *"The Bible itself is virtually silent on abortion."*

First Prohibition

By the early second century, however, the church broke its silence. The Didache, a book of rules considered by some to be teachings of the Apostles, proclaimed: "You shall not kill the fetus by abortion nor destroy the infant already born." What seemed to concern early church leaders most was whether abortion was done to conceal sexual sins and whether it amounted to murder. St. Augustine wrote in the fourth century that abortion could be viewed as murder only if the fetus was judged a "fully formed" human. That stage of development, "hominization," occurred for Augustine some time after conception—40 days for males and 80 days for females. Nonetheless, an early abortion was sinful, Augustine wrote, because it disrupted procreation.

The Catholic Church's early reversals on abortion suggest the difficulty it had coming to a firm position. In 1588, Pope Sixtus V declared that abortion at any stage was murder. Three years later, Pope Gregory XIV reversed that opinion but said abortion could not be used as birth control and was wrong if used to cover up a sexual sin. Finally, in 1869, Pope Pius IX sidestepped hominization and declared that the fetus, "although not ensouled, is directed to the forming of man. Therefore, its ejection is anticipated homicide." He prohibited abortion under all circumstances. That remains the official position of the Roman Catholic Church.

Jews have arrived at a much more tolerant position. The Reform, Conservative and Reconstructionist movements generally consider abortion a matter of individual conscience and oppose most government restrictions on abortion—a position with roots in ancient Jewish writings. The Talmud suggests that the fetus is not fully a person but, rather, is "as the thigh of its mother." Nonetheless, it is worthy of protection as a potential human being. The Mishna, a compilation of Jewish law from the third century A.D., explicitly approves of therapeutic abortions if the mother's life is endangered. And the Responsa, later commentaries on Talmudic law, contain varying opinions as to when a nontherapeutic abortion may be justified. Orthodox Jews today allow abortion only in strictly defined cases involving the health and survival of the mother. "It's nonsense to say a woman has the right to her body," says Rabbi Pinchas Stolper, executive vice president of the Orthodox Union. "No one in this country has that right."

Individual Duty

In Protestantism, positions on abortion have tended to follow each denomination's liberal or conservative outlook on other issues. Most churches place biblical authority above church tradition and emphasize the duty of individuals to interpret scripture for themselves. For some, the abortion issue boils down to a deceptively simple proposition. Even though the Bible does not specifically ban abortion, says theologian Harold O.J. Brown, of Trinity Evangelical Divinity School, it "prohibits the taking of innocent human life. If the developing fetus is shown to be a human being . . . then abortion is homicide." Yet as with abortion itself, the Bible is not explicit on when a fetus becomes fully human or whether it is so from conception.

> *"As with abortion itself, the Bible is not explicit on when a fetus becomes fully human or whether it is so from conception."*

Even so, both sides cite biblical texts to support their arguments. Abortion opponents note such passages as Isaiah 49:1 ("The Lord called me from the womb, from the body of my mother he named my name") and Jeremiah 1:5 ("Before I formed thee in the belly I knew thee: and before thou camest forth out of the womb I sanctified thee and I ordained thee a prophet unto the nations") as showing the fetus as esteemed and ordained by God. Perhaps the most powerful of such passages is in Psalm 139:

> For thou didst form my inward parts,
> thou didst knit me together in my
> mother's womb. . . . Thine eyes have
> beheld my unformed substance;
> in thy book were written, every one
> of them, the days that were ordained
> for me when as yet there
> was not one of them.

That passage, argues Brown in his book *Death Before Birth*, makes it "abundantly clear that God . . . is personally concerned for us *before* birth."

Meanwhile, some abortion-rights supporters find evidence in the book of Exodus that the fetus is something less than fully human. Chapter 21 depicts a fight between two men that results in a pregnant woman's suffering "a miscarriage, but no further injury." If the miscarriage is the only damage, it says, the offender must pay a fine. "But if injury ensues, you shall give life for life, eye for eye, tooth for tooth. . . ." Although Exodus clearly depicts an accidental rather than a willful termination of pregnancy, says Paul Simmons of the Southern Baptist Theological Seminary, "it gives no support to the parity argument that gives equal religious and moral worth to woman and fetus." Deference should be given to the rights and well-being of the woman, Simmons argues, when it comes to abortion.

> *"Some commentators . . . are calling for new dialogue among theologians from various traditions as a step toward common ground."*

Some Christian theologians contend that, given the Bible's silence on abortion and its ambiguity concerning the fetus, the biblical principle of human free will should be emphasized. Prof. Virginia Ramey Mollenkott of William Paterson College in New Jersey, writing for the Religious Coalition for Abortion Rights, argues that in scripture, "God foreknew that Adam and Eve would misuse their power to choose, yet God chose to give them that power. . . . We should follow our Creator's example by giving each other more moral elbow room."

New Dialogue

With theologians as divided as the rest of society over abortion, some commentators, like Anglican clergyman John R. W. Stott, are calling for new dialogue among theologians from various traditions as a step toward common ground and, perhaps, toward a healing of the cultural rift. Others doubt such deliberations would be productive given how deeply entrenched many churches are in their own dogma. "Inevitably," says conservative theologian Carl F. H. Henry, "the theological issue is going to prove central, either by way of a recognition of the moral authority of the Judeo-Christian heritage or by a deliberate rejection of it." If the heritage is rejected, Henry warns, "it is a capitulation to the barbarians." Such dialogue clearly would not be without risk. But it is a risk many are ready to take.

Abortion Is Immoral

by Helen M. Alvaré

About the author: *Helen M. Alvaré is director of planning and information for the secretariat for pro-life activities of the National Conference of Catholic Bishops in Washington, D.C. She has previously worked as a trial lawyer and has written friend-of-the-court briefs on behalf of the U.S. Catholic Conference.*

It is impossible to pick up a newspaper or magazine in January 1993 without reading a coroner's-eye view of the pro-life movement. The word from the community of professional political observers is that the legal struggle is in the can, "pro-choice" has won and what remains is the unresolved moral debate among Americans.

Moral Opposition

Before assessing the possible future for a real public moral conversation on abortion, a few preliminary observations are in order. First, the above observers apparently agree with abortion advocates that the moral discussion is what's left over *after* law and public policy are settled (in their favor). This contravenes common sense and experience. Newcomers to the moral conversation should not be surprised to find that this conversation has been pursued by the pro-life movement for the last 20 years. How on earth could we otherwise account for the enduring abortion controversy 20 years after *Roe v. Wade*? And how otherwise account for the majority sentiment of moral opposition to 98 percent of abortions performed for reasons other than rape, incest or danger to the life of the mother? Only robust moral education could sustain such sentiment in the face of overwhelming support for legal abortion among members of the media, the academy, the entertainment industry and professional societies.

Other benefits of these efforts to sustain a moral discussion include doctors' increasing unwillingness to perform, and hospitals' unwillingness to train for, abortion. And figures from the Centers for Disease Control show that, while absolute numbers of abortions have increased since 1980, the ratio of abortions to live births has declined. More women are opting to carry their pregnancies to term.

Second, with regard to the legal debate, there is in every state in this country,

Helen M. Alvaré, "A Pro-Life R.S.V.P.," *America*, January 30, 1993. Reprinted by permission of the author.

and on the Federal level, a pro-life lobby actively pursuing limited but nonetheless real legal avenues for discouraging abortion. Substantive protections for unborn children are constitutionally off-limits, but efforts proceed to insure full, informed consent for women, parental involvement and health and safety regulations.

Furthermore, the much ballyhooed "Freedom of Choice Act" (FOCA)—which would forbid American people in the 50 states from enacting any regulations on abortion and would permit abortion for any reason through the ninth month of pregnancy—is by no means a "done deal." Likely to the chagrin of abortion advocates, the pro-life movement began the moral debate about FOCA [long] ago. As a result, the same moral misgivings Congressional members evidenced [toward FOCA] are surfacing again. Even President Bill Clinton wavers occasionally on his once limitless support for FOCA, now claiming that he opposes third-trimester abortions unless the mother's life is endangered (whereas the proposed FOCA requires states to permit abortions for "health," including emotional health) and favors parental notification (whereas FOCA requires states to permit any "responsible adult" to substitute for parents) and waiting periods (FOCA forbids them).

The Rebirth of the Moral Debate?

Many politicians and members of the press will continue to deny or ignore these legal and social trends, and insist that the moral debate has only just begun. Given that large segments of the U.S. public are likely to believe what they read in black and white, however, the pro-life movement must consider how best to take advantage of this "new" development—an apparent willingness to enter into true moral conversation about abortion.

What is moral conversation? Classically, of course, morality is concerned with whether behavior is right or wrong, good or bad. The moral inquiry on abortion therefore encompasses questions about the value of unborn human life—whether that life has an equal or lesser right (vis-à-vis the born) not to be killed directly, and whether or where abortion falls on the continuum of humane solutions that could be offered pregnant women and children for the variety of problems they disproportionately face.

Americans seem ready to face these moral questions. It has been said that we are currently trying to recover from two decades of exaggerated individualism. Americans seemed to resonate with President Clinton's

> *"There is in every state in this country, and on the Federal level, a pro-life lobby actively . . . discouraging abortion."*

campaign rhetoric about "a new ethic of mutual responsibility" and about there being "not a single person to waste."

But there is one serious flaw (not to say irony) in all this talk of a return to moral conversation: Abortion advocates HATE to talk about the moral aspects of "choice." Kate Michelman of the National Abortion Rights Action League (NARAL) has gone so far as to suggest that even to *ask the question* whether an abortion is right or wrong is unfairly to question whether women can make moral choices. And who can forget a reporter's unanswered query following Ms. Michelman's televised declaration that every abortion is a tragedy: "Why is it a tragedy, Kate? Kate, why is it a tragedy?"

Daniel Callahan has noted that a growing number in the "pro-choice" movement feel that "to concede that it is a *serious* moral choice and to have a public discussion about that choice is politically hazardous, the opening wedge of a discussion that could easily lead once again to a restriction of a woman's right to an abortion." Consider that Senate Majority Leader George Mitchell (D., Me.), chief sponsor of FOCA, refused even to bring FOCA to the floor because he did not have the 60 votes needed to foreclose public debate or amendments on sticky moral subjects such as abortions in the third trimester and sex-selection abortions. And in perhaps the clearest rejection of moral debate, a founder of the Republican Majority Coalition (the "pro-choice" faction of the Republican Party), Tom Campbell, stated: "Our purpose is to exclude issues of morality and conscience as litmus tests of being a Republican."

> *"Abortion advocates HATE to talk about the moral aspects of 'choice.'"*

In other words, the current calls, mostly by advocates of legal abortion, for a renewed "moral debate" do not really intend public conversation, but one conducted between the ears of each American. Again, Daniel Callahan: "The pro-choice movement has in fact never known quite what to do with the moral issue. For most of its leaders, it is simply set aside altogether, left to the opaque sphere of personal morality, itself a subject of uncertainty and discomfort."

Clearly a Public Matter

To cast abortion as a solely private moral question, however, is to lose touch with common sense: How human beings treat one another is practically the definition of a "public" moral matter. Of course, there are many private aspects of human relations, but the question whether one human being should be allowed fatally to harm another is not one of them. Abortion is an inescapably public matter.

To the extent that abortion advocates are willing to participate in substantive, public moral discussion, they posit the central question as this: How to "minimize the need for elective abortion" (presuming always that it remains legal)? In President Clinton's words, how do we make abortion "rare"?

With all due respect to those supporters of legal abortion who genuinely desire its "rarity," most abortion advocates will not likely be good mediators of the message to "choose life." They have spent 20 years promoting an unfettered "right" to abortion—defending as constitutionally protected (in the Casey reply brief) even sex-selection abortions. And who among us generally feels bad exercising a "right"? More fundamentally, the abortion advocacy movement is best known for promoting choice without reference to object or limits, choice as an *inherent* good. To move to a public stance distinguishing between choices would completely undercut their simple if flawed message.

Abortion advocates have also resorted to demeaning everything the pro-life movement stands for, including one of the best things to come out of this whole abortion debate—crisis pregnancy assistance to women considering abortion. They have also resorted to demeaning the unborn. Dr. Joycelyn Elders, President Clinton's choice for the post of Surgeon General, has said: "[W]e would like for the right-to-live [sic], anti-choice groups to really get over their love affair with the fetus." These are not auspicious beginnings for entering into a serious moral dialogue.

This is not to conclude that no abortion advocate could effectively work to make abortion "rare." Movements are generally known, however, by their loudest voices, and the "pro-choice" voices speaking to the media and filing Supreme Court briefs are best known for their defense of unlimited abortion and for disparaging the motivations and social services that pro-life advocates offer.

Areas of Moral Discourse

But if moral debate were actually to ensue in the public square, the results could be little in doubt. Every poll taken since abortion became legal in the 50 states in 1973 has shown that Americans are morally opposed to the majority of abortions performed in this country—i.e., abortions performed for reasons other than rape, incest or danger to the life of the mother. And women, left by the Federal judiciary with the entire abortion decision, are more morally opposed to abortion than men. In this environment, a reasoned, compassionate moral argument will bear much fruit. Furthermore, pro-life apologists can speak with confidence in three primary areas of moral discourse about abortion: 1) the moral status of each unborn human life; 2) the legitimacy of discriminating between different stages of human life vis-à-vis the right not to be killed, and 3) the choice of abortion among public policy solutions offered to alleviate discrimination against women.

The Moral Status of Unborn Life. The elements of the moral argument on the status of unborn life—facts about fetal development, abortion procedures and prenatal surgery— strongly favor the conclusion that this unborn segment of humanity has a right not to be killed, at least. Without laying out all the evidence here, it is fair to conclude from medicine that the humanity of the life growing in a mother's womb is undeniable and, in itself, a powerful reason for treating the unborn with respect. Put more interestingly by the pollster for NARAL, Harrison Hickman:

> *"How human beings treat one another is practically the definition of a 'public' moral matter."*

Probably nothing has been as damaging to our cause as the advances in technology which have allowed pictures of the developing fetus, because people now talk about the fetus in much different terms than they did 15 years ago. They talk about it as a human being, which is not something that I have an easy answer on how to cure.

Restrictions Against Humanity

Discrimination Against the Unborn. The content of the moral debate about choosing among human lives likewise tilts toward a pro-life conclusion. Few are likely to dispute Phillip Abbott's statement:

> There are very few general laws of social science, but we can offer one that has a deserved claim: the restriction of the concept of humanity in any sphere never enhances a respect for human life. It did not enhance the rights of slaves, prisoners of wars, criminals, traitors, women, children, Jews, blacks, heretics, workers, capitalists, Slavs or Gypsies. The restriction of the concept of personhood in regard to the fetus will not do so either.

Public scrutiny of the reasons ordinarily given for denying to the unborn a "right not to be killed" is quite likely to generate, at the least, an aversion to legal abortion. Few would be proud to make the public case that those who are smaller, who are disabled, who are relatively more dependent, who are not generally visible, who are developing (but not "finished"), who might suffer or cause others to suffer emotionally or otherwise have thereby lost their right not to be directly killed.

The Choice of Solutions for Women and Children. Finally, the pro-life stance also has the edge in the debate about the morality of offering women and children abortion as a public policy "solution" to a host of their problems: problems like poverty, disability, lack of educational opportunities, employers' failures to accommodate working mothers, relative devaluation of pregnancy and mothering (vis-à-vis economic achievements outside the home), non-supporting fathers, etc. The list could go on. A country's choice among possible solutions to persistent problems speaks volumes about its people. When abortion is what we offer a pregnant woman to assuage her suffering or the potential suffering of her child, we know intuitively we have failed. Empirical evidence compiled by constitutional law scholar Mary Ann Glendon of Harvard shows a correlation between countries' willingness to offer substantive pre- and post-natal assistance to women, children and families, and their abortion policies: The lesser assistance offered, the more permissive the abortion policies.

> *"Every poll taken since . . . 1973 has shown that Americans are morally opposed to the majority of abortions."*

Abortion advocates regularly call abortion a "tragedy." Americans adopting the "pro-choice" label regularly claim that their support for legal abortion will disappear with the appearance of more positive options for pregnant women. With each such utterance, the speaker confirms our collective shame over America's willingness to substitute freely available abortion for public policies affirming the equality and dignity of each woman and each child.

Welcoming a Moral Discussion

For the pro-life movement, the return to a moral discussion of abortion in the public square bodes well. Efforts to change the law will continue, whether politicians or members of the press acknowledge them or not. Americans know the awesome moral weight the law carries, and are not at all likely to sever in this one area the natural relationship between the community's mores and its laws.

With this renewed focus on the moral question come exciting new opportunities to help the public articulate why they intuitively recoil from abortion, as well as a chance to consider more creative, humane ways to solve the problems presently leading women to abortion clinics. It is a chance to help every conscientious person answer the question a national abortion advocate left unanswered: "Why is it a tragedy, Kate? Kate, why is it a tragedy?"

Abortion Violates the Fetus's Interests

by Morton A. Kaplan

About the author: *Morton A. Kaplan is the editor and publisher of* The World & I, *a monthly publication covering current events, science, and the arts. Kaplan is Distinguished Service Professor of Political Science Emeritus at the University of Chicago.*

Ronald Dworkin has an exceptionally distinguished reputation, which his book, *Life's Dominion*, can only enhance. It is a beautifully and eruditely reasoned book, which includes the best defense of abortion on demand that I have ever read. It is fatally flawed, however, in both its conclusions and philosophy.

Dworkin believes that antiabortion positions are without constitutional foundation for two reasons: a First Amendment reason based on the argument that beliefs concerning the sanctity of life are quasi-religious, in which case the state has no right to impose its views on individuals; and the claim that the fetus is without interests and, therefore, is not a person and has no rights.

Life and Choice

If the belief in the sanctity of life is religious to some extent, and this may not necessarily be the case, so is the perspective that exalts choice. If life does not have exalted value, if it is a matter only of Hobbesian survival, then neither do choice and dignity. . . . Every society that sanctifies life also sanctifies at least some moral values that are central to character formation. In their absence, both life and choice would have sharply diminished value, a feature of some societies that we would not desire to emulate.

Dworkin's effort to claim on First Amendment grounds that these choices are entirely optional for the individual would fail any constitutional test, as shown by numerous restrictions on religious freedom, which the [U.S. Supreme] Court enforces when very important public policy issues are involved. The courts will order a blood transfusion to save the life of a child even when the parents object

From Morton A. Kaplan, "Personhood, Abortion, and Rights: A Reply to Ronald Dworkin." This article appeared in the September 1993 issue and is reprinted with permission from *The World & I*, a publication of The Washington Times Corporation, copyright ©1993.

on religious grounds. Although I disagree with the Court's decision with respect to the religious use of peyote by some Indian tribes, my disagreement involves only where the line is drawn, not whether the state can impose restrictions under some conditions.

Furthermore, Dworkin's view of the impact that the sanctity of life consideration, if permitted, would have on the constitutionality of abortion is flawed. All religions, except those that accept absolute pacifism, permit life to be taken under some conditions. Except for Roman Catholicism, all religions permit abortion under some conditions. The sanctity of life does not determine decisions concerning whether abortions may be permitted or forbidden, although it may, like any moral consideration, influence them. The extreme position taken in *Roe v. Wade*, however, can best be defended by Dworkin's dichotomous position concerning rights and personhood, not by his First Amendment argument. Except for several sentences that will become relevant later, it is to the flaws in that [dichotomous] position that I now turn.

> *"If life does not have exalted value ... then neither do choice and dignity."*

Dworkin believes that all persons have equal interests and rights and that the state has no constitutional authority to attribute personhood and rights where they do not exist, as in, for instance, a tree. The fetus, he says, does not have interests or rights before it develops certain human capabilities, which will be specified shortly.

Legal Personhood Changes with Age

But are the concepts of personhood, interests, and rights as dichotomous as Dworkin affirms? Consider Section 1 of the Fourteenth Amendment: "Nor shall any State deprive any person of life, liberty, or property, without due process of law." The mere fact that children and adults fit Dworkin's concept of agency does not determine what their rights are or that these rights are equal. These are socially given and depend upon the framework of culture and understanding.

Note that Section 1 also states as follows: "All persons born or naturalized in the United States . . . are citizens of the United States. . . . No State shall make or enforce any law which shall abridge the privileges or immunities of citizens of the United States." Babies and minor children are citizens of the United States. Yet they are not permitted to vote or to sign contracts. The legal personhood of young people changes with age. The courts often determine whether the law makes adequate distinctions by using the doctrines of rationality and compelling grounds, although these also do not function with mechanical precision but depend upon a framework of factual, moral, and legal understandings. Personhood is divisible, and so are interests and rights.

The issue is not whether the fetus is an agent or a person or human in the full sense—even some adults are not and their rights are accordingly changed—but the extent to which it is human or has personhood and the legal implications thereof. This is what rights flow from. The high value our culture places on human life is related to the rights it recognizes, and perhaps someday all life will be accorded some degree of respect.

Dworkin thinks he can show that at an early stage the fetus lacks interests because it lacks a central nervous system and, thus, the ability "to enjoy or fail to enjoy, to form affections and emotions, to hope and expect, to suffer disappointment and frustration." These constitute, according to Dworkin, the prerequisites for interests, personhood, and rights. Thus, the fetus, because it lacks this capacity, lacks personhood. The community may have an interest in preserving it, like a statue, but it has no interests of its own, he says.

It is not clear, at least to me, whether the sufficient criterion for interests and legal personhood, according to Dworkin, lies in the neural structure that permits the specified human abilities or in the contemporaneous ability to exercise them. Therefore, I shall consider each of these possibilities separately. . . .

Let us first assume that the criterion for personhood lies in the ability to exercise the capacities Dworkin specifies. By this argument, an individual in a reversible coma would be without interests. But, like the fetus, which is developing into a human, the individual in a reversible coma, even if kept alive in the interim by machinery, clearly has interests, even in the absence of the complex capacity to which Dworkin refers, because he retains the potentiality to exercise them. He has an interest in recovering and in pursuing additional activities. . . .

> *"Like the fetus, . . . the individual in a reversible coma . . . clearly has interests."*

It would defeat ordinary understanding to argue that the individual has interests before the coma and will have them after he emerges from the coma but lacks them while in the coma. He has interests that derive from his potential agency and from his existence as a continuing being, which are exercised by proxy while in the coma.

The Frankenstein Analogy

In a flawed analogy that is meant to illustrate his claim, Dworkin asserts that the fetus has no more interests or rights than the parts of Frankenstein's monster before apparatus brought the monster to life. Dworkin's analogy of the fetus to Frankenstein's monster is flawed because the parts that are to be combined while subject to Frankenstein's mechanisms have no genetic instructions for combination, and, furthermore, except at the cellular level, are dead.

If, someday, we can create life in the laboratory, that life will acquire interests as a human life-form only when it has reached a stage of self-development that is dependent only upon conditions similar to those of the womb or, like Frankenstein's monster, if it comes fully to life. The proper analogy would have been to the chemical constituents that could be made into DNA while within an artificial womb. They would have no interests in becoming human and no rights. The fetus already is on the path to fully human life. It has an interest in developing its capacities, even though it may be unaware of these interests.

That external means are necessary for the fetus to remain alive is irrelevant, for adults require external support such as food and oxygen to live. Just as nature is the natural environment for children and adults, so is the womb for the fetus. . . .

The fetus is a separate, if not, in the state of current technology, separable, individual, but its intimate connection to the mother creates both a special bond and a potential tragic conflict of interest. If Dworkin's argument had been restricted to the often superordinate importance of the mother's interest, it would have the power his rhetoric and subtlety of argument appear to give it, but only to the extent that it was not counterbalanced by society's interest in preserving human life, even at that stage, because of the impact on human solidarity of massive abortion rates.

No individual has full control over his body. The ingestion of certain drugs is forbidden. If an individual feels such guilt that only the severing of part of a finger would satisfy it, society would still forbid the surgery even though we could say that it would be in the individual's interest. If the surgery involved the amputation of an arm or eye, the surgeon likely would lose his license and be indicted.

If we can accept this, it seems strange that we have difficulty in recognizing some social interest in determining whether an abortion may be performed. It is possible that the consequences of illegal abortions give rise to this perspective. Perhaps if few abortions occurred, this might be a controlling perspective, but the consequences of mass abortions and truckloads of dead fetuses create a counterbalancing interest, even if one believes the fetus is not a person and has no interests of its own. I believe a more nuanced approach is both possible and preferable. If I can show, as I believe I do, that the fetus has a degree of personhood and some interests, the former conclusion is considerably strengthened.

No Rights Without Personhood

Let us now examine whether Dworkin's dichotomous concept of personhood can be saved if the sufficient condition is the mere existence of the neural structure. Suppose a fetus has a genetic defect. Although I would assert that it has an interest in not having a genetic defect, it might seem absurd to claim that it has a right not to have a genetic defect. Suppose, however, that genetic science produces a gene that if inserted into the fetus before the fourth week—and, thus, well before the development of a central nervous system—would correct this defect. Suppose

> *"The fetus already is on the path to fully human life. It has an interest in developing its capacities."*

30

this procedure is free and universally available. Would we not say that the fetus has a right to receive the treatment, and would not a court order it, even if the mother refused consent on grounds both of religion and privacy?

I believe that the court would do so not merely to avoid future expense but also to protect the rights of the fetus. Suppose that a mother ordered a doctor to insert a defective gene into the fetus at this early stage, and the doctor complied. Would they not be subject to criminal law? Yet, if the fetus had no personhood, no interests, and no rights at this stage, then it would acquire rights only after the injury, just as the fetus subject to an ordinary genetic defect would acquire rights only after conception. The issue of the latter could not sue its parents for this defect, even if they knew about it before voluntary conception.

> *"How can it be that the mother can abort the fetus without penalty but not injure it without penalty?"*

In parallel, in the former case, if the early fetus has no personhood or interests, no rights of the individual, or of society, would have been violated. If a suit for parental responsibility in passing on defective genes in the future should be successful, that would only strengthen my case.

How can it be that the mother can abort the fetus without penalty but not injure it without penalty? In part, the answer lies in the fact that the interests and personhood of the fetus are strengthened by the decision not to abort. They cannot be created by this decision. Therefore, they must be present to some extent even from its earliest stage.

In a class sense, however, some degree of moral right can exist even for humans who are not yet possibilities in the minds of possible parents who are not yet born. Do we not recognize the rights of unborn generations to inhabit a livable globe? Are these our interests but not those of succeeding generations? We will not be alive to have interests. We must be confused to believe these are our interests unless our minds permit us human solidarity even with unborn generations, in which case we recognize their interests and also have an interest in their interests. Although I should be wary about the Court's intervening in such decisions, legislation may strike an appropriate balance and create the equivalent of a right.

Attributing Interests

Dworkin is correct when he says that we would not attribute an interest to a building. Linguistic usage restricts the concept of interest to living entities, although whether this is an insuperable barrier is not entirely certain. It already has been shown that knowledge of an interest, or even the capability thereof, is not a requirement for the existence of an interest. A severely retarded orphan may have an interest in an estate without knowing of that fact or even being capable of knowing what it means. It would seem odd to suggest that an animal, or even an insect, has no interest in avoiding a trap, although both creatures would lack some of the elements Dworkin makes essential to the existence of interests. . . .

Personhood is not an either/or proposition. Interests and personhood exist from origin, although perhaps in attenuated forms. Rights, however, do not flow merely from interests but from the recognition of these interests by society. Animals or plants may acquire rights, if society so decides, and these could be exercised on their behalf. They may also lose those rights if society so judges, as may the fetus, infant child, and so forth. Moral arguments enter into the determination of when interests should give rise to rights.

The New Testament Canon Condemns Abortion

by Michael J. Gorman

About the author: *Michael J. Gorman teaches early Christianity and moral theology at the Ecumenical Institute at St. Mary's Seminary in Baltimore. Gorman, a United Methodist, is the author of* Abortion and the Early Church *and is a contributor to* The Church and Abortion: In Search of New Ground for Response.

The 27 books of the New Testament are indisputably silent on the subject of abortion. Yet many Christians feel strongly that opposition to abortion is the biblical position. Many others are confused by this puzzling silence, for they intuitively question the compatibility of abortion and Christian faith. Still others maintain that the New Testament's silence means that abortion was, and must continue to be, a matter of individual conscience.

These polar perspectives, along with the confusion of those caught in the middle, have divided the Christian community for the last 20 years of debate since *Roe* v. *Wade*. For those who take the Bible as their authority in matters of faith and life, the New Testament's puzzling silence on abortion seems indeed to be a serious problem. Given this silence, would it not be most logical—most *biblical*—to affirm freedom of conscience with abortion? Could it be that when it comes to abortion, the New Testament's silence implies neutrality, ambiguity, or even acceptance? Doesn't this *historical* silence also logically lead to the *theological* conclusion that God is neutral about or even accepting of abortion? And if God is, at most, neutral, how can anyone be dogmatically opposed?

The Bible and Fetal Personhood

The "individual-conscience" interpretation of the New Testament's silence has been vigorously advocated by one very significant and powerful organization, the Religious Coalition for Abortion Rights (RCAR). [The organization is now called the Religious Coalition for Reproductive Choice.] RCAR, their literature states, is "a national, nonprofit, nonpartisan coalition of 35 Protestant,

Michael J. Gorman, "Why Is the New Testament Silent About Abortion?" *Christianity Today*, January 11, 1993. Reprinted by permission of the author.

Jewish, and other denominations and faith groups" that are "religiously and theologically diverse . . . [but] unified in [their] commitment to preserve reproductive freedom." It is clear that one of RCAR's goals is to convince or reassure people that the Bible neither affirms the personhood of the fetus nor condemns abortion. Especially devoted to this goal are two publications written by professors of theology: a short pamphlet, *Is the Fetus a Person—According to the Bible?* by Miami University of Ohio's Roy Bowen Ward, and a booklet entitled *Personhood, the Bible, and the Abortion Debate*, by Southern Baptist Theological Seminary's Paul D. Simmons.

Ward writes, "One thing that the Bible does not say is 'Thou shalt not abort.'" The biblical writers "did not choose to condemn" abortion. Why not? Because, Ward contends, the

> *"Many Christians feel strongly that opposition to abortion is the biblical position."*

Jews and early Christians did not believe the fetus is a person. According to Ward, the biblical notion of a person—in Hebrew, *nephesh*—is a living, *breathing* being. Since the fetus is not such a being, it is not a person, biblically speaking, and is therefore not entitled to the rights and protection granted to persons. Ward claims that because this was the Jewish view at the time the New Testament writings were composed and collected, it was also the view of such eminent New Testament writers as the apostle Paul.

Simmons agrees that the New Testament does not teach fetal personhood. He claims that the "most plausible explanation" for the Bible's silence on abortion is that early Christians saw abortion as "a private, personal and religious matter, not subject to civil regulation." The apostle Paul's failure to name abortion in his vice lists, argues Simmons, means that he "apparently . . . regarded abortion as a matter to be dealt with on the basis of faith, grace and Christian freedom."

The "Sacredness" of Choice

What, then, are the moral and social implications of this interpretation of the silence? Ward maintains abortion is clearly not murder according to the New Testament, and says that if the New Testament is silent on abortion, then Christians should also be silent: "Speak where the Bible speaks. Be silent where the Bible is silent." But Ward's own pamphlet is hardly silent; it is a clarion call to support individual conscience and choice.

Simmons concludes his booklet more forthrightly by claiming that

> Abortion is never to be taken lightly but it is not a forbidden option. . . . Contemporary Christians will do well to follow the biblical pattern in treating the subject of elective abortion. . . . The biblical writers' silence [on abortion] reveals a becoming reticence to judge too quickly concerning the morality of another person's choice. It is eloquent testimony to the sacredness of this choice for women and their families and the privacy in which it is to be considered.

It is clear, then, that Ward, Simmons, and RCAR believe the Bible's silence on abortion speaks quite clearly in support of the "sacredness" of choice. As persuasive as these arguments may seem to be, an alternative explanation better accounts for the silence.

The Jewish Perspective

As Professor Ward indicates in his pamphlet, many of the first Christians, including all but one (Luke) of those whose writings are preserved in the New Testament, were *Jewish* Christians with a basically Jewish morality. We can therefore rightly expect, as Ward does, that if a Jewish consensus on fetal personhood and/or abortion existed at that time, the writers of the New Testament would almost certainly have held the common Jewish view.

Ward implies that the Jewish consensus in the early part of the Christian era was not antiabortion, but he has incorrectly interpreted texts that are only marginally relevant, and he has failed to discuss Jewish documents that explicitly mention induced abortion. Early Judaism was, in fact, quite firmly opposed to induced abortion.

The popular Jewish wisdom of the *Sentences of Pseudo-Phocylides* (written between 50 B.C. and A.D. 50) says that "a woman should not destroy the unborn babe in her belly, nor after its birth throw it before the dogs and vultures as a prey." So, too, the apocalyptic *Sibylline Oracles* includes among the wicked two groups: women who "produce abortions and unlawfully cast their offspring away"

> *"The apocalyptic* Sibylline Oracles *includes among the wicked . . . women who 'produce abortions.'"*

and sorcerers who dispense abortifacients. The apocryphal, first- or second-century B.C. 1 Enoch says that an evil angel taught humans how to "smash the embryo in the womb."

In his exposition of the commandment against murder, the Hellenistic Jewish philosopher Philo of Alexandria (25 B.C.–A.D. 41) rejected the common notion that a fetus is merely a part of its mother. He taught that anyone who induces abortion must be fined if the fetus is unformed and given the death penalty if it is formed. Similarly, the first-century Jewish historian and apologist Josephus wrote, "The Law orders all the offspring to be brought up, and forbids women either to cause abortion or to make away with the fetus." A woman convicted of this was regarded as having committed an infanticide, because she destroyed a soul and diminished the race.

No contradictory early Jewish texts about abortion have been discovered, thus suggesting that a Jewish antiabortion consensus did exist in the first century. (Later, some rabbis pronounced an exception—abortion to save the mother's life.) This consensus is acknowledged even by more liberal scholars, such as William Countryman, who find the New Testament's silence on abortion puzzling and problematic.

Given the Jewish consensus on abortion, the most logical supposition is that the Jewish-Christian writers of the New Testament would have shared the antiabortion posture of their Jewish heritage and ethos, even if they did not mention abortion explicitly in the preserved writings of the New Testament canon.

Silent Witness

Why, then, is abortion not mentioned in any of the 27 books of the New Testament? As scholars such as Yale Divinity School's Leander Keck have emphasized, neither the New Testament as a whole, nor any of the individual documents, constitutes a comprehensive manual of ethics. Rather, Keck reminds us, each document deals only with ethical matters that had become, or were becoming, *problems.* That the New Testament never directly addresses abortion (or exposure or infanticide) does not mean that the first-century churches were ignorant of this practice or that they believed it to be a matter of "individual conscience." On the contrary, the silence simply tells us that abortion was not an issue in need of resolution. The silence indicates that there was little or no deviation from the norm inherited from Judaism. Imbued with a profound Jewish respect for unborn and newborn human life as the gift of God, and inspired by Jesus' welcoming of children, the earliest Christians were not tempted to end or endanger the life of their children before or after birth. When the abortion temptation—or at least the question—arose explicitly, the church answered with an unequivocal *no.*

If this interpretation of the silence is correct, should we not expect *some* hint of this Jewish and Christian consensus in the New Testament itself? The question is more complex than it first appears, but there is one important hint at the consensus in the New Testament.

In the birth narrative of the gospel according to Matthew, one of the most thoroughly Jewish of the New Testament documents, the story is told of Joseph's reaction to the news of his teenage fiancée's premarital pregnancy. The solution that comes to Joseph's mind is divorce, not abortion. Divorce for unfaithfulness was acceptable; abortion unthinkable.

The "Other" New Testaments

Another dimension for understanding the New Testament's silence is to note that although it *is* silent, it once was *not* silent. While the New Testament in nearly universal use for 1,600 years contains no texts on abortion, many of the New Testaments produced and used by the earliest Christians *did* contain such texts. Even though the books containing these texts were

> *"Divorce for unfaithfulness was acceptable; abortion unthinkable."*

eventually excluded from the official New Testament, they first expressed and spread their opposition to abortion throughout the Christian church.

The 27 books of our New Testament were not the only Christian writings considered by early Christian congregations to be inspired. Nor was the New Testament assembled and published all at once, at some time in the late-first or early-second century. Its formation was gradual, beginning perhaps in the early-second century and ending, more or less, in the late-fourth. As a collection, in other words, the 27-book New Testament is not really a *first*-century publication but a *fourth*-century publication of first-century writings.

> *"Three writings [prohibiting abortion] remained popular and, in some cases, semiauthoritative among Christians."*

For almost three centuries, each congregation, each theologian, each area, and finally each major region of Christianity had its own collection of authoritative writings, its own "canon." Although the core of these canons—the four Gospels and Paul's letters—was essentially the same from the mid-second-century onward, the other contents varied from place to place and from time to time.

Early Works Condemning Abortion

Among the frontrunners of the several early Christian works that eventually lost their bid for canonicity were three popular documents that condemned abortion—the *Didache*, the Epistle of Barnabas, and the Apocalypse of Peter. These widely distributed writings were all of Jewish-Christian origin and were composed during the late-first or early-second century from even earlier Jewish moral traditions. These now-obscure documents were part of the authoritative writings read and preached in many Christian congregations throughout the Roman Empire during the second, third, and fourth centuries.

The texts on abortion in these three documents are brief but very significant:

> Love your neighbor as yourself. . . . You shall not murder a child by abortion nor shall you kill a newborn. (*Didache*)

> You shall love your neighbor more than your own life. You shall not murder a child by abortion nor shall you kill a newborn. (Barnabas)

> [In a vision of hell] I saw . . . women . . . who produced children out of wedlock and who procured abortions. (Apocalypse of Peter)

These three texts bear witness to the general Jewish and Jewish-Christian attitude of the first and second centuries, thus confirming that the earliest Christians shared the antiabortion position of their Jewish forebears. Each of the three writings containing these texts appears in some of the early church's lists of its New Testament canon.

As time went on, for varied reasons these writings came to be known as "disputed" books—those not universally read in worship and whose authority and place in the canon were in question. Writing in the early-fourth century, Eusebius notes that although these three books were not universally accepted, they were "recognized by most writers in the church" and "publicly read by many in most churches." Even when they were permanently excluded from the church's official canon in the late-fourth or early-fifth century, each of these three writings remained popular and, in some cases, semiauthoritative among Christians. This clearly suggests that their antiabortion position was never deemed deviant from the Christian norm.

The Significance of the Silence

When we ask, "Why is abortion not mentioned in the New Testament?" we must realize that it *was* mentioned, and *prohibited*, in many of the "New Testaments" in use for several centuries. The antiabortion statements of the (now) noncanonical books do not veer from the central early Christian path; they maintain it. The writers of these documents also laid the groundwork for further statements against abortion and for the early church's universal acceptance of the inherited position.

Furthermore, the lack of any attempt to safeguard an antiabortion text for the New Testament canon suggests that the Christian antiabortion position was so universally accepted that its absence from the emerging canon was not noticed, nor was its presence deemed necessary. Not only had moralists, apologists, and theologians—without a dissenting voice—condemned abortion, but by the early-fourth century early canon-law documents had begun to prescribe punishment for abortion.

> *"The New Testament canon did indeed speak, and still does speak, against abortion."*

When the New Testament is understood in its historical, developmental context, as a fourth-century Christian collection of first-century Jewish-Christian documents, its silence on abortion testifies to the antiabortion stance of its original Jewish-Christian writers, its later compilers, and its earliest hearers and readers. In a very real sense, then, the New Testament canon did indeed speak, and still does speak, against abortion.

The Christian community was, and must continue to be, a place where the most vulnerable are welcomed and protected. Christians recognize two neighbors present in every pregnancy, and they must seek mercy, love, and justice for both of these neighbors. That, quite simply, is the way of the New Testament, the way of Christ.

Thus, the New Testament calls us to welcome children, to protect God's gift of life, to be a community of merciful hospitality to women in need. Those seeking a religious defense of abortion "rights" or "individual conscience" must search for it in texts and communities other than those of early Judaism and early Christianity, including the Christianity of the New Testament.

Donating to Abortion Providers Is Immoral

by Paul V. Mankowski

About the author: *Paul V. Mankowski is a Jesuit priest who teaches New Testament studies at the Pontifical Biblical Institute in Rome, Italy. He previously taught Old Testament studies at Harvard University in Cambridge, Massachusetts.*

The deliberate destruction of the life of an innocent human being is always and everywhere wicked. I will take this principle (in shorthand: murder is wicked) as the linchpin of everything that follows. I believe that there are conclusive reasons for acknowledging this principle to be an exceptionless moral norm, but I will not attempt to sketch them here. I am simply nailing my colors to the mast, convinced that those are unlikely to profit from this particular exercise who deny that killing the innocent is wrong.

Forbidden Regardless of Circumstances

By "exceptionless moral norm" I mean this: a rule of human conduct that excludes a class of action in such a way that, as soon as we can identify a given act as belonging to that class, we understand that the choice to perform it is morally forbidden, regardless of the attendant circumstances. For example, if we acknowledge that the rule forbidding treachery is an exceptionless moral norm, once we admit that a certain action (conniving to steal military secrets in order to sell them to a hostile power, say) falls under the category of treachery, no circumstances or complicating factors can make this choice a moral one. As the Oxford philosopher John Finnis reminds us, there are many moral norms that are true, but not "absolute" in this sense:

> "Feed your children," for example. This moral norm is true, forceful, but not absolute. When the only food available is the body of your neighbor's living child, one (morally) cannot apply that norm in one's action; nor does one violate it by not applying it.

Paul V. Mankowski, "Funding Abortion the United Way," *Human Life Review*, Fall 1993. Reprinted with permission.

The norm forbidding killing the innocent is, however, absolute precisely in the sense that it is exceptionless.

I am myself a convinced Roman Catholic, and I believe that the universe of moral reason is only brought to fullness and clarity by faith. Yet the remarks that follow presume no faith, no Catholic or Christian conviction. I am making a minimalist argument directed to persons of any religion or no religion at all who are willing to admit the truth of the claim that killing the innocent is wrong.

So much for the major premise. The minor premise is simply that abortion is an occasion of the destruction of innocent human life.

The objections to this claim are not formidable. No one has been able to argue convincingly that a fetus is not innocent in the relevant sense, or that it is not human, or that it is not alive, or that the procedure in question does not end this life. Most of the objectors have had to abandon the language of philosophy and resort to the language of law, and have been pushed into the position of maintaining that one and the same entity, the child, has a full franchisement of human rights on one side of the uterine wall, but not even the most fundamental human right on the other.

The feebleness of this position is so glaring that most abortion proponents have shifted their rhetorical spotlight from the object of the moral act to the independence and freedom of the moral agent. They insist, through a kind of numbing repetition, on a generalized Right to Choose, leaving the thought unfinished, sensing quite rightly that the Right to Choose the moral object in dispute—the death of the innocent—is indefensible.

Responsibility for Wickedness

So I maintain: the deliberate destruction of innocent human life is wicked. Abortion is deliberate destruction of innocent human life. Therefore, abortion is wicked. If the major premise holds exceptionlessly, and if the minor premise is true, then the conclusion must hold exceptionlessly as well. But the question before us today is: who counts as a moral agent in the act of abortion? Who shares the responsibility for its wickedness? And the answer is the same as for any other action: those who knowingly and freely conduct themselves so as to make this action possible, those who participate, who take part, who collaborate, in the action.

You notice that I did not say: those who *desire* a given action to take place are morally responsible for it. Desire that an action occur does not implicate one in its occurrence unless one chooses to do something that will

> *"The Right to Choose the moral object in dispute—the death of the innocent—is indefensible."*

help it occur. By the same token, if a man desires that a certain action not occur, but freely and knowingly acts in such a way that it will, he does share moral responsibility for the action. An officer in the Nazi SS may have been "personally opposed" to the Holocaust, he may have desired that the destruction of innocent Jews not happen; but if he served in the machinery of destruction, knowing the purpose to which the machinery was put, he was complicit in the act, he was morally responsible.

Sentimentally perhaps it makes a difference whether the SS officer operated a gas chamber at Auschwitz or simply rubber-stamped papers in a well-lit office in Berlin to the sound of Wolfgang Mozart coming over the radio; morally it makes no difference whatsoever. The pertinent categories for moral responsibility are knowledge and freedom: Do I know what's going on? Am I free to oppose wrongdoing?

Who Shares Responsibility?

Who then shares moral responsibility for abortion? Those who freely and knowingly act in a way that will make it possible. Even if a person desires that abortions not occur, should he deliberately provide a condition for abortions to happen, he shares responsibility for them. Providing funds for abortion providers to operate abortion services or to counsel abortion is obviously supplying a condition for abortions to happen, because abortions and abortion counseling cost money. Those who freely and knowingly fund abortion providers must accept moral responsibility for the death of the innocent.

At this point the objection will be raised to my treatment: What you say may be true as far as it goes, but this is not a fair description of funding that derives from global, umbrella charitable organizations. You have

> *"Should [someone] deliberately provide a condition for abortions to happen, he shares responsibility for them."*

wrongly described the act of the financial contributor. If I donate some money to an organization in order that it will do good things with my contribution, and I make my wishes plain about which things I consider good, and the good things the charity funds far outnumber the bad, how can I be responsible for the bad actions I reject? Now this is a serious objection that an intelligent person can make with good will, but it involves the rejection of a principle that is absolutely central, crucial, to a system of universal reasoned morality.

The traditional axiom that expresses this principle runs in Latin: *malum ex quocumque defectu*, which means "wrong comes from any defect whatever." That is, when we are contemplating the action of some agent, we are obliged to judge it wrong as soon as we identify a morally significant defect in the agent's motivation—either in his means or his ends—and here the term "defect" means an intention to act contrary to a relevant and forceful moral norm. No amount of good motivations and good intentions can outweigh a single significant flaw in the contemplated action.

Think of it this way. Suppose we're dealing with a notorious wife-beater who lives next door. One day he approaches us to ask for $20 with which to buy a baseball bat. Suspicious, we ask him whether he intends to harm his wife with the bat. He admits that he intends to kill her with it, but goes on to say that he intends to use it for many other purposes as well, purposes we admit to be innocent and even wholesome, such as hitting fungoes to kids during Little League practice: moreover, he insists, the amount of time and the number of occasions he will spend working with youth will *far* outweigh the time and exertion spent engaged in actions we object to, so we have no moral ground for withholding the $20. Now obviously this is moral nonsense, and it is no good making a little speech to ourselves ("I am giving this money for Little League") that absolves us of complicity in wickedness. If we freely and knowingly engage in an act that makes evil possible, there is no aggregate of attendant good effects that removes or diminishes our complicity and our blame.

> *"We cannot segregate good from bad by inspecting our own desires and concluding that . . . we did not* **wish** *those abortions to occur that we helped make possible."*

By the same token, if we contribute money to keep open an abortion clinic, even if that clinic performs services that are morally neutral or good (such as pregnancy testing or Pap smears) in addition to abortions, we cannot segregate good from bad by inspecting our own desires and concluding that, after all, we did not *wish* those abortions to occur that we helped make possible.

Now suppose, after we've refused to buy a bat for our wife-beating neighbor, he comes to us again and says, "Alright, I agree that there are differences of moral opinion about wife-battering and I won't ask you to buy me a bat. Could you please give me $20 to pay my heating-oil bill?" Obviously there is nothing immoral about heating a house, and contributing financially to heating expense might seem innocent enough. But when we quiz our neighbor on his intent to bat his wife to death he admits his plan is still on. "But you needn't worry about your own involvement," he assures us, "I promise the bat won't be paid for out of my utilities account but out of my recreation budget. In fact, you can bring in any auditor you want to prove to your own satisfaction that your $20 won't go toward the bat."

Paying for Death

Do we accept this dodge? Of course not. Provided the murderer perseveres in his stated intention to kill, and needs money to accomplish his end, ANY expense we relieve him of (that he'd have to pay anyway) makes us complicit in the contemplated murder. It is folly to pretend that strictly audited accounting procedures have any moral bearing whatsoever in this case. As long as a murderer has any discretion over his income, and has any income besides what we give him, any donation we directly or indirectly provide to him helps to make his murders possible. All villains, after all, have innocent expenses as well as nefarious ones.

I hope the application to charitable funding of abortion providers is clear enough. Morally it makes no difference whether an agency relieves an abortionist of his light bill or his secretarial expense or the cost of the apple juice for the post-surgical blood sugar boost. If you pay for his Kleenex you're paying for death. To claim otherwise is a scam and a scandal. Nor is it reasonable to think that channeling monies from charitable agencies solely into referral or counseling or family-planning offices makes the slightest difference from pumping them directly into dilation and curettage. This is important: we do *not* have to assume there will be any fiddling of accounts; the financial procedures may be flawlessly and scrupulously observed. But if there are any sources of funding shared between the soft end and the sharp end of a reproductive health service, and any discretion in the use of income, avoidance of moral culpability for funding is a fiction.

But wait a minute: Is it not the case that we have a moral duty to act charitably, to provide for the poor and the weak according to our means? And isn't it the case that financial donation to agencies engaged in serving the poor and unfortunate is an exercise of this charity, a way of discharging this duty? The answer to both questions is yes. Does it follow, however, that our duty to charity permits us to discharge our responsibilities by directing our alms through funding agencies that disburse monies to organizations engaged in systematic homicide? By no means. It is good to remember here that while a negative moral norm (like, "You shall not kill the innocent") holds *semper et ad semper*, always and on every occasion, positive moral norms (e.g., "Provide for the poor") hold *semper sed non ad semper*; they are always in force but require further moral judgment as to the times, places, and circumstances of their application.

> *"If you pay for [an abortionist's] Kleenex you're paying for death. To claim otherwise is a scam and a scandal."*

In particular, a positive moral norm can never be honored in such a way that an exceptionless negative moral norm is violated. You cannot observe the positive moral norm that says Feed Your Children by slaying your neighbors and violating the negative norm forbidding homicide of the innocent. By the same token, you cannot morally provide for the poor and disabled in a way that involves, directly or indirectly, the taking of unborn life through abortion.

An Erroneous Assumption

The waters are muddied here by the erroneous assumption, sometimes abetted by the propaganda of the charitable organizations themselves, that the poor and vulnerable will suffer if donations are re-routed because of moral objections to the executive policy of the charity. There are two responses to be made here. On the one hand, it should be pointed out that this consideration cuts two ways, that it ought to make directors of the charity loath to fund a morally defective or questionable agency out of their putative concern for the greater good. On the other hand it must be said that, as an inducement for potential donors to pony up their contributions in defiance of their own ethical objections, this consideration would be plausible if and only if there were no way of directing alms to the needy except through the umbrella organization in question—and of course this simply isn't the case.

Everyone has the freedom to discharge his obligations to charity by "rifle-shot" donation, that is, by targeting a specific agency with a wholesome, beneficent, morally praiseworthy purpose and giving money and other kinds of assistance directly to that agency. In addition, rifle-shot donation has the twin effect of making the recipient agency more responsive to the moral and social concerns of the donor than is possible through donation by means of pooled funds, while it heightens the interest and knowledge of the donor in the social goods served by his targeted agency. And of course, nothing whatsoever prevents a moral dissenter from a pooled-fund program from giving as much or more than his customary money to meals-on-wheels, or to programs for the retarded, or to a cancer-research hospital.

To accuse those who choose alternate funding routes for their alms of neglecting the needy, when the choice for the alternate route is motivated by ethical repugnance to institutionalized homicide, is stark moral nonsense.

Moral Pressure

Is it really so difficult? If any other instance of institutionalized homicide were involved—if the controversy concerned social agencies that aspired to execute runaway children, or eliminate the homeless by putting them through gas chambers, or reduce non-European races by paramilitary death squads—would we even hesitate in our deliberation? Would we let ourselves even for a moment be inclined toward a donor-designation program that funded these procedures but allowed us to earmark our own contributions for non-homicidal purposes? Wouldn't the smallest taint, the remotest hint of association with such enterprises utterly damn any organization that solicited our donations, regardless of the nobility of the causes for which they promised to apply them? Would we accept anything less than full repudiation and compensation before we even consented to listen to such an appeal?

> *"You cannot morally provide for the poor and disabled in a way that involves . . . the taking of unborn life."*

It wasn't that long ago that the heaviest moral pressure was brought to bear on public institutions such as universities to divest themselves of stocks they held in companies that did business in South Africa, because of South Africa's policy of racial apartheid, even though appeals were made by many opposed to apartheid that divestiture would cause great economic distress to precisely those people the moral activists were trying to help. The standard response was that no price can be put on moral integrity. If this reasoning applies to the injustice of apartheid, surely it must apply *a fortiori* [more certainly] to abortion?

> *"If the controversy concerned social agencies that aspired to execute runaway children . . . would we even hesitate in our deliberation?"*

Is there not a fundamental inconsistency at the bottom of this controversy? On one hand we have appeals made to our humanity, our sense of compassion for the handicapped and our protectiveness toward the weak; on the other monies are asked for the elimination of human problems through the elimination of problem humans. On the one hand, our hearts are warmed by pictures and stories of those who have struggled against adversity in heroic ways to better not only their lives but ours; on the other we are asked to help ensure that some never even have the chance to struggle. Charitable solicitations bring us face to face with people who are less than perfect physically, mentally, and emotionally, and who challenge us to expand our notion of community and our own generosity; our vision of humanity is thereby enlarged.

On the other hand we are offered a picture of what Planned Parenthood foundress Margaret Sanger called "a race of thoroughbreds": that is, life, happiness and prosperity for the fit, an early surgical death for those who aren't; our vision of humanity is narrowed, brutally. If someone were to try to make us believe that we can't say yes to one picture without saying yes to another, would we really want to listen to him at all? Would we trust him with the things and persons we loved? Would we *pay* him to fix our broken world for us?

Donations to charity are not compulsory. They are free acts, deliberate choices, for which we must accept full moral responsibility—because, after all, we become the people we are, for better or for worse, through our morally significant free choices. When we freely choose to fund abortionists, we have freely joined ourselves to their inequity. It's unsettling, but true: morally speaking, you become what you pay for.

Abortion Is a
Moral Choice

by Paul Savoy

About the author: *Paul Savoy is an appellate attorney in Walnut Creek, California, and a former law professor at Southwestern University in Los Angeles and the University of California at Davis.*

Not since the Civil War has a conflict of moral values so radically transformed the social role of an entire class of Americans or so dramatically shifted the tectonic plates of national politics. Unlike the issues of slavery or segregation, however, the abortion dilemma has acquired all the attributes of a spiritual enigma. It is as if the morality of abortion ultimately depended on answers to the most baffling and perhaps unanswerable questions about "the concept of existence, of meaning, of the universe, and of the mystery of human life," as Justices Sandra Day O'Connor, Anthony Kennedy, and David Souter put it in 1992 in a joint opinion announcing a 5-to-4 decision that reaffirmed *Roe v. Wade*, while sidestepping "the profound moral and spiritual implications of terminating a pregnancy."

Rethinking Basic Assumptions

Confronting these moral and spiritual issues will pose the most serious challenge yet to the new politics of meaning articulated by [Hillary Rodham Clinton] in a speech at the University of Texas in which she summoned the nation to embrace what is "morally and ethically and spiritually correct" as a basis for public policy. If a woman's right to terminate a pregnancy is to be based on widely shared notions of morality and social justice, as it must if universal access to abortion services is to become public policy [within a national health care plan], abortion rights advocates will have to rethink the most basic assumptions about what it means for a woman to claim such a right.

Contrary to the prevailing orthodoxy of abortion rights doctrine, the right to terminate a pregnancy actually has very little to do with a right of procreation or

Excerpted from Paul Savoy, "The Coming New Debate on Abortion," *Tikkun*, September/October 1993. Reprinted from TIKKUN MAGAZINE, A BI-MONTHLY JEWISH CRITIQUE OF POLITICS, CULTURE, AND SOCIETY. Subscriptions are $31.00 per year from TIKKUN, 251 West 100th Street, 5th floor, New York, NY 10025.

reproductive freedom, or what the Supreme Court has broadly characterized as "the right of the individual, married or single, to be free from unwarranted governmental intrusion into matters so fundamentally affecting a person as the decision whether to bear or beget a child." Except in cases of coercive sex, women in America did not need a ruling from the Supreme Court to establish a right to decide "whether to bear or beget a child." Women were always free to decide not to have children by not having sex. Indeed, the feminists who preceded Margaret Sanger advocated reproductive freedom primarily through sexual abstinence, although given the extent to which women have long been subjected to unwanted sex, abstinence all too often has been an unrealistic alternative.

What the Supreme Court, in effect, has recognized over the last quarter of a century in its rulings on birth control and abortion is a constitutional right of women to have sex for pleasure rather than procreation as part of a more general freedom from sexual subjugation. To be sure, no lawyer was about to get up before the Supreme Court and argue that what the Constitution protects is a fundamental right of women to a more liberated sex life, if the Court pleases. But sexual equality for women is exactly what legal access to the Pill was all about. (Condoms had always been available to men as a means of preventing sexually transmitted diseases.) And, aside from cases of rape and other kinds of coercive sex, or when a pregnancy threatens a woman's life or health, what else is abortion but a bloody and messy means of insuring a woman's right to have sex without having any more children than she wants?

The Right to Sexual Happiness

Since there is no fail-safe method of contraception (43 percent of unintended pregnancies occur in women using birth control, according to the Alan Guttmacher Institute), the only way, other than abortion, that women could participate equally with men in the economic life of the nation would be to submit to sterilization or to live as secular nuns. How, in the wake of the sexual revolution of the sixties, state bans on birth control and abortion could have escaped scrutiny as a discriminatory restraint on the erotic life of American women would be incomprehensible without the benefit of insight into the ability of the legal mind to contemplate two inextricably linked ideas without ever relating one to the other. Within a period of less than ten years—between 1965, when the Supreme Court handed down its first birth control decision, and 1973, when *Roe* was decided—the Court had legalized the sexual revolution without so much as a nod of acknowledgment that its rulings had anything to do with the liberation of women as sexual beings.

"What the Supreme Court... has recognized... is a constitutional right of women to have sex for pleasure."

Talk about a right to "procreate," or a right to "bear" or "beget" a child, or a right of women to "control their reproductive systems" gives an aura of respectability to the underlying right to sexual pleasure and autonomy by wrapping arguments about birth control and abortion in the sanitized language of a standard medical text on gynecology and obstetrics. But it is all beside the

> *"Treating the unborn child as a person . . . actually exposes the abortion-is-murder argument as a radical failure of moral reasoning."*

point. However artfully the justices may have packaged the right to abortion as an aspect of privacy under the Fourteenth Amendment, the real meaning of *Roe* and its reaffirmation in 1992 in *Planned Parenthood v. Casey* is inescapable: Life, liberty, and the pursuit of happiness must include—as Sigmund Freud argued so convincingly in *Civilization and Its Discontents*—the right to *sexual* happiness.

The extent to which the issue of female sexuality has been obscured [since *Roe*] in legal and political debates about "privacy" and "choice" attests to our continuing inability as a society to talk openly about sexual behavior, particularly the sexual behavior of women. But most of all, the suppression of the sexual issue suggests that for all the energy both sides have spent on debating the right to an abortion, we will simply not talk about it honestly, at least not in public, and certainly not in court. Finding a new and more honest way of thinking and talking about the abortion issue is important for reasons beyond the legal scholar's demand for intellectual candor. If the country is ever to find a common moral ground for resolving the abortion issue, the people will have to take back the conversation from the lawyers and the professional advocates, and start talking about sex and murder.

A Failure of Moral Reasoning

Is abortion murder? It is generally assumed, even by pro-choice advocates, that if the fetus is a person with an individual right to life, then abortion is murder. Justice Harry Blackmun, in his opinion for the Court in *Roe*, had no doubt about the validity of this assumption. "If this suggestion of personhood is established," Blackmun wrote, "the [pro-choice] case collapses, for the fetus' right to life is then guaranteed specifically by the [Fourteenth] Amendment." Yet it is not exactly clear how one gets from the premise that a fetus is a person to the conclusion that abortion is murder. Perhaps the step appears so simple and obvious those on both sides of the debate assume that no explanation is required. The step is neither easy nor obvious, however. And if we subject it to closer moral scrutiny, we shall find that we are not only inclined to reject it, but that treating the unborn child as a person with an individual right to life, far from conceding victory to the pro-life lobby, actually exposes the abortion-is-murder argument as a radical failure of moral reasoning. Indeed, it is the unwillingness of abortion rights advocates to face up to the issue of abortion in the moral terms that pro-lifers have posed it that has substantially contributed to the moral vulnerability of the pro-choice position.

More than twenty years ago, before the Supreme Court decided *Roe v. Wade*, Judith Jarvis Thomson, a philosophy professor at the Massachusetts Institute of Technology, offered an analogy to counter the image of woman as Terminator. In an article in *Philosophy and Public Affairs*, Thomson asked the reader to imagine waking up one morning and finding oneself in bed with a famous and unconscious violinist suffering from a fatal kidney ailment.

You discover, to your dismay, that the circulatory system of the unconscious violinist has been connected to your healthy kidneys by means of a tube, a feat accomplished while you slept so that you had in no way consented to the procedure. You had simply been selected by the Society of Music Lovers, because of your blood type and other favorable conditions, to serve as a kind of human dialysis machine. If you were then to demand that you be immediately disconnected from the violinist, the attending physician might reply with an argument that is familiar to participants in the abortion debate: The violinist is a *person*, and since disconnecting his circulatory system from your kidneys would result in his death, it cannot be permitted. Moreover, you cannot plead self-defense since the violinist is unconscious and not personally guilty of any aggression against you. Unplugging him would therefore constitute murder.

Such an argument, Professor Thomson suggested, would strike most readers as ridiculous. Yet it is,

> *"No one has the right to use another's body as a life support system without her consent."*

in principle, indistinguishable from the abortion-is-murder argument. Whatever the imperfections in Thomson's lucid analogy—some might argue that a woman who voluntarily engages in intercourse is responsible for the life she conceives—the metaphor of pregnant woman as human dialysis machine succeeds in making one point perfectly clear: An abortion is closer to the refusal to allow one's body to be used as a life support system than it is to an ax murder by the local butcher.

The Alien Metaphor

Another metaphor that counters the devaluation of women by anti-abortion forces can be found in *Alien*, that ultimate sci-fi horror story of the reproductive cycle. In the film, the offspring of an unwanted pregnancy is portrayed as an intruder into the last frontier of inner space, resembling a penis with teeth bursting out of the chest cavity in a kind of equal-opportunity Caesarean. Has there ever been a more graphic statement of the unspoken facts of fertility? "Many women, good mothers, who become unwillingly pregnant, speak of the fetus they carry as an invader, a tumor, a thing to be removed," Sallie Tisdale wrote in a sobering meditation in *Vogue* on the reproductive experience as an act of invasion as much as love. Whatever moral status may be ascribed to an unborn child—alien invader, innocent human being, or a person with a right to life—no one has the right to use another's body as a life support system without her consent. It is time to recognize the murder case against abortion for what it is: a stupendous vaudeville of moral folly.

But are pro-choice advocates, in their strenuous defense of the right not to sustain unborn life, committing another kind of moral folly? Those of us who oppose legal restrictions on abortion but wish to address the issue as a moral question, as a decision

> *"The abortion debate must become part of the larger national conversation about the right to guaranteed health care."*

made in the context of a morally lived life, must ask ourselves whether failing to nurture the life of an unborn child simply perpetuates the pervasive ethos of selfishness in our society. How can communities of care and mutual aid treat the refusal of aid to unborn life as a choice worthy of moral respect?

One answer is that the question mistakenly assumes that acting selfishly is always immoral. To deny the ailing violinist the benefit of my kidneys is no doubt a selfish act. It would be a marvelous act of caring, if not saintliness, were I to spend the next nine months keeping the violinist alive by letting him remain hooked up to my body. But should I decide to unplug the violinist, my decision could hardly be characterized as immoral, even though disconnecting him resulted in his death.

This is not to deny the value of nurturing human life. It is merely to say that the debate about the morality of abortion must undergo a change of venue: from the ethical framework that governs the duty to refrain from killing, to the community of values that informs the duty of self-sacrifice. If the kind of self-sacrifice that pro-life ethics would impose on a pregnant woman were enforced in a nondiscriminatory manner by a Uniform Code of Altruism, we would have to construct a barbed-wire fence around the United States and declare it a federal penitentiary.

A Perversion of Health Policy

Defending abortion as a moral choice means understanding a woman's right to terminate a pregnancy not merely as a "negative" freedom from involuntary servitude, but also as an affirmative right to the doctor a pregnant woman needs to make her choice real. The objection to denying public funding for abortion or excluding abortion coverage from national health care is not only that it discriminates against indigent women. The more glaring objection is that it involves an unprecedented perversion of public health policy. No rational legislator would seriously consider denying public funding for the medical treatment of injuries resulting from a failure to use seat belts as a means of promoting highway safety, or denying smokers treatment for lung cancer as a way of discouraging the use of tobacco. Yet Congress and state legislatures, with the approval of the Supreme Court, continue to use public health policy as a means of promoting childbirth over abortion by funding the former but not the latter.

This depraved use of health policy escapes moral scrutiny because the prevailing model of rights theory treats abortion as a "private" decision, or a matter of conscience, like choosing prayer over surgery. The penchant for privatizing reproductive choice has rendered the right to abortion virtually meaningless for women who are poor, or who live in communities where abortion services are simply unavailable. If abortion is to become accessible to all women without regard to economic status or geographic location, the abortion debate must become part of the larger national conversation about the right to guaranteed health care. The argument for abortion coverage as part of a national health plan is unlikely to prevail, however, until a convincing case can be made for abortion as a moral choice. And this will not happen until moral discourse moves from the metaphor of abortion as physician-assisted killing to the idea of abortion as medical emancipation from forced labor.

The overarching issue, as then-Judge Ruth Bader Ginsburg [now a U.S. Supreme Court justice] noted in a 1984 speech at the University of North Carolina Law School, is not only coercion of a woman's body for a span of nine months. "Also in the balance is a woman's autonomous charge of her full life's course . . . her ability to stand in relation to man, society, and the state as an independent, self-sustaining, equal citizen." Addressing the issue of public funding and the Supreme Court's failure to require public financing of abortions for poor women, Judge Ginsburg said, "If the Court had acknowledged a woman's equality aspect . . . to the abortion issue, a majority might have seen the public assistance cases as instances in which, borrowing a phrase from Justice John Paul Stevens, the sovereign had violated its 'duty to govern impartially.'"

The Rights of Men

A new conversation about abortion, if it is to focus on equal rights for women, must also address the rights of men. Reframing the right to an abortion in terms that make explicit the issues of sexual pleasure and personal responsibility—as a right to choose whether to assume responsibility for a human life conceived out of sexual desire without the desire for children—makes clear that men too must be afforded rights with respect to some aspects of choice.

> *"There are many single males who have sex for pleasure, without procreative intent. Requiring child support from these men is unfair."*

The most neglected matter of choice for men— perhaps the only major crisis men go through today without receiving any support—is the dilemma a man faces when his sexual partner decides to continue an unplanned pregnancy to term and he does not wish to become a father. The idea that a man should have the right to refuse to support a child he did not choose to bring into the world has not only been rejected by the courts; it is a notion that is regarded as morally incorrect on both sides of the political aisle. When it comes to defending voluntary motherhood and the right to an abortion, thoughtful men and women reach for the Bill of Rights and Justice Blackmun's scholarly opinion in *Roe*. When the principle at stake is one of voluntary fatherhood, a man who chooses not to support a child resulting from an unplanned pregnancy which a woman decides to carry to term is indicted as a member of the class of "deadbeat dads" and remanded to that rogue's gallery of sexual stereotypes and cultural prejudice that includes the unborn-baby killer and the murderous mom.

To be sure, as the Supreme Court has noted, "it is the woman who physically bears the child and who is the more directly and immediately affected by the pregnancy." Because men and women are not similarly situated with respect to pregnancy, the Court has correctly concluded that a husband has no right to veto or even receive notice of his wife's decision to abort a pregnancy. When what is at stake is not a woman's choice regarding motherhood, but a man's choice not to become a father, however, control of the woman's body is not at issue.

The considerations that militate against allowing a man power over his partner's decision whether to become a parent, therefore, do not provide a justification for denying a man the power to control his own destiny as a parent and to choose whether he will support the child his partner unilaterally decides to bear. What makes the issue of prenatal choice problematical for men is whether society's strong interest in assuring adequate financial support for dependent children is sufficient to outweigh a man's claim to an equal voice in the decision to become a father.

> *"The prevailing model of fatherhood gives too much power to women over men's procreation."*

Unmarried Men

However defensible the system of child-support laws may be for divorced men who married with the intention of having children, the system is frequently discriminatory and unjust when unmarried men are involved. Although there are substantial numbers of unmarried males—including adolescents—who engage in sex with the intention of impregnating women as a source of male pride, with little or no consideration for the consequences, there are many single males who have sex for pleasure, without procreative intent. Requiring child support from these men is unfair, and for those who can hardly command more than the minimum wage and face going to jail whether working or not, the penalty for sexual liberation is excessively harsh. While there are no perfect answers to the question of how and when during the course of his partner's unplanned pregnancy a man can effectively manifest a choice not to become a parent, the prevailing model of fatherhood gives too much power to women over men's procreation, just as the old model gave too much power to men over women's procreation.

Thinking in Terms of Duties

The entire debate about reproductive freedom needs to be recast in terms of duties and mutual responsibilities, a language that is closer to the way ordinary people think about this issue than the strident rhetoric of rights and clashes of rights crafted by lawyers and judges. It is one of the inherent deficiencies of traditional rights theory that it makes reproductive freedom sound like a right of women to murder and men to abandon innocent children rather than freedom from a duty of compulsory parenthood. As Harvard law professor Mary Ann Glendon has suggested in her book *Rights Talk* and elsewhere, we need a well-developed public language of responsibility to match our language of rights.

Indeed, it is far more common and natural today to talk about responsibilities rather than rights in the bedroom. We have gone beyond the idea of a right to contraceptives introduced by the Supreme Court in 1965 and come to think of contraception as more of a duty than a right. What we mean now by a "right" to contraception actually refers to the duty of government to provide access to birth control so that men and women can make responsible decisions about sex.

With respect to the "right" to an abortion, it makes far more sense to ask whether a woman is willing and prepared to assume responsibility for another human being, with all that implies for a lifetime of being a parent, than it does to ask whether a woman has the right to terminate an unwanted pregnancy, as if she were seeking a license for fetal assassination. If there is a "right" to choose, it is the right of access not only to abortion services as part of a comprehensive national health-care plan, but to a broad spectrum of social supports including child care, paid parental leave, family allowances, and other benefits for parents and children that are essential to making the choice about motherhood—and fatherhood—real. In place of the existing adversarial framework of legal theory that pits the rights of the fetus against the rights of the woman, the rights of women against the rights of men, in isolated spheres of privacy, we need to start a new conversation about our responsibilities to one another and how as a society we can build communities of care and concern capable of sustaining the idea of parenthood—for both men and women—as a voluntary relationship based on bonds of love, not biology.

> *"We need to start a new conversation about our responsibilities to one another."*

The debate over abortion will continue, not because its resolution depends upon the answers to some spiritual mystery about when life begins, but because abortion has become the Gettysburg of sexual politics. It is the battlefield for establishing sex as a basic human need and a human right without regard to gender, for redefining the nature of parenthood, and ultimately for rethinking the limits of individual and collective responsibility for nurturing human life. It is easy for Americans to talk about rights. It is harder to talk about responsibilities, and most difficult to talk about them in a way that frees the moral imagination from the prejudices and illusions that affect our thinking about sex and parenthood, about gender and equality, about the giving and taking of human life.

Abortion Can Be a Moral Sacrifice

by Frederick Turner

About the author: *Frederick Turner is Founders Professor of Arts and Humanities at the University of Texas at Dallas.*

Before we talk, let's get something clear. I'm a doctor, and the facts I'll be mentioning are backed up by my expertise as a doctor. But the intent of the law under which we're going to be talking is basically moral, and I'm no more an expert on morality than you are. That isn't to say morality isn't important, or that you and I can't get it right; in fact, we may be better at it than the authorities.

I'm supposed to give you some facts, so let's get it over with. You're in the early part of the second trimester, so that if we do the abortion, we'll be killing an organism inside you that is potentially human and is shaped like a human baby but has a degree of organized sensitivity and awareness somewhere between that of a sheep and that of your own lower spine. It's pretty small—smaller than your fist—and once it's dead, we'll remove it.

Two Ends of the Scale

Those are the facts. Now for the difficult part. Suppose your baby were at term and in the birth canal. What you'd have there would be a human being, with rights that need to be protected. Some premature babies can survive when they're three months early. If we killed a preemie, the law would call it murder. They'd be right, wouldn't they? But let's look at the other end of the scale. I'm scratching my hand, as you can see. I just removed, and killed, some hundreds of skin cells. Each of them has a full set of my chromosomes. In a few decades we'll probably have the biotechnology to clone up one of those skin cells into a perfect baby twin of me. So in a sense, I've just killed a potentially viable human life—and yet we both know that it was a completely trivial act.

In the hours after conception, abortion is utterly trivial; nine months later it's as serious a crime as there is. And for all our wishful talk of "trimesters" and "viability," the process between the beginning and the end is completely smooth—there is no dramatic moment of metamorphosis from scrap of tissue to human being. Many classical cultures abandoned babies even after they were born: they drew the line between what's human and what's not in a different place. And they weren't bad people.

Drawing a Moral Line

So how do *we* draw the line? Right now it's up to you. You're the best judge; you're the one on the ground, in the trenches, dealing with the situation.

Have you noticed that when the pro-life people are talking about near-term babies and murder, you can see the honesty in their eyes and hear it in their voices? But then when you ask them about two-day-old embryos, you see their eyes shift to and fro and their faces get hard and their voices get that honking sound, and you know they're lying, and ashamed, and ashamed of their shame. And you know that if they had the chance they could be cruel, even bloody, in defense of their assertions—because they fear they'd fall apart without them. And the same thing with pro-choice activists—talk to them about the first trimester and you can see all the decent truth and honor and courage in them. But then you ask about the last couple of months, and you get the scared eyes, the twisted mouth, the willingness to lie and lie, the pretended casualness in the tone of voice, the false air of certainty, the shame, the sadistic cruelty in defense of their weakness, in defense of what those poor folks think are their nasty secrets.

> *"In the hours after conception, abortion is utterly trivial; nine months later it's as serious a crime as there is."*

The point is, people sometimes just can't deal with the idea of morality as a gradual slope. They have to draw a line; they have to be sure. Both sides want it to be easy. As you already know, it's not.

But I think there is a way to understand it— a way that's helped me, anyway. I was visiting my sister's lab at the National Institutes of Health [NIH] one time—her research has probably saved dozens of lives—and they were using a cat that would not survive the procedure. It was a crucial experiment, the cat was going to be put to sleep at the pound anyway, and it was unconscious and feeling no pain. The people at the lab were very businesslike. But something went wrong with the equipment, and it looked as if they weren't going to get any usable results from the experiment. My sister didn't make a big deal of it but just said quietly, "It's tough on the cat." The point was, the experiment was worth doing even if experiments sometimes fail; the cat, though it didn't have any choice in the matter, was contributing to an advance that was in the interests of all life, human and otherwise. The scientists who work in these labs call the use of these animals a "sacrifice."

See, at some point we have to connect with the rest of nature, and it always in-

56

volves death. Our immune systems are killing billions of little beasties right now. When we eat, we must kill, even if we're vegetarians. Animals kill and eat one another—the prey is sacrificed to the generally faster metabolism, smarter intelligence, and more sensitive social system of the predator. There's no getting away from the food chain. That doesn't mean we can't make distinctions. I think most people these days would agree that one wouldn't kill a higher animal—a chimp or a dolphin—without a pretty big reason, like saving human lives. With lower animals, like cows or pigs, most of us

> *"There's a stage when the human fetus has something like a gill; perhaps it has as much of a soul then as a fish does."*

feel that it's permissible to eat them, though some of us have qualms and others will eat them only on important or festive occasions, believing that one shouldn't sacrifice them for nothing. Eating a still lower animal, like a chicken or a fish, doesn't bother most of us, and we feel even less anxiety about eating eggs and milk and vegetables.

In other words, nature—and our own inherited common sense—makes distinctions of value according to how high an organism is on the scale of evolution, and implicitly recognizes that the lower can be legitimately sacrificed to the higher. Biologists used to believe that the stages of fetal growth mimicked the stages of evolution by which our ancestors became human. It doesn't work as a usable scientific idea anymore, but it still makes sense in some other ways. There's a stage when the human fetus has something like a gill; perhaps it has as much of a soul then as a fish does. Later there's a stage when it's still pretty hard to distinguish a photo of it from one of a chicken embryo. Maybe it's about as important as a live chicken at that point. And so on.

The Sacrifice of Abortion

It might help if you think of abortion as a sacrifice—the later the abortion, the heavier and graver the reason had better be, and the more sacred the whole thing is. And maybe it's sacred because of its connection with sex and reproduction—all of nature seems to rise to a pitch of beauty and intensity and expense when it comes to reproduction. Think of the mating colors and mating dances of fish and birds and mammals. But just because reproduction is sacred, that doesn't mean that it's not wasteful. The male human wastes millions of sperm, and the female wastes a valuable egg every month. Spontaneous miscarriages are wasteful natural sacrifices. If you abort a fetus intentionally for a good reason, you're in accord with nature's own tradition of sacred sacrificial waste.

But the way I look at it, a sacrifice demands respect. It had better be done in a good cause, or it will come back to haunt us. That's why we often make a beautiful communal ritual out of sacrifice, even if it's a highly symbolic one; think of a Buddhist burning a candle or a Catholic priest breaking a bit of bread—or a

scientist at NIH giving a curt little epitaph for a cat. And there's another implication to the idea of abortion as a sacrifice: if it's done right and done in a good
cause, it can be something much better than just making the best of a bad situation, a nasty episode to be forgotten as soon as possible. What traditional religious ritual tells us is that sacrifice can be enriching, creative, evoking powers
and values that can contribute great gifts to human existence. Isn't it possible
that abortion, in the right circumstances, for the right reasons and intentions,
could be like that?

Our society doesn't provide us much in the way of ritual to deal with this difficult moment you have before you. But maybe you—and I—can take advantage of this blundering, well-intentioned law, and make our little talk into the
beginning of a proper rite of sacrifice. Maybe you—and I—can take on a bit
more moral and spiritual weight through this work we're doing.

The Roman Catholic Church Historically Condoned Early Abortions

by Stephen T. Asma

About the author: *Stephen T. Asma is a humanities professor at Columbia College in Chicago.*

On a street corner in downtown Chicago, an elderly woman lurches toward me with pious intensity and presses a pamphlet into my hand. Such an occurrence is so frequent that one fails to register the event until later. Eventually, I take stock of the day's "literature." In fact, nothing quite lifts the spirits like perusing the abusive ultimatums and grave injunctions contained in these propaganda leaflets.

A few days ago, I was enjoying my three-by-five-inch "Practical Guide for the Sacrament of Penance in the '90s" when an irony of the strongest magnitude struck me. The "guide" is a series of questions that the devotee must inquire of his or her own conscience. Just after asking myself whether I had "physically injured or killed anyone" recently, I read that "regarding abortion, check with your priest to see if you were automatically excommunicated." Apparently, canon 1398 states that persons party to an abortion are automatically excommunicated. Like most other people forced to endure the interminable discourse concerning abortion, I understand that the Catholic church forms a crucial flank of pro-life ideology. But as I read the pamphlet, Saint Thomas Aquinas leapt to mind—and therein crept the irony.

The *Webster* Case

What does a thirteenth-century saint have to do with contemporary debates over abortion? O ye of little faith: we need look no further than the controversial 1989 Supreme Court case of *Webster* v. *Reproductive Health Services*.

The *Webster* case, you recall, questioned the constitutionality of certain

From "Abortion and the Embarrassing Saint," by Stephen T. Asma, *The Humanist*, May/June 1994. Reprinted with the permission of the American Humanist Association, ©1994.

statutes regulating abortions in Missouri. The restrictions upon abortions (for example, public facilities may not be used for abortions even if no public funds are spent) were upheld by a five-to-four Supreme Court vote. Media coverage of the dissenting votes focused around Justice Harry Blackmun's cryptic "I fear for the future" sermon. But the key passage in the Missouri law was quietly and persistently targeted by Justice John Paul Stevens. The crucial passage—actually contained in the preamble of the Missouri statute—set forth "findings" which stated that the life of each human being "begins at conception" and that "unborn children have protectable interests in life, health, and well-being." In other words, zygotes are people too.

> *"How many . . . 'pro-life' Roman Catholics know that the entire history of their church* **denies** *that the zygote is a person?"*

Justice Stevens argued that the Missouri "findings" were unconstitutional, and he appealed to a remarkable (yet little noticed) argument. At first, his reasoning seems rather academic—indeed, this is undoubtedly why the media centered on Blackmun's more dramatic comments. Had we given Stevens' "illustrational" argument closer examination, however, we would have found it to expose the irony lurking just beneath the surface of pro-life ideology. And guess who Stevens appeals to in his subtle dissent? Why, Saint Thomas Aquinas, of course.

The irony, quite simply, is this: how many clinic-blocking, doctor-harassing, "pro-life" Roman Catholics know that the entire history of their church *denies* that the zygote is a person? Since history can be so painfully embarrassing, I suppose we should all be thankful for that most soothing of afflictions, the short memory.

Official Church Positions

The current official position of the Catholic church is published in the 1987 Vatican-issued *Instruction on Respect for Human Life in Its Origin and on the Dignity of Procreation*. In the *Instruction*, it is stated that "every human being" has a "right to life and physical integrity from the moment of conception until death." Now contrary to most writers and readers of abortion-related discourse, I am not going to line up on either side of this insoluble question (sorry to disappoint the simpleminded dichotomy purveyors). In fact, to leap in at this point, boldly asserting or denying the personhood of the zygote and then weighing that conviction against the woman's personal rights, is precisely the move that has consistently clouded the clear argument of thinkers like Justice Stevens. What I wish to point out, as Stevens subtly attempts to do, is that the official position of the church—from the church's very conception up until Pope Pius IX's 1869 decree [declaring the fetus a person]—held that the fetus did *not* become a person until late in the course of gestation. And this tradition (lasting almost two millennia) of church "findings" should give the modern Catholic some pause over the "eternal veracity" of their current findings. Ask almost any Roman Catholic if the saints believed in personhood at conception, and they will scoff, "Of course." But they would be wrong.

I wish to focus primarily on Saint Thomas, but even earlier church fathers held that "personhood" developed late in the pregnancy. Saint Augustine and Saint Jerome, for example, both believed that destruction of a fetus could not be considered homicide until the fetus had fully formed. Prior to this "full formation," the fetus held no greater moral significance than an irrational animal. That is not to say that the fetus held *no* moral status, for all living things, according to the faithful, are products of God's handiwork and consequently deserving of reverential respect. But this line of thinking (which Ronald Dworkin, in his book *Life's Dominion*, finds more intelligible than other abortion-related arguments) must be understood as quite different from the "personhood argument." It is different because the criteria for moral respect widen radically from the sanctity of "persons" to the sanctity of "life." Moreover, such a broadening of the criteria for moral respect opens the door too widely for the pious believer, who must now sin nightly as he devours his sacred sirloin.

In dredging up the uncomfortable past creeds of Augustine, Jerome, and Aquinas, I am not suggesting that changes in dogma automatically manifest church fallibility. Rather, to expose the irony—indeed, the contradiction—in church doctrines is a crucial first premise in a wider and more important argument about the relation between church and state. It is for this reason that we must visit the embarrassing saint.

> *"The 'soul,' according to Aquinas, is not a friendly ghost that enters the body at birth and departs after death."*

Thomas Aquinas has been the official Catholic theologian for the past 600 years. Aquinas was given the thankless job of making the potentially heretical ideas of Aristotle (then only newly discovered by European intellectuals) consistent with church doctrine. Anyone who doubts his current influence on Christianity need only visit a Catholic college campus, where the mandatory core-curriculum is drenched in Thomistic ideas, or simply ask any priest to recite one of Aquinas' proofs for the existence of God (he will no doubt be able to recite five). The pope himself [John Paul II], in his October 1993 encyclical, cites Aquinas no less than six times.

The Views of Thomas Aquinas

Aquinas, writing in that encyclopedic manner so beloved by philosophical types, has much to say (and many distinctions to draw) concerning just about everything. In his magnum opus, the *Summa Theologica*, he tackles (among many other issues) the formation of the human soul.

Generally speaking, Aquinas has three basic strategies. Faced with a vexing question, he either appeals directly to his reasoning skills (which were, make no mistake, quite awesome), or he appeals to scripture, or he appeals to "The Philosopher." By "The Philosopher," Aquinas—and everybody else at that time—meant Aristotle. In the case of the formation or genesis of the human soul, Aquinas quite rightly defers to the wisdom of "The Philosopher." Appealing to Aristotle on this issue is not merely falling back on the authority of antiquity; it is, in fact, a respectful submission to a renowned specialist. While Aquinas spent most of his time cloistered in classrooms and monks' cells, Aristotle spent most of his time elbow deep in the entrails of animal specimens. In fact, much of Aristotle's careful embryological observations are still completely accurate and insightful. So when Aquinas turned to the issues of fetal development, he did so with Aristotle's biological texts close at hand.

> *"Human ensoulment occurs, according to [Saint Thomas Aquinas], not at conception but at six or eight weeks."*

In the Thomist-Aristotelian tradition, it is the faculty of "reason" that distinguishes humans from all other animals. Reason, then, is the defining essence of what it means to be a human person. The "soul," according to Aquinas, is not a friendly ghost that enters the body at birth and departs after death; it is a principle of life that all animated creatures possess in varying degrees. For example, plants have souls but they are "nutritive souls"—they have the power of growth. Animals have souls that are not only nutritive but also allow them the powers of sensation and locomotion. Human beings, in Aquinas' view, have the nutritive level of soul (because they are alive), the sensate and locomotive levels of soul (because they are animals), and, finally, the rational level of soul (which makes them human—something "more" than animal).

Body and Soul

This Thomistic view of the soul is not the sort of thing most Christians envision when they consider such matters; it seems that the "ghost in the machine" metaphor has taken stronger root in the common consciousness. But the idea of the soul as inseparable from the body (the animating principle of the body) is still very much the official church doctrine. Pope John Paul II, in [his] encyclical, reiterated the Thomist position on the relationship between body and soul. The pope states that a person's "rational soul is *per se et essentialiter* [through itself and in its essence] the form of his body." He then states that "reason and free will are linked with all the bodily and sense faculties." Aquinas draws out this principle to its conclusion when he observes that, if the "bodily and sense faculties" do not develop until the eighth week, then "reason and free will" also do not develop until that time. Consequently, if reason and free will are the defining properties of human persons, then in the first eight weeks of pregnancy no human person per se exists. Obviously, this conclusion remains undrawn for the contemporary Catholic.

The "levels" of soul, according to the Thomist position, develop from lower to higher through the course of fetal development. This temporal development follows the basic embryological law of *epigenesis* (which Aristotle argued for and which modern biology currently affirms). Epigenesis means that embryological development occurs in a pathway from the less specific to the more specific. In other words, in the chronological order of gestation, I was alive (a nutritious blob) before I was an animal (capable of sensation and self-movement), and I was both these things before I developed into a human being (having the faculty of reason). The more "specific" (species-defining) traits develop last in the order of time. Now all this may sound quite antique in tone, but it is only a different way of stating what current biology asserts. Human capacities develop at different times in the course of embryological growth; the finished product is not all there at the outset. Regarding the powers of soul, Aquinas states that "the more imperfect powers precede the others in the order of generation, for the animal is generated before the man."

To be blunt, Aquinas believed that in the course of gestation we are first plants, later become animals, and finally become human persons. If we arrest the development of a human zygote early on, we find, according to Aquinas, a nonspecific animal—or, if the arrest is very early, a nonspecific plant. Human ensoulment occurs, according to the saint, not at conception but at six or eight weeks. This discrepancy—between classical and contemporary Catholic theories of personhood-development—is enough to make the pope cringe.

> *"Christians cannot so easily shout 'heretic' and consign [Aquinas] to burn in some obscure level of hell."*

The Renaissance church even codified the saint's "findings" into laws at the Council of Trent [1545–1563], stating that an individual would not be committing homicide if he or she aborted a fetus prior to its human ensoulment (six to eight weeks). Justice Stevens makes note of the Trent council in his dissenting *Webster* opinion and uses this embarrassing chapter of Catholic theology to make the crucial point about the separation of church and state.

Having acquainted ourselves with Aquinas' theory of "person formation" (a theory which, I hasten to add, might currently land Aquinas in the company of heretics rather than saints), we can turn to the wider and more significant argument. We must ask not whether women's rights outweigh fetuses' rights but whether religious ideology should ever be allowed to dictate law.

Ideology and Secular Law

The current church ideology holds that personhood begins at conception. This ideological (not scientific) "finding" has been written into Missouri law—a secular law which governs not only Christians but Jews, atheists, Muslims, Hindus, and others. But if we want to infuse secular laws with religious convictions, let us see what an alternative set of convictions might produce. We won't pick a different faith, like Hinduism or Buddhism, for that will be too easily dismissed by the Christian right as pagan confusion. Instead, we will pick our alternative set of ideological commitments from the church fathers themselves. Saint Thomas Aquinas' "findings" could just as easily be dressed up into the form of legal statutes (as they in fact were at the Council of Trent), with the added attraction of being founded—unlike the Missouri findings—on some empirical study of biological development. And if the saint's findings were now codified and sanctioned by the state, then abortion up until the eighth week would be entirely justified and protected.

> *"What is currently grounds for automatic excommunication . . . was, under the Council of Trent, entirely permissible."*

Christians, it seems, want *their* religious ideology sanctioned by the state; when "outside" (non-Christian) ideologies are posed, they are often dismissed as heathen and godless. But when a Catholic ideologist of Saint Thomas Aquinas' stature pronounces against the current personhood credo, Christians cannot so easily shout "heretic" and consign him to burn in some obscure level of hell.

Pope John Paul II, in a November 1993 anti-abortion speech given to the U.S. bishops, stated: "Fundamental moral principles, in fact, are an essential ingredient of the formation of public policy, as was clearly understood and intended by your nation's Founding Fathers." But if we take the pope seriously on this point, then we must recognize that the official Catholic "moral principle" at the time of our nation's founding was that abortion was permissible up to the sixth or eighth week of pregnancy. This is in direct conflict with the "fundamental moral principles" of current Catholic thinking—yet the pope seems to suggest that those earlier principles should have been written into law. We must conclude either that the pope is unaware of church history (which is very unlikely) or that he does not mean what he says here.

Therefore, it seems, Christians do not *really* want their ideology sanctioned by the state, for that would entail the inclusion of an embarrassing contradictory tradition. Rather, they really want to have only their most recent visceral responses and intuitional moral impressions stamped onto the gavel of state authority. Opening the door to this sort of idiosyncratic contingency is death to the secular state.

Changes in Sacred Dogma

Of course, today's Catholic, steeped in the American faith in "progress," might simply bite the bullet and dismiss the entire history of the church as wrong and the current belief in "sacred conception" as correct. This attitude to-

The Abortion Controversy

ward church fathers is akin to our position regarding early scientists (for example, geocentrists), thinking them naive and uninformed about later discoveries (heliocentrism). But then the question arises as to how one justifies a complete reversal in church dogma. In science, such a justification is easier to understand, for new instruments are developed, new observations made, new tests devised, and so on. But the "findings" of religious groups have no such tie to empirical data, because religion has to do with matters of the spirit and these are, by definition, not open to scientific method. Science can "progress" because it admits all along that it is only tentative, that new findings can influence commitments; but religious tenets are supposed to be "absolute." When they contradict each other from one era to the next, we cannot call that "progress" but, rather, plain old "politics."

If jurisprudence is based upon religious creed rather than secular reasoning, an alternative and opposing creed—one which, in this case, runs counter to pro-life ideology—could just as easily rise to the level of law. The sweet irony of this particular issue lies in the fact that the alternative creed comes not from *outside* but from *within* the sacred dogma.

What is currently grounds for automatic excommunication, as my Catholic instructional pamphlet assures me, was, under the Council of Trent, entirely permissible. Not only is it impossible for the secular state to mandate the inconsistent beliefs of different faiths (for example, should we all eat pork or abstain?), but the radical inconsistencies *within* a single tradition prove too perilous for constitutionality. If the state took its lead from religious ideology, on what grounds could it arbitrate between, say, Aquinas' abortion-tolerant position and the pope's abortion-intolerant position?

65

The Early Fetus Has No Interests

by Ronald Dworkin

About the author: *Ronald Dworkin is a law professor at New York University and university professor of jurisprudence at Oxford University in England.*

The public argument over abortion has failed to recognize an absolutely crucial distinction. One side insists that human life begins at conception, that a fetus is a person from that moment, that abortion is murder or homicide or an assault on the sanctity of human life. But each of these phrases can be used to describe two very different ideas.

Two Objections to Abortion

First, they can be used to make the claim that fetuses are creatures with interests of their own right from the start, including, preeminently, an interest in remaining alive, and that therefore they have the rights that all human beings have to protect these basic interests, including a right not to be killed. Abortion is wrong in principle, according to this claim, because abortion violates someone's right not to be killed, just as killing an adult is normally wrong because it violates the adult's right not to be killed. I shall call this the *derivative* objection to abortion because it presupposes and is derived from rights and interests that it assumes all human beings, including fetuses, have. Someone who accepts this objection, and who believes that government should prohibit or regulate abortion for this reason, believes that government has a derivative responsibility to protect a fetus.

Familiar Rhetoric

The second claim that the familiar rhetoric can be used to make is very different: that human life has an intrinsic, innate value; that human life is sacred just in itself; and that the sacred nature of a human life begins when its biological life begins, even before the creature whose life it is has movement or sensation or interests or rights of its own. According to this second claim, abortion is wrong in principle because it disregards and insults the intrinsic value, the sacred character, of any stage or form of human life. I shall call this the *detached* objection to abortion, because it does not depend on or presuppose any particular rights or interests. Someone who accepts *this* objection, and argues that abortion should be prohibited or regulated by law for *this* reason, believes that government has a detached responsibility for protecting the intrinsic value of life. . . .

Confusion in Objections Toward Abortion

The idea that abortion is sinful or wicked because human life is sacred is very different from the claim that it is sinful or wicked because a fetus has a right to live. The former offers an argument against abortion that does not in any way presume that a fetus is a person with rights or interests of its own. For just as someone can think it wrong to remove life support from a permanently vegetative patient or to assist a dying cancer patient to kill himself, whether or not death is in the patient's interests, so one can think it wrong to destroy a fetus whether or not a fetus has any interests to protect. The belief that human life in any form has intrinsic, sacred value can therefore provide a reason for people to object violently to abortion, to regard it as wicked in all circumstances, without in any way believing that a tiny collection of cells just implanted in the womb, with as yet no organs or brain or nervous system, is already something with interests and rights. Someone who does not regard a fetus as a person with rights and interests may thus object to abortion just as strenuously as someone who insists it is. But he will object for a different reason and, as I shall try to show, with very different implications for the political question of whether and when the state ought to prohibit or permit abortion.

> *"The idea that abortion is sinful or wicked because human life is sacred is very different from the [derivative] claim."*

The confusion that I believe has poisoned the public controversy about abortion, and made it more confrontational and less open to argument and accommodation than it should be, is the confusion between these two kinds of reasons for believing that abortion is often, perhaps always, morally wrong. The scalding rhetoric of the "pro-life" movement seems to presuppose the derivative claim that a fetus is from the moment of its conception a full moral person with rights and interests equal in importance to those of any other member of the moral community. But very few people—even those who belong to the most vehemently anti-abortion groups—actually believe that, whatever they say. The disagreement that actually divides people is a markedly less polar disagreement about how best to respect a fundamental idea we almost all share in some form: that individual human life is sacred. Almost everyone who opposes abortion really objects to it, as they might realize after reflection, on the detached rather than the derivative ground. They believe that a fetus is a living, growing human creature and that it is intrinsically a bad thing, a kind of cosmic shame, when human life at any stage is deliberately extinguished. . . .

Life Does Not Mean Interests

It is very hard to make any sense of the idea that an early fetus has interests of its own, in particular an interest in not being destroyed, from the moment of its conception.

Not everything that can be destroyed has an interest in not being destroyed, of course. A beautiful sculpture can be smashed, and that would be a terrible insult to the intrinsic value that great works of art embody and also very much against the interests of people who take pleasure in seeing or studying them. But a sculpture has no interests of its own; a savage act of vandalism is not unfair to *it*. Nor is it enough, for something to have interests, that it be alive and in the process of developing into something more mature—it is not against the interests of a baby carrot that it be picked early and brought to the table as a delicacy—nor even that it be something that will naturally develop into something different or more marvelous: a butterfly is much more beautiful than a caterpillar, but it is not better for the *caterpillar* to become one. Nor is it enough, for something to have interests, that it might, if treated in the right way, grow or develop into a human being. Imagine that (as some scientists apparently think conceivable) doctors were able to produce a child from an unfertilized ovum, by parthenogenesis [development of an egg without fertilization]. Menstruation would still not be against an ovum's interests; a woman who used contraception would not be violating some creature's fundamental right every month.

Nor is it even enough, for something to have interests, that it be actually en route to becoming a full human being. Imagine that, just as Dr. Frankenstein reached for the lever that would bring life to the assemblage of body parts on his laboratory table, someone appalled at the experiment smashed the apparatus. That act, whatever we think of it, would not have been harmful or unfair to the assemblage, or against its interests. It might be objected that a newly conceived fetus, unlike an unfertilized ovum or a collection of spare body parts, is growing into a full human being on its own, with no outside help needed. But that isn't true—external help, either from a pregnant woman or from scientific ingenuity, is essential. In any case, the difference is irrelevant to the present question; the collection of body parts wouldn't have interests—stopping the experiment before it came to life wouldn't be harmful to it— even if Dr. Frankenstein had designed the procedure to work automatically unless interrupted, and that automatic procedure had already begun. It makes no sense to suppose that something has interests of *its own*—as distinct from its being important what happens to it—unless it has, or has had, some form of

> *"It is very hard to make any sense of the idea that an early fetus has interests of its own."*

consciousness: some mental as well as physical life.

Creatures that can feel pain have an interest in avoiding it, of course. It is very much against the interests of animals to subject them to pain, in trapping them or experimenting on them, for example. It is also very much against the interests of a fetus with a nervous system sufficiently developed to feel pain to inflict pain on it. But a fetus cannot be aware of pain until late in its mother's pregnancy, because its brain is not sufficiently developed before then. True, electrical brain activity arises in a fetus's brain stem, and it is capable of reflex movement, by approximately the seventh week after conception. But there is no ground for supposing that pain is possible before a connection is made between the fetus's thalamus [which helps integrate sensory information], into which peripheral nerve receptors flow, and its developing neocortex [a part of the brain that helps coordinate sensory information]; and though the timing of that connection is still uncertain, it almost certainly takes place after mid-gestation. (One recent study concluded that "thalamic fibers pass into the human neocortex at about 22–23 weeks' gestation.") These thalamic fibers do not begin to form synapses [transmission points] with cortical neurons until some later time, moreover, which has been estimated to be at about twenty-five weeks. According to a leading embryologist [Clifford Grobstein], "This process of vastly enhanced connectivity among cortical neurons presages a change in the electrical patterns observed in the brain via electroencephalograms. The

> *"It makes no sense to suppose that something has interests of its own . . . unless it has . . . some mental as well as physical life."*

patterns tend to become more regular and to show resemblance to adult patterns associated with sleeping and waking states. Such criteria lead some investigators to suggest that an adequate neural substrate for experienced pain does not exist until about the seventh month of pregnancy (thirty weeks), well into the period when prematurely born fetuses are viable with intensive life support. . . . To provide a safe margin against intrusion into possible primitive sentience," that expert continued, "the cortical maturation beginning at about thirty weeks is a reasonable landmark until more precise information becomes available. Therefore, since we should use extreme caution in respecting and protecting possible sentience, a provisional boundary at about twenty-six weeks should provide safety against reasonable concerns. This time is coincident with the present definition of viability."

More Complex Capacities

Of course, many acts that cause people no physical pain are against their interests. Someone acts against my interests when he chooses someone else for a job I want, or sues me, or smashes into my car, or writes a bad review of my book, or brings out a better mousetrap and prices it lower than mine, even when these actions cause me no physical pain and, indeed, even when I am unaware that they have happened. My interests are in play in these circumstances not because of my capacity to feel pain but because of a different and more complex

> *"A provisional boundary at about twenty-six weeks [of pregnancy] should provide safety against reasonable concerns."*

set of capacities: to enjoy or fail to enjoy, to form affections and emotions, to hope and expect, to suffer disappointment and frustration. Since a creature can be killed painlessly, even after it has the capacity to feel pain, it is these more complex capacities, not the capacity to feel pain, that ground a creature's interests in continuing to live. It is not known when these more complex capacities begin to develop, in primitive or trace or shadowy form, in human beings. But it seems very unlikely that they develop in a human fetus before the point of cortical maturation, at around thirty weeks of gestational age, at which cortical electrical activity becomes more complex and periods of wakefulness can be distinguished by electroencephalogram from periods of sleep. [According to Grobstein,] "Electrical activity of the brain begins to show intermittent patterns resembling some of those seen in normal adults" only at that point.

Embryology has much more to discover about the development of the fetal nervous system, of course. As the expert I just quoted remarked, "The designation of twenty-six weeks as a safe barrier against the invasion of sentience . . . almost certainly will change as more sophisticated and penetrating information accumulates on the time of advent of sentience. That time is far more likely to be later than twenty-six weeks than earlier." But it seems beyond challenge that a fetus does not have the neural substrate necessary for interests of any kind until some point relatively late in its gestation.

This important point—that an immature fetus cannot have interests and therefore cannot have an interest in surviving—is often overlooked because people are mistakenly drawn to an argument to the contrary something like this: It is very much in my interests that I am alive now and was not killed at any moment in the past. So when I was a just-conceived fetus, it must have been in my interests not to be aborted. Therefore any fetus has interests from the moment of its conception, and abortion is against those interests. This argument is fallacious, but we will have to take care to see why.

Interests and Existence

Once creatures with interests exist, then it makes sense to say, in retrospect, that certain events would have been against those interests if they had happened in the past. But it doesn't follow that if these events had happened they would have been against anyone's interests when they did. It is in the interests of every human being now alive, we might assume, that the earth did not explode in a collision with a gigantic meteor millions of years ago. But it does not follow that it would have been against any human being's interests if the earth had exploded then, because there would then never have been any human beings against whose interests that *could* have been. It is in my interests that my father didn't go on a long business trip the day before I was conceived. But it would not have been against anyone's interests, in that way, if he had done so because, once again, there would never have been anyone whose interests it could have harmed.

Of course, when a fetus is aborted, there is a creature for whom someone might think this bad; there is at least a candidate for that role. But the fetus's existence before it is aborted makes no difference to the logical point. If Frankenstein's monster were actually brought to life, and felt and acted like a real person, then it would have interests like any other such person, and it would plainly have been against those interests, in retrospect, if Frankenstein's apparatus had been smashed before the monster was created. But it doesn't follow that the collection of body parts on the laboratory table had interests before the switch was thrown, even though those body parts did exist, as just body parts, at that time. Whether abortion is against the interests of a fetus must depend on whether the fetus itself has interests at the time the abortion is performed, not whether interests will develop if no abortion takes place.

> *"An immature fetus cannot have interests and therefore cannot have an interest in surviving."*

That distinction may help explain what some observers have found puzzling. Many people who believe that abortion is morally permissible nevertheless think it wrong for a pregnant woman to smoke or otherwise behave in ways injurious to the child she intends to bear. Critics find that contradictory; they say that because killing something is worse than injuring it, it cannot be wrong to smoke and yet not wrong to abort. The mistake in this criticism is just the mistake we have been analyzing. If a woman smokes during her pregnancy, a human being may later exist whose interests will have been seriously damaged by her behavior; but if she aborts, no one will exist whose interests her behavior will have damaged. This does not mean, of course, that there is nothing wrong with abortion, nor even that abortion is not morally worse than risking the health of a child who will be born. But it does mean that if early abortion is wrong, it is not for this reason; it is not because abortion is against the interests of the fetus whose life it terminates. . . .

Multiple Ambiguities

We must be careful not to be misled by emotionally charged descriptions about human life and persons and murder that reveal strong emotions but are not a clear guide to the beliefs that people are emotional about. We must be especially careful about the highly ambiguous claims that human life begins at conception and that a fetus is a person from that moment. When someone makes one or the other of these claims, we cannot tell whether he means to make the derivative claim—that a fetus already has interests and rights of its own from the instant of conception, and that abortion is wrong for that reason—or the detached claim—that from the moment of conception a fetus embodies a form of human life which is sacred, a claim that does not imply that a fetus has interests of its own.

> *"Whether abortion is against the interests of a fetus must depend on whether the fetus itself has interests at the time the abortion is performed."*

The familiar questions about when life begins and whether a fetus is a person are not simply but multiply ambiguous, and because these questions have become such familiar parts of the abortion debate, it is important that we understand the multiple ambiguities. Consider the question of whether human life begins at conception. Scientists disagree about exactly when the biological life of any animal begins, but it seems undeniable that a human embryo is an identifiable living organism at least by the time it is implanted in a womb, which is approximately fourteen days after its conception. It is also undeniable that the cells that compose an implanted embryo already contain biological codes that will govern its later physical development. When an opponent of abortion insists that a fetus is a human being, he may mean only to report these undeniable biological facts.

But it does not follow from those facts that a fetus also has rights or interests of the kind that government might have a derivative responsibility to protect. That is plainly a further question, and it is in large part a moral rather than a biological one. Nor does it follow that a fetus already embodies an intrinsic value that government might claim a detached responsibility to guard. That is also a different question, and also a moral rather than a biological one. The question of whether a fetus is a human being, either at conception or at some later point in pregnancy, is simply too ambiguous to be useful. The crucial questions are the two moral ones I have just described, and we should consider these directly and unambiguously. When does a human creature acquire interests and rights? When does the life of a human creature begin to embody intrinsic value, and with what consequences? We do not have to decide whether a fetus is a full human being at conception, or at what point it becomes one, or whether that process is gradual or abrupt, in order to answer those crucial questions.

The Questions That Count

Is a fetus a person? That is an even more treacherous question, because the term "person" has a great many uses and senses that can easily be confused. Suppose it is discovered that pigs are much more intelligent and emotionally complex than zoologists now think they are, and someone then asks whether a pig should therefore be considered a person. We might treat that as a philosophical question, asking us to refine our conception of what a person really is to see whether pigs, on the basis of our new information, qualify for that title. Or we might treat the question as a practical one, asking whether we should now treat pigs as we treat creatures we regard as people, acknowledging that pigs have a right to life so that it is wrong to kill them for food and a right not to be enslaved so that it is wrong to imprison them in pens. Of course, we might think that the two questions are connected: that if pigs are persons in the philosophical sense, they should be treated as other persons are, and that if they are not, they should not. But that does not necessarily follow, in either direction. We might believe philosophically that pigs are persons but that human beings have no reason to treat them as we treat one another; or, on the contrary, we might decide that pigs are not persons according to our best understanding of that complex concept but that nevertheless their capacities entitle them to the treatment persons give one another.

Once again it would be wise, therefore, to set aside the question of whether a fetus is a person, not because that question is unanswerable or metaphysical, as many judges and commentators have declared, but because it is too ambiguous to be helpful. Once again, we must ask, instead, the key moral questions I distinguished. Does a fetus have interests that should be protected by rights, including a right to life?

> *"We must be especially careful about the highly ambiguous claims that human life begins at conception."*

Should we treat the life of a fetus as sacred, whether a fetus has interests or not? Once again, we do not need to decide whether a fetus is a person in order to answer these questions, and these are the questions that count.

Chapter 2

Should Abortion Rights Be Protected or Restricted?

CURRENT CONTROVERSIES

Abortion Rights and Laws: An Overview

by Joan Biskupic

About the author: *Joan Biskupic is a staff writer for the* Washington Post *daily newspaper.*

Wanda Franz remembers where she was on January 22, 1973, when the Supreme Court handed down *Roe v. Wade*. She was in the cafeteria at West Virginia University, and a woman who knew Franz had spoken out against abortion shouted at her, "You can go home now. It's over."

Hardly.

Meant to solve a problem, *Roe v. Wade*, the monumental ruling that made abortion legal nationwide, incited a war that has shut down legislatures, divided political parties and splintered families. It took on a woman's intensely personal dilemma and made it the focus of an enduring and glaringly public debate.

Strife over the issue has been so bitter and sustained that the only comparison that comes close is the country's conflict over race. Upwards of 75,000 abortion opponents marched to the Supreme Court and Capitol on Jan. 22, 1993, part of what has become their yearly anniversary ritual.

Abortion Battles

The war is far from over. Battles have only shifted venues since 1973, from the Supreme Court, to statehouses, Congress, back to the court. It has been fought in front of clinics, at political conventions, always in homes.

In *Roe*, the court ruled 7 to 2 that state laws making abortion a crime infringed upon the 14th Amendment's due process guarantee of personal liberty, which, the majority said, protects a woman's decision whether to have a child.

But the ruling only led to more questions. Should the government pay for abortions for poor women? Must a husband or parents be told? Could the tissue of aborted fetuses be used in important medical research?

Each issue raises more dilemmas. Choice vs. life. Equality vs. responsibility.

Symbolic coat hangers vs. pictures of developing fetuses.

Now, a whole new era of abortion conflict is beginning.

The election of President Clinton, a supporter of abortion rights, and a 1992 court ruling affirming most of *Roe* but inviting state regulation, changed the battleground once again.

Even as demonstrators marched outside the White House, Clinton overturned several restrictions on abortion, including reversing the

> *"Now, a whole new era of abortion conflict is beginning."*

Bush administration's "gag order" restricting abortion counseling in clinics that receive federal funds and lifting the ban on funding for research on fetal tissue.

Abortion opponents are bracing for a fight. "People are really ready to work now," says Franz, who is president of the National Right to Life Committee, a group that plans to step up its lobbying of state legislatures for more abortion limits. Franz, a student at West Virginia University in 1973, is now a professor of child development there.

Meanwhile, abortion rights advocates still are reeling from 12 years of Republican administrations that opposed abortion and a conservative Supreme Court that, despite affirming *Roe*, made it easier for states to restrict abortion.

"We have to recoup a lot of losses from the last 12 years," says Janet Benshoof, who in 1992 began a new advocacy organization in New York City dedicated to preserving abortion rights. "We're just realizing how far back we are."

A New Standard

The future of abortion rights hangs on how far states push restrictions and how the Supreme Court assesses whether those limits are an "undue burden" on women seeking abortions. The court, in the 1992 ruling, said an undue burden exists if substantial obstacles are placed in the path of a woman seeking an abortion before the fetus is viable, that is, can live outside the womb.

It is a new standard and one not yet defined. Fearing that states might pass laws that significantly impede access to abortion, abortion rights supporters have been lobbying Congress to pass the proposed Freedom of Choice Act [FOCA], which would greatly limit state abortion regulation.

"While there is a mood among the laity that maybe things have calmed down," says syndicated columnist Nat Hentoff, who switched sides to oppose abortion in 1984, "they haven't."

What is it about abortion that the issue remains salient at a time when [seven] of the nine *Roe* justices have died or retired?

Abortion raises questions about the beginnings of life and equally profound questions about individualism and privacy.

To many people, abortion means equality for women; and to many women, it invokes conflicts about motherhood, control of one's own body and destiny. In the background is sexuality, challenging the country's Puritan origins.

Abortion rouses strong feelings about religious convictions and lifestyle differences. Some conservatives equate abortion with loose morals and a lack of "family values." Liberals say the need for abortion is a human reality and that the country must allow for a safe and accessible option to end a pregnancy.

Polls—including one conducted by the *Washington Post* the week before the 1993 anniversary—show that most people fall into a conflicted middle, believing in a right to abortion but also saying it should be exercised rarely, such as when a woman's health is threatened or in cases of rape or incest. The Alan Guttmacher Institute, which collects national statistics on abortion, reports that no single reason predominates in women's choices to have an abortion. Most women who end their pregnancies say having a baby would conflict with work, school or other responsibilities and that they could not afford a child.

Supreme Court Decisions

Since 1973, more than 22 million legal abortions have been performed, with the current annual count estimated at 1.6 million. The aging of the baby-boom generation and increased use of birth control appear to have contributed to a leveling off of the abortion rate and a downward trend in the ratio of abortions to live births, according to the Guttmacher Institute.

From the start, the Supreme Court has steered the debate, either by shutting out lawmakers or, now, by enticing their involvement in defining abortion rights.

> *"Abortion raises questions about the beginnings of life and equally profound questions about individualism and privacy."*

Roe v. Wade said a state could interfere with a woman's "fundamental" right to abortion only if it had a "compelling interest." During the first three months of pregnancy, the court said, states must leave the abortion decision to a woman. During the second trimester, a state could impose restrictions intended to safeguard the mother's health. Only after the sixth month of pregnancy could abortion be prohibited, but not if it is necessary to save the mother's life or health.

Under that framework, most restrictions on abortion were found invalid.

The first departure from *Roe* came in the court's 1989 ruling in *Webster v. Reproductive Health Services*. In a 5 to 4 ruling, the court upheld a Missouri abortion law that an appeals court had found inconsistent with *Roe*. The law's preamble said that "the life of each human being begins at conception" and "unborn children have protectable interests in life, health and well-being."

The law barred using public employees and facilities for abortion and required that before a woman who may have been pregnant 20 or more weeks could obtain an abortion, a physician first had to determine whether the fetus could survive outside the womb.

The Supreme Court did not produce the five votes needed to overturn *Roe*, although a majority criticized it and Justice Harry A. Blackmun, the author of *Roe*, said the court was implicitly inviting state legislatures to enact more restrictions on abortion.

Pennsylvania, under the leadership of its anti-abortion Gov. Robert P. Casey, a Democrat, adopted new abortion limits in 1989, and its law came to the court in 1992's *Planned Parenthood of Southeastern Pennsylvania v. Casey.*

There, justices upheld requirements that women seeking abortions be given information discouraging the procedure and that physicians wait at least 24 hours before performing an abortion; that minors obtain parental permission; and that clinics collect and make public certain information on abortions performed. (Polling has shown that a large majority of Americans support parental and spousal notification laws and waiting periods.)

Most significantly in the *Casey* ruling, the court by 7 to 2 discarded the trimester framework of *Roe* and its strict test for state regulation. The plurality in *Casey* said the standard now should be whether a regulation puts an "undue burden" on a woman seeking an abortion.)

At the Local Level

Activists on both sides of the abortion debate expect the so-far loosely defined "undue burden" standard to lead states to test the outer limits, the lower courts to craft their own interpretations, and the Supreme Court ultimately to decide—again—how far states may go.

"What happened with *Casey*," Franz says, "is that the courts finally opened the door to some protective legislation. As soon as we saw that opportunity, we immediately went to work developing legislation."

Kathryn Kolbert, who works with Benshoof in the Center for Reproductive Law & Policy, agrees that states will become the focus of activity. "After *Webster*, there were some 600 bills introduced," she says. "I personally think I went to 22 states. And I think [1993], frankly, will be one of the worst."

Members of the anti-abortion community insist that state regulations are "protections" that should not be resisted by women's advocates. They say women are being exploited by the "billion-dollar abortion industry" that wants to keep their business, and abortion opponents especially advocate requiring physicians to detail fetal development and make women wait at least 24 hours before having an abortion.

Abortion rights advocates say such laws are a burden on poorer women in rural areas who must drive long distances and stay overnight to obtain an abortion. "*Casey* divides the country into women who are rich and women who are poor," Benshoof says.

> *"Under [Roe's trimester] framework, most restrictions on abortion were found invalid."*

Sarah Weddington, the lawyer who defended the "Jane Roe" in the landmark abortion case, adds, "The 24-hour waiting period comes into a new focus . . . when you hear about a young woman who went into a clinic and the [other side] copied down her license plate and they called her parents that night and created a real family ruckus."

> *"The plurality in Casey said the standard now should be whether a regulation puts an 'undue burden' on a woman seeking an abortion."*

Weddington, who was 27 when she heard she had won the case, wrote a book about her experience representing a young carnival worker who claimed she was raped and wanted an abortion. (Rape was not an issue in the legal challenge to the Texas abortion ban, and the woman later disclosed that she had not been raped.)

In the book, Weddington also described for the first time her own abortion, as "a scared graduate student in 1967 in a dirty, dusty Mexican border town . . . fleeing the law that made abortion illegal in Texas."

Abortion and Politics

The jousting between the states and courts does not mean that Congress can avoid this emotional issue.

In an attempt to roll back state restrictions and cut off new regulation, abortion rights activists have asked Congress to pass a bill [FOCA] that would significantly limit state abortion laws and try to capture the essence of *Roe*. The lead proponents are Democratic Rep. Don Edwards of California and Senate Majority Leader George J. Mitchell. . . .

Abortion is always there in politics, lying in wait. Even legislation that touches abortion only tangentially—or not at all—has been derailed with an abortion-related amendment. Conservative activists use abortion as an effective club against Democrats, invoking Democrats' tolerance of abortion and homosexuality to complain about a lack of "family values."

Despite the antagonism and passion that infuses the debate, the rhetoric from some leaders has mellowed. During 1992's [presidential] campaign, Vice President Quayle, who was vocally opposed to abortion rights, resisted advocating an abortion ban. Quayle deflected questions about a ban, insisting the issue was: "How are we going to handle the tragedy of abortion?"

Also in 1992, New York Democratic Gov. Mario M. Cuomo called on both sides to reach a "common ground" to try to reduce the number of abortions. Cuomo, who backs abortion rights, said more attention should be given to adoption and preached sexual abstinence, education and contraception.

In an interview with the Catholic News Service, Clinton agreed, saying, "We should . . . try to find ways that people who disagree over what the law should be on abortion can work together and reduce the number of abortions."

That might be the politically expedient route. After two decades of heavy lobbying, militant protests and expensive advertising campaigns, neither side in the abortion battle has convinced the country that abortion should be either outright illegal or an unqualified right.

Some on the front lines are not talking compromise at all.

George Weigel, president of the Ethics and Public Policy Center, is troubled by what he calls a blithe acceptance of abortion: "No one really has to have an abortion."

Across the trenches, Planned Parenthood general counsel Eve Paul says, "Either a woman can get an abortion or not. I don't see how abortion can ever be compromised."

Roe v. Wade Is Reaffirmed

by Sandra Day O'Connor, Anthony Kennedy, and David Souter

About the authors: *Sandra Day O'Connor, Anthony Kennedy, and David Souter are United States Supreme Court justices and authors of the joint opinion in* Planned Parenthood of Southeastern Pennsylvania v. Casey. *They were joined in judgment of* Casey *by Justices Harry A. Blackmun and John Paul Stevens.*

Liberty finds no refuge in a jurisprudence of doubt. Yet 19 years after our holding that the Constitution protects a woman's right to terminate her pregnancy in its early stages, *Roe v. Wade*, 410 U. S. 113 (1973), that definition of liberty is still questioned. Joining the respondents as *amicus curiae* [friend of the court], the United States, as it has done in five other cases in the last decade, again asks us to overrule *Roe*.

Pennsylvania's Abortion Control Act

At issue in these cases are five provisions of the Pennsylvania Abortion Control Act of 1982 as amended in 1988 and 1989. The Act requires that a woman seeking an abortion give her informed consent prior to the abortion procedure, and specifies that she be provided with certain information at least 24 hours before the abortion is performed. For a minor to obtain an abortion, the Act requires the informed consent of one of her parents, but provides for a judicial bypass option if the minor does not wish to or cannot obtain a parent's consent. Another provision of the Act requires that, unless certain exceptions apply, a married woman seeking an abortion must sign a statement indicating that she has notified her husband of her intended abortion. The Act exempts compliance with these three requirements in the event of a "medical emergency," which is defined in [section] 3203 of the Act. In addition to the above provisions regulating the performance of abortions, the Act imposes certain reporting requirements on facilities that provide abortion services.

Before any of these provisions took effect, the petitioners, who are five abor-

Sandra Day O'Connor, Anthony Kennedy, David Souter, Supreme Court decision in *Planned Parenthood of Southeastern Pennsylvania v. Robert P. Casey*, June 29, 1992 (#112 S.Ct. 2791).

tion clinics and one physician representing himself as well as a class of physicians who provide abortion services, brought this suit seeking declaratory and injunctive relief. Each provision was challenged as unconstitutional on its face. The District Court entered a preliminary injunction against the enforcement of

the regulations, and, after a 3-day bench trial, held all the provisions at issue here unconstitutional, entering a permanent injunction against Pennsylvania's enforcement of them. The Court of Appeals for the Third Cir-

> *"The essential holding of* Roe v. Wade *should be retained and once again reaffirmed."*

cuit affirmed in part and reversed in part, upholding all of the regulations except for the husband notification requirement. We granted certiorari [a writ to obtain a lower court's records].

Casting Doubt on *Roe*

The Court of Appeals found it necessary to follow an elaborate course of reasoning even to identify the first premise to use to determine whether the statute enacted by Pennsylvania meets constitutional standards. And at oral argument in this Court, the attorney for the parties challenging the statute took the position that none of the enactments can be upheld without overruling *Roe v. Wade*. We disagree with that analysis; but we acknowledge that our decisions after *Roe* cast doubt upon the meaning and reach of its holding. Further, the Chief Justice [William Rehnquist] admits that he would overrule the central holding of *Roe* and adopt the rational relationship test as the sole criterion of constitutionality. State and federal courts as well as legislatures throughout the Union must have guidance as they seek to address this subject in conformance with the Constitution. Given these premises, we find it imperative to review once more the principles that define the rights of the woman and the legitimate authority of the State respecting the termination of pregnancies by abortion procedures.

After considering the fundamental constitutional questions resolved by *Roe*, principles of institutional integrity, and the rule of *stare decisis* [let the decision stand], we are led to conclude this: the essential holding of *Roe v. Wade* should be retained and once again reaffirmed.

It must be stated at the outset and with clarity that *Roe*'s essential holding, the holding we reaffirm, has three parts. First is a recognition of the right of the woman to choose to have an abortion before viability and to obtain it without undue interference from the State. Before viability, the State's interests are not strong enough to support a prohibition of abortion or the imposition of a substantial obstacle to the woman's effective right to elect the procedure. Second is a confirmation of the State's power to restrict abortions after fetal viability, if the law contains exceptions for pregnancies which endanger a woman's life or health. And third is the principle that the State has legitimate interests from the outset of the pregnancy in protecting the health of the woman and the life of the fetus that may become a child. These principles do not contradict one another; and we adhere to each. . . .

Philosophic Questions

Men and women of good conscience can disagree, and we suppose some always shall disagree, about the profound moral and spiritual implications of terminating a pregnancy, even in its earliest stage. Some of us as individuals find abortion offensive to our most basic principles of morality, but that cannot control our decision. Our obligation is to define the liberty of all, not to mandate our own moral code. The underlying constitutional issue is whether the State can resolve these philosophic questions in such a definitive way that a woman lacks all choice in the matter, except perhaps in those rare circumstances in which the pregnancy is itself a danger to her own life or health, or is the result of rape or incest.

It is conventional constitutional doctrine that where reasonable people disagree the government can adopt one position or the other. That theorem, however, assumes a state of affairs in which the choice does not intrude upon a protected liberty. Thus, while some people might disagree about whether or not the flag should be saluted, or disagree about the proposition that it may not be defiled, we have ruled that a State may not compel or enforce one view or the other.

> *"Our obligation is to define the liberty of all, not to mandate our own moral code."*

Our law affords constitutional protection to personal decisions relating to marriage, procreation, contraception, family relationships, child rearing, and education. Our cases recognize "the right of the *individual*, married or single, to be free from unwarranted governmental intrusion into matters so fundamentally affecting a person as the decision whether to bear or beget a child." *Eisenstadt* v. *Baird* (1972) (emphasis in original). Our precedents "have respected the private realm of family life which the state cannot enter." *Prince* v. *Massachusetts* (1944). These matters, involving the most intimate and personal choices a person may make in a lifetime, choices central to personal dignity and autonomy, are central to the liberty protected by the Fourteenth Amendment. At the heart of liberty is the right to define one's own concept of existence, of meaning, of the universe, and of the mystery of human life. Beliefs about these matters could not define the attributes of personhood were they formed under compulsion of the State.

Liberty and Sacrifice

These considerations begin our analysis of the woman's interest in terminating her pregnancy but cannot end it, for this reason: though the abortion decision may originate within the zone of conscience and belief, it is more than a

philosophic exercise. Abortion is a unique act. It is an act fraught with consequences for others: for the woman who must live with the implications of her
decision; for the persons who perform and assist in the procedure; for the
spouse, family, and society which must confront the knowledge that these procedures exist, procedures some deem nothing short of an act of violence
against innocent human life; and, depending on one's beliefs, for the life or potential life that is aborted. Though abortion is conduct, it does not follow that
the State is entitled to proscribe it in all instances. That is because the liberty of
the woman is at stake in a sense unique to the human condition and so unique
to the law. The mother who carries a child to full term is subject to anxieties, to
physical constraints, to pain that only she must bear. That these sacrifices have
from the beginning of the human race been endured by woman with a pride
that ennobles her in the eyes of others and gives to the infant a bond of love
cannot alone be grounds for the State to insist she make the sacrifice. Her suffering is too intimate and personal for the State to insist, without more, upon its
own vision of the woman's role, however dominant that vision has been in the
course of our history and our culture. The destiny of the woman must be
shaped to a large extent on her own conception of her spiritual imperatives and
her place in society. . . .

Roe's Central Rule

In this case we may inquire whether *Roe*'s central rule has been found unworkable; whether the rule's limitation on state power could be removed without serious inequity to those who have relied upon it or significant damage to
the stability of the society governed by the rule in question; whether the law's
growth in the intervening years has left *Roe*'s central rule a doctrinal anachro-
nism discounted by society; and whether *Roe*'s premises of fact have so far
changed in the ensuing two decades as to render its central holding somehow irrelevant or unjustifiable in dealing with the issue it addressed.

Although *Roe* has engendered opposition, it has in no sense proven "unworkable," representing as it does a simple limitation beyond which a state law is
unenforceable. . . .

For two decades of economic and social developments, people have organized
intimate relationships and made
choices that define their views of
themselves and their places in society, in reliance on the availability of
abortion in the event that contraception should fail. The ability of women
to participate equally in the economic

> *"The liberty of the woman is at stake in a sense unique to the human condition and so unique to the law."*

and social life of the Nation has been facilitated by their ability to control their
reproductive lives. The Constitution serves human values, and while the effect
of reliance on *Roe* cannot be exactly measured, neither can the certain cost of

overruling *Roe* for people who have ordered their thinking and living around that case be dismissed.

No evolution of legal principle has left *Roe*'s doctrinal footings weaker than they were in 1973. No development of constitutional law since the case was decided has implicitly or explicitly left *Roe* behind as a mere survivor of obsolete constitutional thinking.

> *"No evolution of legal principle has left* Roe*'s doctrinal footings weaker than they were in 1973."*

It will be recognized, of course, that *Roe* stands at an intersection of two lines of decisions, but in whichever doctrinal category one reads the case, the result for present purposes will be the same. The *Roe* Court itself placed its holding in the succession of cases most prominently exemplified by *Griswold* v. *Connecticut* [legalizing contraception]. When it is so seen, *Roe* is clearly in no jeopardy, since subsequent constitutional developments have neither disturbed, nor do they threaten to diminish, the scope of recognized protection accorded to the liberty relating to intimate relationships, the family, and decisions about whether or not to beget or bear a child.

Roe, however, may be seen not only as an exemplar of *Griswold* liberty but as a rule (whether or not mistaken) of personal autonomy and bodily integrity, with doctrinal affinity to cases recognizing limits on governmental power to mandate medical treatment or to bar its rejection. If so, our cases since *Roe* accord with *Roe*'s view that a State's interest in the protection of life falls short of justifying any plenary override of individual liberty claims. . . .

Viability Is the Critical Fact

We have seen how time has overtaken some of *Roe*'s factual assumptions: advances in maternal health care allow for abortions safe to the mother later in pregnancy than was true in 1973, and advances in neonatal care have advanced viability to a point somewhat earlier. But these facts go only to the scheme of time limits on the realization of competing interests, and the divergences from the factual premises of 1973 have no bearing on the validity of *Roe*'s central holding, that viability marks the earliest point at which the State's interest in fetal life is constitutionally adequate to justify a legislative ban on nontherapeutic abortions. The soundness or unsoundness of that constitutional judgment in no sense turns on whether viability occurs at approximately 28 weeks, as was usual at the time of *Roe*, at 23 to 24 weeks, as it sometimes does today, or at some moment even slightly earlier in pregnancy, as it may if fetal respiratory capacity can somehow be enhanced in the future. Whenever it may occur, the attainment of viability may continue to serve as the critical fact, just as it has done since *Roe* was decided; which is to say that no change in *Roe*'s factual underpinning has left its central holding obsolete, and none supports an argument for overruling it.

The sum of the precedential inquiry to this point shows *Roe*'s underpinnings unweakened in any way affecting its central holding. While it has engendered disapproval, it has not been unworkable. An entire generation has come of age free to assume *Roe*'s concept of liberty in defining the capacity of women to act in society, and to make reproductive decisions; no erosion of principle going to liberty or personal autonomy has left *Roe*'s central holding a doctrinal remnant; *Roe* portends no developments at odds with other precedent for the analysis of personal liberty; and no changes of fact have rendered viability more or less appropriate as the point at which the balance of interests tips. Within the bounds of normal *stare decisis* analysis, then, and subject to the considerations on which it customarily turns, the stronger argument is for affirming *Roe*'s central holding, with whatever degree of personal reluctance any of us may have, not for overruling it. . . .

A Clear Duty

The Court's duty in the present case is clear. In 1973, it confronted the already-divisive issue of governmental power to limit personal choice to undergo abortion, for which it provided a new resolution based on the due process guaranteed by the Fourteenth Amendment. Whether or not a new social consensus is developing on that issue, its divisiveness is no less today than in 1973, and pressure to overrule the decision, like pressure to retain it, has grown only more intense.

> *"The attainment of viability may continue to serve as the critical fact, just as it has done since* Roe *was decided."*

A decision to overrule *Roe*'s essential holding under the existing circumstances would address error, if error there was, at the cost of both profound and unnecessary damage to the Court's legitimacy, and to the Nation's commitment to the rule of law. It is therefore imperative to adhere to the essence of *Roe*'s original decision, and we do so today.

From what we have said so far it follows that it is a constitutional liberty of the woman to have some freedom to terminate her pregnancy. We conclude that the basic decision in *Roe* was based on a constitutional analysis which we cannot now repudiate. The woman's liberty is not so unlimited, however, that from the outset the State cannot show its concern for the life of the unborn, and at a later point in fetal development the State's interest in life has sufficient force so that the right of the woman to terminate the pregnancy can be restricted.

That brings us, of course, to the point where much criticism has been directed at *Roe*, a criticism that always inheres when the Court draws a specific rule from what in the Constitution is but a general standard. We conclude, however, that the urgent claims of the woman to retain the ultimate control over her destiny and her body, claims implicit in the meaning of liberty, require us to perform that function. Liberty must not be extinguished for want of a line that is clear. And it falls to us to give some real substance to the woman's liberty to determine whether to carry her pregnancy to full term.

We conclude the line should be drawn at viability, so that before that time the woman has a right to choose to terminate her pregnancy. . . .

Roe's Difficult Question

The woman's right to terminate her pregnancy before viability is the most central principle of *Roe* v. *Wade*. It is a rule of law and a component of liberty we cannot renounce.

On the other side of the equation is the interest of the State in the protection of potential life. The *Roe* Court recognized the State's "important and legitimate interest in protecting the potentiality of human life." The weight to be given this State interest, not the strength of the woman's interest, was the difficult question faced in *Roe*. We do not need to say whether each of us, had we been Members of the Court when the valuation of the State interest came before it as an original matter, would have concluded, as the *Roe* Court did, that its weight is insufficient to justify a ban on abortions prior to viability even when it is subject to certain exceptions. The matter is not before us in the first instance, and coming as it does after nearly 20 years of litigation in *Roe*'s wake we are satisfied that the immediate question is not the soundness of *Roe*'s resolution of the issue, but the precedential force that must be accorded to its holding. And we have concluded that the essential holding of *Roe* should be reaffirmed.

Yet it must be remembered that *Roe* v. *Wade* speaks with clarity in establishing not only the woman's liberty but also the State's "important and legitimate interest in potential life." That portion of the decision in *Roe* has been given too little acknowledgement and implementation by the Court in its subsequent cases. Those cases decided that any regulation touching upon the abortion decision must survive strict scrutiny, to be sustained only if drawn in narrow terms to further a compelling state interest. Not all of the cases decided under that formulation can be reconciled with the holding in *Roe* itself that the State has legitimate interests in the health of the woman and in protecting the potential life within her. In resolving this tension, we choose to rely upon *Roe*, as against the later cases.

> *"The woman's liberty is not so unlimited . . . that from the outset the State cannot show its concern for the life of the unborn."*

Roe established a trimester framework to govern abortion regulations. Under this elaborate but rigid construct, almost no regulation at all is permitted during the first trimester of pregnancy; regulations designed to protect the woman's health, but not to further the State's interest in potential life, are permitted during the second trimester; and during the third trimester, when the fetus is viable, prohibitions are permitted provided the life or health of the mother is not at stake. . . .

87

The very notion that the State has a substantial interest in potential life leads to the conclusion that not all regulations must be deemed unwarranted. Not all burdens on the right to decide whether to terminate a pregnancy will be undue. In our view, the undue burden standard is the appropriate means of reconciling the State's interest with the woman's constitutionally protected liberty.

The concept of an undue burden has been utilized by the Court as well as individual members of the Court, including two of us, in ways that could be considered inconsistent. Because we set forth a standard of general application to which we intend to

> *"The immediate question is not the soundness of* **Roe's** *resolution of the issue, but [its] precedential force."*

adhere, it is important to clarify what is meant by an undue burden.

A finding of an undue burden is a shorthand for the conclusion that a State regulation has the purpose or effect of placing a substantial obstacle in the path of a woman seeking an abortion of a nonviable fetus. A statute with this purpose is invalid because the means chosen by the State to further the interest in potential life must be calculated to inform the woman's free choice, not hinder it. And a statute which, while furthering the interest in potential life or some other valid state interest, has the effect of placing a substantial obstacle in the path of a woman's choice cannot be considered a permissible means of serving its legitimate ends. To the extent that the opinions of the Court or of individual Justices use the undue burden standard in a manner that is inconsistent with this analysis, we set out what in our view should be the controlling standard. In our considered judgment, an undue burden is an unconstitutional burden. Understood another way, we answer the question, left open in previous opinions discussing the undue burden formulation, whether a law designed to further the State's interest in fetal life which imposes an undue burden on the woman's decision before fetal viability could be constitutional. The answer is no.

Guiding Principles

Some guiding principles should emerge. What is at stake is the woman's right to make the ultimate decision, not a right to be insulated from all others in doing so. Regulations which do no more than create a structural mechanism by which the State, or the parent or guardian of a minor, may express profound respect for the life of the unborn are permitted, if they are not a substantial obstacle to the woman's exercise of the right to choose. Unless it has that effect on her right of choice, a state measure designed to persuade her to choose childbirth over abortion will be upheld if reasonably related to that goal. Regulations designed to foster the health of a woman seeking an abortion are valid if they do not constitute an undue burden.

Even when jurists reason from shared premises, some disagreement is inevitable. That is to be expected in the application of any legal standard which must accommodate life's complexity. We do not expect it to be otherwise with respect to the undue burden standard. We give this summary:

(a) To protect the central right recognized by *Roe* v. *Wade* while at the same time accommodating the State's profound interest in potential life, we will employ the undue burden analysis as explained in this opinion. An undue burden exists, and therefore a provision of law is invalid, if its purpose or effect is to place a substantial obstacle in the path of a woman seeking an abortion before the fetus attains viability.

(b) We reject the rigid trimester framework of *Roe* v. *Wade*. To promote the State's profound interest in potential life, throughout pregnancy the State may take measures to ensure that the woman's choice is informed, and measures designed to advance this interest will not be invalidated as long as their purpose is to persuade the woman to choose childbirth over abortion. These measures must not be an undue burden on the right.

(c) As with any medical procedure, the State may enact regulations to further the health or safety of a woman seeking an abortion. Unnecessary health regulations that have the purpose or effect of presenting a substantial obstacle to a woman seeking an abortion impose an undue burden on the right.

(d) Our adoption of the undue burden analysis does not disturb the central holding of *Roe* v. *Wade*, and we reaffirm that holding. Regardless of whether exceptions are made for particular circumstances, a State may not prohibit any woman from making the ultimate decision to terminate her pregnancy before viability.

> *"In our considered judgment, an undue burden is an unconstitutional burden."*

(e) We also reaffirm *Roe*'s holding that "subsequent to viability, the State in promoting its interest in the potentiality of human life may, if it chooses, regulate, and even proscribe, abortion except where it is necessary, in appropriate medical judgment, for the preservation of the life or health of the mother."

Abortion Rights Should Not Be Restricted

by Marlene Gerber Fried and Loretta Ross

About the authors: *Marlene Gerber Fried, author of* From Abortion to Reproductive Freedom, *is a reproductive rights activist for the Boston Reproductive
Rights Network. Loretta Ross, a longtime civil and reproductive rights activist,
is the program director for the Center for Democratic Renewal, an Atlanta organization that works to end bigotry and hate crimes.*

We women have always fought to control our fertility. We have always
wanted to have sex and children on our own terms and we have resisted efforts—whether by individual men, governments, judges, or antiabortionists—to
prevent us from having that control.

The persistence of this struggle reveals its importance. At stake is nothing
less than the power to shape our own lives. It is not rhetoric but reality to say
that if we cannot control whether, when, and under what conditions we will
have sex and children, there is little else in our lives that we can control.

Real Gains

During the 1960s and 1970s, the women's movement and other
progressive/liberation movements in the United States made real gains. Even
though what we won was so much less than what we wanted, or needed, those
gains were a threat to the systems of power that control our lives. We challenged traditional hierarchies and rejected fundamental forms of social control.

The civil rights movement and the women's movement indelibly changed our
society, and by the 1980s, these movements presented a formidable front
against ongoing assaults. We saw this coalition during presidential campaigns
and in fights against conservative Supreme Court nominees.

Defenders of the status quo have responded to these sweeping social changes
with a consistent effort to reverse the gains that our movements fought so hard
to win. This effort includes campaigns of repression—legal, illegal, and in-

creasingly violent.

This is the context of the current battles over abortion in the United States. Not only are we fighting to win back funding and abortion rights for teenage women, today we must also resist the effort to overturn *Roe v. Wade*. *Roe* had a profound impact on the daily lives of women. Without legal abortion, thousands of women died in back alleys, thousands more suffered serious medical complications, and all women's health was threatened. After *Roe*, for those women who had access to legal abortion, a dangerous and desperate experience was transformed into a safe and legitimate health care option.

Together with legalizing contraception, abortion legitimized the separation between biology and procreation. This is a necessary step in the struggle for sexual freedom—heterosexual women could choose to have sex and choose not to be pregnant. And by breaking the link between sexuality and reproduction, it opened the door to sexual self-determination for lesbians and gay men.

On the Brink

Now we are on the brink of losing legal abortion in the United States. In its 1992 decision (*Planned Parenthood v. Casey*), the Supreme Court upheld *Roe* by a narrow, 5 to 4 majority (with four justices ready to overturn *Roe*). At the same time, the Court dealt severe blows to abortion rights by allowing states to place restrictions such as mandatory waiting periods, biased "informed consent" requirements, parental consent regulations, and by weakening the standard against which further constraints will be judged. As with all of the previous erosions of abortion rights, these restrictions hit hardest at the most vulnerable women in our society—low-income women among whom women of color are disproportionately represented, young women, any women who depend on the state for their health care.

As we plan our strategies for resistance, we find that the popular focus on the judicial arena obscures our own history of struggle. Legal abortion wasn't a gift from the Supreme Court, but a victory of a women's movement that was fighting on many fronts for a range of rights and freedoms. And this is what it will take again to protect legal abortion and to win other reproductive freedoms.

> *"Legal abortion wasn't a gift from the Supreme Court, but a victory of a women's movement that was fighting on many fronts."*

We write as activists and participants in this struggle, hoping to contribute to the dialogue. We are angered by the state of siege under which we must live. We are pained by the militaristic terms we must use to describe this assault. But when women are singled out to die, especially poor women, it feels like a war, complete with bombs and terrorists.

We are not going to allow Supreme Court justices, legislators, or antiabortion terrorists to make fundamental decisions about our reproductive lives. We are going to do whatever is necessary to help women get safe abortions and to save women's lives. . . .

Eroding Abortion Rights

The goal of the antiabortion movement is to outlaw all abortions—not to stop abortions or save lives as they self-righteously claim. They want to punish women who have abortions. If abortion is recriminalized, they will succeed. Women will continue to have abortions as they did before *Roe*. Abortions will not be stopped; they will once again be made dangerous, life-threatening operations. And once again, women trying to control their *own* lives will be criminals.

The antiabortionists are pursuing their long-range goal of criminalization by working on several fronts to make abortion increasingly less accessible for increasing numbers of women. They attack public funding of abortions, try to close down clinics and attempt to pass as many restrictive laws as possible. They have also tried to control the imagery surrounding abortion, shrouding it in messages of guilt and shame. In all of these areas, the attacks have come first against the most vulnerable women—poor women, young women, women of color.

> *"[Antiabortionists] . . . tried to control the imagery surrounding abortion, shrouding it in messages of guilt and shame."*

The most dramatic erosion came soon after *Roe v. Wade.* In 1977 Congress passed the Hyde Amendment prohibiting the use of federal Medicaid funding for abortion. For low-income women, Hyde effectively undermined *Roe*—if you cannot access abortion, it might as well be illegal. Because a disproportionate number of low-income women are women of color, curtailing access to abortion hits this group the hardest. Rosie Jiménez has become the symbol of this discrimination. She was the first woman known to have died from an illegal abortion after the Hyde Amendment was passed. She was, of course, not the last.

State funding has also been attacked. Only thirteen states and the District of Columbia continue to fund abortions. These restrictions affect all women who depend on the federal government for health care. This includes women on Medicaid, Native American women on reservations, women in the military, and federal employees. The Supreme Court has upheld these funding restrictions.

Access to abortion has also been undermined for young women. Thirty-four states have parental consent or notification laws. The Supreme Court has upheld their constitutionality.

Antiabortion Strategy

The antiabortion movement's legislative strategy is to try and pass as many restrictive laws as possible. In the first year after [the 1989 *Webster* Supreme Court case], 400 such laws were passed, 300 in the following year. Although most of these efforts failed, those that did pass have provided the courts with opportunities to weaken and perhaps even overturn the constitutional protection.

Their judicial strategy has involved gaining the appointment of large numbers of judges and Supreme Court justices who oppose abortion. As of 1992, over 70 percent of the sitting federal judges and a majority of Supreme Court justices were appointed during the Reagan/ Bush era in which opposition to abortion was used as a litmus test qualification for appointment.

This has resulted in eroding the constitutional right piecemeal through court cases that chip away at it. And these decisions invite further antiabortion legislation like the Pennsylvania law upheld [in *Casey*] by the Court. There are several other cases already in the pipeline, any of which could be used to overturn *Roe v. Wade* or at the very least, to continue to weaken it.

Negotiating so much of the abortion battle in the courts tends to hide the real impact that these decisions have had. Courts and judges are far removed from the world they control. In that world millions of women have already been harmed by these decisions and laws. For example, before Hyde, one-third of all abortions were Medicaid funded. Without federal and state funding, low-income women with unwanted pregnancies are forced to have babies, be sterilized, or have abortions using money really needed for food, rent, and other necessities. The illegal and extralegal attacks on abortion clinics are an especially outrageous part of the antiabortionists' strategy.

Over 80 percent of all abortion and family planning clinics have experienced some form of harassment—anything from picketing and bomb threats, to kidnapping doctors and death threats against doctors, other clinic personnel, and Supreme Court justices. Fanatical groups like Operation Rescue and the Lambs of Christ have kept up a steady assault on clinics, clinic personnel, and women seeking abortions.

An Ideological Offensive

In addition to these highly visible attacks on abortion, there has been an ideological offensive. The antiabortion movement has been successful in making fetuses prominent in the moral, legal, and political debates surrounding abortion. In fact, fetuses have more legitimacy and reality than pregnant women. Fetuses are projected as independent beings, deserving of full human rights and endangered by "selfish" women seeking abortion on demand. In the antiabortion moral calculus, fetuses, not women, deserve empathy, legal protection and societal resources. The church and the state project the voices of fetuses, while suppressing those of women. Fetuses after all are innocent; sexually active women are not. The National Council of

> *"There are several other cases already in the pipeline, any of which could be used to overturn* **Roe v. Wade** *or . . . to weaken it."*

Catholic Bishops is currently spending $3–4 million in a propaganda campaign aimed at "persuading" women of the immorality of abortion. This doesn't count other monies spent in their antiabortion work.

This array of strategies placed the pro-choice movement on the defensive. The movement was forced to protect gains already won rather than advancing women's reproductive freedoms.

The Pro-Choice Movement Responds

A strong, multi-issue women's liberation movement fought for abortion rights as part of a broader agenda for women's freedom. The feminist movement fought for women to be able to control their own reproductive lives. Legal abortion was a necessary step toward this goal, but only the first step.

By comparison with this vision, *Roe v. Wade* was a compromise. It did give us legal abortion. But abortion that was controlled by doctors and the state, and protected [only] by the right to privacy. . . .

Our analysis of the abortion struggle leads us to the need for transforming the agenda, the strategies, the membership, and the leadership of the pro-choice movement. The current crisis is full of possibilities for accomplishing these changes. There is a need for many forms of political activism and for activists working in different arenas to find ways to support each other's activities. After all, it is the ability to translate our collective rage, vision, and hope into collective action that is our power.

New leadership is emerging among women of color and young women. This leadership is creating a far-reaching agenda for reproductive freedom, providing a chance to include women who have not traditionally been in the forefront of this struggle. The abortion rights movement should look for ways to directly support these efforts. We can bring this agenda into all of the organizations and arenas in which we work.

> *"We must continue to resist efforts to criminalize abortion even as we prepare ourselves for that eventuality."*

Acknowledging that the judicial system will no longer be an avenue of relief for the foreseeable future requires political action on every front. We must continue to resist efforts to criminalize abortion even as we prepare ourselves for that eventuality. And we must emphasize access to abortion and fight to restore funding, even as the legal right itself is in question. As we fight for specific goals we will also be working toward our larger vision.

Government Should Fund Abortions for the Poor

by Stephanie Mencimer

About the author: *Stephanie Mencimer writes frequently for the Sunday Out-look section of the* Washington Post, *a daily newspaper.*

As [a response to] the Clinton administration's welfare reform plan, the op-ed pages of America have zeroed in on a familiar villain: the overly fecund welfare mother.

At the heart of the debate has been the morally charged and highly compli-cated issue of illegitimacy—a category into which 68 percent of all black ba-bies and 22 percent of white babies are born.

The centrality of the illegitimacy issue to current thinking about America's "underclass" is best captured by American Enterprise Institute scholar Charles Murray, who is lately enjoying a resurgence in popularity for ideas he put forth in his 1984 book, *Losing Ground.* As he wrote in the *Wall Street Journal* "Ille-gitimacy is the single most important social problem of our time—more impor-tant than crime, drugs, poverty, illiteracy, welfare or homelessness, because it drives everything else."

Welfare and Illegitimacy

Through various ideological prisms, writers such as Charles Krauthammer, George Will and Mickey Kaus have echoed Murray's sentiments: Illegitimacy is at the root of what's wrong with the underclass. And each believes that wel-fare benefits are a sharp spur to this careless procreation. Undereducated and sometimes drug-addled welfare mothers (unlike ordinary, white, middle-class moms) are willing to bear another child just to milk the government for an extra $65 a month.

Our pundits argue that the government would be doing the poor a favor by cutting off additional AFDC [Aid to Families with Dependent Children] bene-fits to women who have children while on welfare. But what none of the men

Stephanie Mencimer, "Ending Illegitimacy as We Know It," *The Washington Post National Weekly Edition*, January 17-23, 1994. Reprinted by permission of the author.

dominating this debate has acknowledged (and what women's groups have been strangely silent about pointing out) is that welfare benefits probably have far less impact on illegitimacy than does poor women's lack of access to contraception and abortion.

For example, according to a recent Census Bureau study, white, college-educated women give birth to only 4 percent of all illegitimate kids; women with family incomes of $75,000 or more only 1 percent (Murphy Brown notwithstanding).

> *"Welfare benefits probably have far less impact on illegitimacy than . . . lack of access to contraception and abortion."*

Obviously, the reason rich white women don't have kids out of wedlock is not just because they can't collect welfare benefits for doing so. They have a deep understanding of how an unwanted pregnancy could impinge on their standard of living.

More important, though, they have the *means* to do something about it—more resources, better reproductive health care, education, access to contraception and better access to abortion. In fact, that small percentage of women with household incomes of more than $50,000 obtain more than 10 percent of all abortions performed in this country each year.

The Plight of the Poor

Poor women aren't so lucky. Between 1980 and 1990, federal spending on family planning plummeted by a third in inflation-adjusted dollars. And while the abortion rights movement has successfully kept abortion legal, it hasn't managed to keep it cheap. In the District of Columbia, for example, an abortion performed at a no-frills clinic averages $265—that's half the rent for some poor women, or twice the monthly budget for food.

And they can't rely on the government to cover that bill. In the mid-70s, Republican Rep. Henry Hyde of Illinois sponsored an appropriations rider that banned the use of federal funds for poor women's abortions. After the amendment took effect in 1978, the number of federally funded abortions dropped from 294,600 in 1977 to 165 in 1990—financing permitted because the mothers' lives were in danger.

You don't have to be Pythagoras to see the math here. While some of these 300,000 women every year manage to come up with enough cash for an abortion, studies by the family-planning research group the Guttmacher Institute, estimate that 20 percent of Medicaid-eligible American women now carry their unwanted children to term. States that have also banned public financing for abortion have found similar results.

After the state of Michigan banned the use of state Medicaid funds for abortions in 1988, the number of abortions the next year dropped by 10,300—that's 23 percent. The number of births rose by 7,600 (5.4 percent), and the number of children enrolled for welfare before birth by mothers on Medicaid rose by 3,000—a fiscally horrifying 31 percent increase.

By 1990, Detroit-area adoption agencies were telling the *Detroit Free Press* that they had seen a 50 percent increase in the newborn children of poor black women being put up for adoption since the ban went into effect. This should hardly come as a surprise considering that in 1990 a woman with three children in Michigan received $150 a month in welfare benefits. An abortion there cost $318.

Why Punish Poor Women?

Obviously, not all women on welfare would opt for abortion if it were publicly funded, but it's clear that they choose abortion more often when it's federally funded—or free. But the economics aren't so clear-cut when it comes to what Charles Murray & Co. would have you believe: that generous welfare benefits increase birth rates. Significantly, states with high AFDC benefits have no more out-of-wedlock births than states with low benefits.

Furthermore, reducing welfare benefits in the past hasn't reversed the rise of illegitimacy. Far from it. In fact, in his 1992 book, *Rethinking Social Policy*, sociologist Christopher Jencks notes that between 1976 and 1988, the purchasing power of welfare benefits fell 16 percent and the percentage of all single mothers on AFDC dropped from more than 60 percent to 45 percent. Nonetheless, Jencks notes, between 1975 and 1990, out-of-wedlock births (for all races) doubled.

Illegitimacy obviously poses a serious, burgeoning problem for American culture; it further stacks the deck against millions of children in poverty. But punishing poor women for bearing kids without providing them the same family planning options that middle- and upper-class women have isn't only unjust. It's inept policy. Welfare reform is based on the idea that government should help people become self-sufficient and make better lives for their families. Providing a range of reproductive health alternatives for poor women is one way to help them be responsible.

Thus if Clinton really wants to "end welfare as we know it," as he has said, his smartest step might be to work to repeal the Hyde amendment—a move likely to have a far larger effect on welfare rolls than the kind of expensive, low-results welfare-to-work programs so celebrated lately. (For example, Florida's $30-million-a-year Project Independence reduced the welfare rolls by only 5 percent. California's Greater Avenues for Independence program, at $120 million a

> *"Twenty percent of Medicaid-eligible American women now carry their unwanted children to term."*

year, reduced the welfare rolls by only 4 percent to 5 percent.) But so far the Clinton administration has been bold enough only to fund the abortions of women impregnated through rape or incest—an act it took by administrative fiat Jan. 1, 1994.

Of course, making-lazy-welfare-mothers-work is a politically delicious position. Giving-welfare-mothers-free-abortions is not. Polls show that even people who are in favor of abortion often vote against referendums on public funding because they don't want their tax dollars spent on wayward women. Then again, taxpayers don't want to pay for welfare benefits, foster care, Medicaid, food stamps or prison construction, either.

Net Savings for the Nation

In the cold cost-benefit analysis, publicly financed abortion makes a lot of sense. For every tax dollar spent on abortions for poor women, the public saves at least four dollars in public medical and welfare expenditures in the first two years of the child's life alone. If abortions were fully funded in every state, the Guttmacher Institute estimates that the net savings for the nation as a whole over a two-year period would total between $435 million and $540 million—four to six times the $95 million to $125 million it would cost to publicly fund abortions for all Medicaid-eligible women who want one.

In this light, there may be more support for public funding of abortion than the abortion-rights movement has chosen to exploit. Yet as this one-sided debate over welfare reform has flourished, feminists have been suspiciously quiet on these issues. (Where are you Susan Faludi, Naomi Wolf?) Could it be that women's groups have as low a view of welfare mothers as Charles Murray does?

> *"Providing a range of reproductive health alternatives for poor women is one way to help them be responsible."*

This possibility is deeply troubling, because welfare reform is a distinctly woman's issue. Not only are political leaders and analysts placing the responsibility for urban poverty squarely on the shoulders of women, but the reform effort involves every social issue we've struggled with for the past 20 years: economic equality, child care, health care and reproductive freedom.

If nothing else, abortion-rights advocates could certainly use a little of their considerable leverage to remind legislators that before they embark on Draconian efforts to cut off AFDC for poor mothers, they ought to do a lot more to help welfare moms avoid motherhood in the first place. Talk about politically palatable. For the right reasons or the wrong ones, that's a goal even crabby old Charles Murray would approve of.

Laws Should Protect Reproductive Rights

by Janet Benshoof

About the author: *Janet Benshoof is the president of the Center for Reproductive Law & Policy, a New York City organization formed in 1992. The center seeks to ensure access to abortion and reproductive health care for all women—particularly low-income, minority, rural, and young women—through litigation and public education.*

In 1973, when the United States Supreme Court first recognized a woman's right to reproductive autonomy in the landmark decision *Roe v Wade*, it altered irrevocably the face of the American political landscape by galvanizing a movement whose sole purpose was to either overturn *Roe* or render it irrelevant. Sadly, 20 years later, that movement has been successful in a number of ways. Although the right to terminate a pregnancy before fetal viability was reaffirmed in *Planned Parenthood of Southeastern Pennsylvania v Casey*, many women remain unable to exercise that constitutional right. Access to reproductive health care has been limited to such an extent that there are no abortion providers in 83% of the counties in this nation, forcing many women to travel hundreds of miles to obtain their medical care. Other legal and logistical obstacles designed to prevent women from choosing abortion, combined with a new wave of violence and harassment of women and abortion providers, merely exacerbate this problem. As a result, only some women may exercise their constitutional right to make personal, private childbearing decisions.

The Impact of *Casey*

Many believed that the US Supreme Court was poised to overturn *Roe*. Yet, on June 29, 1992, in an extremely divided opinion in *Casey*, the High Court preserved what it deemed the central tenets of *Roe*. Although expressly holding that states are not free to ban abortion, the justices upheld several other Pennsylvania provisions. Based on the record before it, the Court found constitutional a requirement that all women delay at least 24 hours after receiving a state-scripted lecture discouraging abortion; a requirement that a woman under the age of 18 obtain the "informed" consent of one parent; onerous and unnecessary provider reporting requirements; and a vague definition of "medical emergency."

At the same time, the justices changed the legal standard by which federal courts are to judge the constitutionality of such restrictions, radically changing the legal protections previously afforded women and abortion providers in *Roe*. Rejecting the "strict scrutiny" standard granted all other fundamental rights—such as freedom of speech and freedom of religion—the justices adopted an "undue burden" standard that allows states to impose abortion restrictions so long as they do not have "the purpose or effect of placing a substantial obstacle in the path of a woman seeking an abortion." Whereas the strict scrutiny standard required courts to strike down *all* restrictions that interfered with a woman's ability to choose to terminate her pregnancy prior to fetal viability (unless the state proved that the restrictions would actually promote maternal health), the new standard places the initial burden on women to demonstrate "undue" harm. Federal courts are then directed to measure the *degree* to which each restriction interferes with a woman's ability to exercise her right to choose abortion. Given the federal judiciary's increasing tendency to interpret the Constitution narrowly, providing less protection on issues of privacy and due process, judges may be reluctant to find abortion restrictions unconstitutional under the new standard. Although all women will feel the effects of these new restrictions in the form of reduced access to care, the women with the fewest resources and least political clout in our society—low-income women, young women, battered women, women of color, and women living in rural areas—will be the ones to pay the greatest price.

> *"The women with the fewest resources and least political clout . . . will be the ones to pay the greatest price."*

Reproductive Autonomy

Two other concepts codified in *Casey* will also have a profound impact on women's right to reproductive autonomy. First, in revising the protections of *Roe*, the High Court found the promotion of "fetal life" to be a legitimate state interest *throughout pregnancy*. The plurality thus rejected *Roe*'s trimester framework, under which a state's interest in preserving the fetus did not become "compelling," and thus a basis for restrictions, until after the fetus was viable. Second, the *Casey* opinion represents the first time that the Court abandoned the principle of government neutrality in an abortion case that did not involve the issue of funding. Prior to *Casey*, the Court recognized a governmental interest in allocating monies based on a policy preference for childbirth over abortion and upheld restrictions on abortion funding. But the Court had also previously found unconstitutional state attempts to influence a woman's decision to terminate her pregnancy, which were virtually identical to those at issue in *Casey*. By abandoning governmental neutrality, the Court goes far in permitting states to discourage the abortion choice. Since *Casey* was decided, several courts and numerous state legislatures have grappled with measures designed to restrict a woman's ability to make personal, private childbearing decisions.

Supreme Court Action Since *Casey*

Although it technically takes four "votes" on the High Court to grant a hearing in a case, a quartet will seldom support consideration unless it believes it can garner another justice in the final opinion. Since the *Casey* ruling, the Supreme Court has refused to review three cases involving "facial" challenges [filed before a law or regulation takes effect] to outright bans on abortion. The Court's decision to reject these cases implies that the *Casey* plurality—which reaffirmed the previability right to choose abortion, albeit with restrictions that do not impose an undue burden—remains unchanged. The High Court also refused to review a case from Mississippi involving a mandatory 24-hour delay and biased counseling requirement for women seeking abortions. Without comment, the justices let stand a ruling by the US Court of Appeals for the Fifth Circuit narrowly interpreting *Casey* to render any such laws constitutional on their face. Lifting an injunction that had prevented the requirement from taking effect, the appeals court denied women and abortion providers an opportunity to present evidence about the restriction's likely effects under the Supreme Court's newly minted undue burden standard. Mississippi began enforcing the onerous law in August 1992, resulting in an immediate and marked decline in the number of women obtaining abortions in the state.

> *"Pro-choice congress members advanced a measure making it a federal crime to interfere with access to reproductive health care facilities."*

A second case involving a mandatory 24-hour delay and biased counseling provision came to the High Court in an emergency application filed after the US Court of Appeals for the Eighth Circuit refused to stay a district court ruling on a North Dakota law. After finding the law constitutional on its face in light of *Casey* and granting the state's motion for summary judgment, the lower court vacated a preliminary injunction against enforcement. Denied a trial during which they had hoped to demonstrate the undue burdens that mandatory delays and biased counseling would place on women seeking abortions in North Dakota, plaintiffs sought a stay from the appeals court and then from Justice Harry Blackmun. Two days after Justice Blackmun blocked enforcement, the full Court vacated his emergency stay. However, in a concurring opinion, Justices Sandra Day O'Connor and David Souter asserted that plaintiffs need not show in a facial challenge that abortion restrictions would be unconstitutional in all circumstances—the position taken by both the district court and the court of appeals. These two critical members of the *Casey* plurality also stated that lower courts must consider evidence about how a law affects women when determining whether it imposes an undue burden; those that impose substantial obstacles on the right to choose must be invalidated. The appeals court has since issued a stay pending its ruling on the merits of the case. . . .

Federal Legislative Efforts

Not surprisingly, pro-choice activities in Congress have reflected the legal battles over a woman's right to make reproductive choices.

The Freedom of Choice Act. Following the *Casey* decision, the Freedom of Choice Act, a measure designed to codify *Roe* by providing federal statutory protection to women's childbearing decisions, was reintroduced. Having advanced through the respective Congressional committees, the Freedom of Choice Act is [as of book publication date] awaiting floor action in both the House and Senate. Unfortunately, during the committee process, several amendments were attached to both versions of the measure, causing some pro-choice advocates to raise questions about the bill's ability to provide adequate protection for the abortion choice. In particular, both measures include language allowing states to impose some restrictions on young women's access to abortion services. The Senate version furthermore permits states to decline to fund abortion services for low-income women. In addition, the Senate measure contains language allowing states to protect not only individuals, but also institutions that refuse to provide abortion services because it conflicts with their religious or moral beliefs.

The Freedom of Access to Clinic Entrances Act. In the only abortion-related case decided by the High Court in 1993, *Bray v Alexandria Women's Health Clinic*, the justices limited the ability of women's health centers to prevent antichoice blockades under a federal civil rights statute. The Court held that Operation Rescue activities in the Washington, DC, area did not violate civil rights law because clinics failed to prove antichoice demonstrators were motivated by "animus" against women, a finding needed to invoke the protections of the "prevention" clause of 42 USC §1985(3) (the "Ku Klux Klan Act"). Moreover, relying on the 1974 decision in *Geduldig v Aiello*, the majority concluded that discrimination against abortion, as with discrimination based on pregnancy, is not gender-based discrimination. Recognizing the need to counteract this decision and the escalating violence against and harassment of abortion providers, pro-choice congress members advanced a measure making it a federal offense to interfere with access to reproductive health care

> *"Since the federal government first cut off funding for low-income women's abortion services 15 years ago, many states have followed suit."*

facilities. [President Clinton signed the bill into law in May 1994.]

Mandatory Delays and Biased Counseling. Of the 26 state legislatures that considered measures to impose mandatory delays and biased counseling requirements in 1993, only Nebraska, South Dakota, and Utah have passed such measures so far. Both the Utah and South Dakota statutes have been temporarily enjoined, and a challenge to the Nebraska law is expected. Meanwhile, such legislation remains active in only a handful of states.

Women seeking abortions are currently subjected to delays in only two states: Mississippi (24 hours) and Kansas (8 hours). In North Dakota, Pennsylvania, South Dakota, and Utah, 24-hour delays are enjoined pending the outcome of facial challenges in federal court, whereas a 24-hour provision in Ohio and a 72-hour delay in Tennessee have been blocked by state courts. Laws in Kentucky and Massachusetts were permanently enjoined prior to *Casey* and no attempt has been made to reopen these cases. In Idaho, the Attorney General recently issued an opinion finding valid, after *Casey*, a 24-hour delay that has not been enforced for many years. Mandatory delays remain on the books but unenforced in Delaware and Indiana.

Restrictions on Young Women's Access to Abortion. Although at least 17 states considered provisions in 1993 to mandate the involvement of parents in young women's abortion decisions, only South Dakota has enacted a new measure, which requires one-parent notification at least 48 hours prior to an abortion. After a state trial court struck down a Michigan parental consent provision because the medical emergency definition was invalid under the state constitution, the legislature reenacted the statute using the definition upheld in *Casey*; that law took effect in April 1993. Although laws in 35 states currently include requirements that young women notify or obtain the consent of one or both parents prior to an abortion, these restrictions are in effect in just 22 states.

> *"We must also work to guarantee* **access** *to comprehensive reproductive health services for all women."*

Legislation Concerning Funding for Low-Income Women's Abortions. Since the federal government first cut off funding for low-income women's abortion services 15 years ago, many states have followed suit in their state Medicaid and medical assistance programs. In 1993, efforts to decrease or prohibit funding were introduced in six states, but only a restrictive West Virginia provision has passed. So far, proposals to increase funding in seven states have not yet been enacted. Currently, 13 states provide funds for low-income women's abortions that are necessary to protect a woman's physical or mental health.

Unnecessary Regulations on Abortion Services. Reporting requirements have been adopted in South Dakota and Utah in 1993, although at least 13 other states have considered reporting or licensing requirements or other regulations on the provision of abortion services.

Protective Measures. So far, at least nine states have considered proposals to provide greater protection for reproductive rights. This type of legislation remains active in Massachusetts and has been enacted in Maine. The Maine Privacy Act prohibits the state from restricting access to abortion prior to viability and thereafter if necessary to preserve a woman's life or health; it also includes an "informed consent" requirement and leaves intact a requirement that young women obtain the consent of one parent or adult family member, or seek judicial waiver, prior to an abortion. Finally, the law repealed a 48-hour mandatory delay that had remained on the books but was unenforced.

Due to an increase in antichoice violence and harassment, including the murder of Florida doctor David Gunn in March 1993, efforts to protect reproductive health care providers and access to women's health clinics were introduced in 24 states and the District of Columbia. As of Fall 1993, five states have enacted such measures or amended current law to add more protection.

A Basic Human Right

In his dissenting opinion in *Casey*, Chief Justice William Rehnquist stated: "*Roe* continues to exist, but only in a way a storefront on a western movie set exists: a mere facade to give the illusion of reality." For too many women, this prediction has been and continues to be proven true. Our opposition knows that to prevent women from obtaining abortions, they must wage their battle on many fronts—the courts, the legislatures, the clinics, and the court of public opinion. Whether they are legislating to ban abortion outright, placing impossible roadblocks in the path of women seeking abortions, or terrorizing reproductive health care providers, our opposition has learned this lesson well. For this reason, the struggle for women's reproductive autonomy must not only assure constitutional *protection* for the right to choose, we must also work to guarantee *access* to comprehensive reproductive health services for all women.

Laws Should Not Require Parental Involvement in Abortion Decisions

by The Center for Population Options

About the author: *The Center for Population Options (now called Advocates for Youth) is a Washington, D.C., educational organization that works to reduce unwanted teenage pregnancies and increase minors' access to legal abortion.*

While a majority of Americans believes that abortion should be legal and available to teenagers, a strong majority also favors laws requiring parental consent for a minor's abortion. Most teens, however, believe that while parent-child communication regarding sex is beneficial, communication about abortion should be voluntary rather than mandated through parental involvement laws. Many states have passed, or are considering, laws that would *mandate* parental consent for, or notification of, a young woman's decision to obtain an abortion. The question is whether laws compelling parental involvement achieve the goal of improved family communication and decision-making by young women facing crisis pregnancies.

About Mandatory Parental Involvement

Who is affected by consent and notification laws?

Most mandatory parental consent and notification laws affect women 17 years old and younger. Eighteen- and 19-year-olds are not subject to mandatory parental involvement. Specifically, these laws affect only those young women who, for some reason, feel they cannot tell their parents about a pregnancy.

What's the difference between mandated parental consent and parental notification?

Parental consent laws require that an abortion provider obtain the consent of a young woman's parent before the abortion can be performed. Consent of either one or both parents may be mandated.

Excerpted from *Adolescent Abortion and Mandated Parental Involvement: The Impact of Back Alley Laws on Young Women* by the Center for Population Options (now Advocates for Youth), Washington, DC, 1993. Reprinted with permission.

Parental notification laws require that an abortion provider inform a minor's parent (or parents) that she plans to have an abortion. Although the parents cannot technically veto this procedure, the abortion cannot occur without the parent's knowledge. To enforce this requirement, some states insist upon a waiting period between notification of the parent and performance of the abortion.

In practice, therefore, consent and notification laws have a similar impact, giving parents authority over the abortion decision. In the minds of most teenagers, parental consent and notification laws are identical.

Is there a federal law mandating parental involvement?

There is currently no federal requirement for parental involvement in abortion decisions. The "Bliley Amendment" was introduced in the 103rd Congress to require programs that receive federal Health and Human Services funds and which also perform (privately funded) abortions to notify one parent before a minor can obtain an abortion. This Amendment was stricter than any enforced state law in the nation and would have affected virtually all health care facilities nationwide. The 103rd Congress [rejected] this and other legislation mandating parental involvement.

The Freedom of Choice Act (FOCA) would codify into law the principles established in *Roe v. Wade*. FOCA—as introduced—allows states to mandate parental involvement for minors' abortions. Thus the current version of FOCA would not guarantee access to abortion as a fundamental right for young women. [FOCA had not come to a vote as of publication of this book.]

Parental Involvement Laws Among States

Which states require parental consent or notification for abortion?

Parental involvement laws are currently on the books in a total of 36 states, and enforced in 22 states.

Parental consent laws are [as of 1993] *enforced* in 12 states: Alabama, Indiana, Louisiana, Massachusetts, Michigan, Mississippi, Missouri, North Dakota, Rhode Island, South Carolina, Wisconsin and Wyoming.

Enforcement of parental consent laws is blocked by a court (*enjoined*) pending the outcome of constitutional challenges in four states: Colorado, Illinois, Kentucky and Pennsylvania. Consent laws in Arizona, California and Florida have been declared unconstitutional under state constitutions, and therefore cannot be enforced. Alaska, Delaware and New Mexico have parental consent requirements which

> *"Consent and notification laws have a similar impact, giving parents authority over the abortion decision."*

are neither enjoined nor enforced. Tennessee's parental consent law has been "impliedly repealed" by a new interpretation of the state's parental notice law.

Parental notification laws are *enforced* in 10 states: Arkansas, Georgia, Kansas, Maryland, Minnesota, Nebraska, Ohio, Tennessee, Utah and West Virginia.

Parental notification laws are *enjoined* in three states: Illinois, Nevada and South Dakota. Notification laws in Idaho and Montana exist, but are generally not enforced. An unconstitutional 1979 Maine notification law was repealed when the state codified *Roe* in 1992. Tennessee's notification law prohibits minors from obtaining an abortion until 48 hours after both parents have received notice; no judicial bypass provision exists in the law. A state court interpreted this law as requiring only one parent's notification and allowing a physician to waive involvement if the minor's physical, psychological or emotional health is in jeopardy. This new interpretation is being enforced while under appeal.

Informing Parents

Does a young woman usually need to involve her parents in order to get contraception, reproductive health care or other sensitive services?

No. Because people are reluctant to seek treatment for problems related to sex or sexuality, confidentiality is a vital component in encouraging prompt medical care. This is especially true for adolescents. Federal regulations do not require parental involvement for contraceptive services provided by federal programs.

Some parents feel that, since their consent is required for activities such as ear piercing and school trips, consent should be required for abortion. While schools and other organizations often require parental permission, they do so to protect themselves from potential liability rather than to comply with specific state statutes. No state law *requires* consent for participation in these activities. Most importantly, there is no constitutionally protected right involved in these examples, nor are there lasting or irreversible consequences for the minor if consent is withheld.

> *"Confidentiality is a vital component in encouraging prompt medical care."*

In 1965, the Supreme Court determined in *Griswold v. Connecticut* that the right to prevent pregnancy through the use of contraceptives is protected by the right to privacy. This right was recognized for unmarried individuals in 1972 by the ruling in *Eisenstad v. Baird*, and explicitly applied to minors in 1977 by *Carey v. Population Services International*. Therefore, states cannot forbid minors' access to contraception.

States generally treat services relating to sexual or reproductive health as private and confidential for adults and minors. Parental involvement as a requirement for such treatment is either forbidden or not required in a majority of states. In addition, many states allow minors to consent for pregnancy-related care, medical care of their own children and treatment for drug or alcohol abuse. Furthermore, no state has a law requiring a young women who decides to bear a child to inform her parents, nor to receive their consent to continue a pregnancy.

Are adolescents able to make reasoned decisions about abortion?

Yes. Young women are capable of consenting to their own reproductive health care. A 1992 study of women seeking pregnancy tests found those aged 14–17 to be as competent as adult women to make an informed, voluntary and independent decision about abortion and to understand the risks and benefits of the procedure.

Many organizations recognize this fact, and explicitly support adolescents' right to confidential access for sensitive services, including abortion. Such groups include the American Medical Association, the American Public Health Association and the Society for Adolescent Medicine.

Teens Choose to Inform Parents

Do young women usually tell their parents about a crisis pregnancy and their desire for abortion?

Regardless of whether or not state law forces them to do so, over 60 percent of all pregnant teens who choose to terminate their pregnancy *do* inform at least one parent. The younger the teen, the more likely she is to involve either a parent or another trusted adult in her decision. In a recent study conducted in states without mandated parental involvement, 74 percent of the teens under 15 had voluntarily told a parent and 80 percent of those under 16 were accompanied to the clinic by their mother.

In the above study, 81 percent of the teens under 18 reported at least one adult was involved in their abortion decision. Of those under 16, 90 percent involved a parent or another adult in their decision. Over half the minors whose parents did not know of the decision reported that they had discussed the situation with another adult such as a health professional, guidance counselor or teacher. Another study found fewer than 5 percent of young pregnant women failed to involve an adult in their decision.

Young women choose not to involve their parents for numerous reasons, including fear of being rejected, abused or of disappointing the parent. Young women are more likely to inform a parent of their abortion decision if they are younger, live a greater distance from the abortion provider, have established good communication with their mother and anticipate a supportive reaction.

> *"Over 60 percent of all pregnant teens who choose to terminate their pregnancy* **do** *inform at least one parent."*

Do more young women talk to their parents because of these laws?

No. A comparison of a state with parental involvement laws (Minnesota) and one without (Wisconsin) revealed no significant difference in the proportion of young women who involved their parents in the abortion decision.

Factors other than parental involvement laws were deemed to be more important in a young woman's decision to discuss her situation with a parent. The researchers concluded that mandated involvement does not, in fact, increase family communication.

There will always be instances in which a law convinces a young woman to inform her parents of a crisis pregnancy. Many young women who are reluctant to involve their parents voluntarily in an abortion decision are, however, equally reluctant when required to do so by law. These young women will go to great lengths to retain privacy and autonomy in their decision making.

A nationwide survey by the Alan Guttmacher Institute indicated that 23 percent of abortion patients under 18 would be reluctant to seek parental involvement in their decision. If parental involvement were required, 39 percent of this group reported that they would self-abort, 86 percent said they would leave home and 13 percent were unsure about their course of action.

> *"Young women are significantly more satisfied with the pregnancy outcome when they make the decision themselves."*

In one study, young women who chose not to inform their mother of their abortion decision stated that they feared her disappointment (74 percent), anger (55 percent) or adding to her stress (25 percent).

Many judges, health care providers and counselors who work with young women seeking abortions agree that when a teen believes she cannot involve her parents in her decision, she is usually right. Long-term studies of abusive families indicate an increase in the incidence of violence during adolescence and/or when a family member is pregnant. In a recent study, 4 percent of teens under 18 who voluntarily informed a parent about their pregnancy reported physical violence in response. The same study found that 13 percent of women under 18 whose parents had discovered her pregnancy some other way reported violence.

Research indicates that young women are significantly more satisfied with the pregnancy outcome when they make the decision themselves, rather than having it made for them. One study assessed whether the satisfaction of minors who experienced either abortion or childbirth was affected by whether or not she had talked with her mother before making the decision. The researchers concluded that the young woman's satisfaction was not related to whether the minor had consulted her mother. Satisfaction was highly related, however, to the support the minor received from her mother.

About Judicial Bypass

What is a judicial bypass procedure?

In 1979 the Supreme Court ruled in *Bellotti v. Baird* that any mandatory parental consent law must include a procedure by which young women may obtain a waiver of the requirement in a confidential and expeditious manner. At a minimum, the law must allow teens to go to court and ask a judge's permission to obtain the abortion without parental involvement.

In theory, the judge is required to grant a waiver if (1) the young woman is "mature" enough to make her own decision, or (2) if the abortion is deemed to be in her "best interest." In practice, however, comments from judges charged with making these determinations suggest that, in many cases, the judges' personal moral beliefs about abortion are as much a factor in the bypass decision as are the young woman's maturity or her best interest.

In effect, judicial bypass provisions merely substitute consent or notification of a judge for that of a parent. A few states (Maryland, Maine, Connecticut) have expanded the bypass procedure so that adults other than judges may serve as parental substitutes for the purposes of approving the young woman's decision. The majority of states with parental involvement laws, however, require a young woman to involve either a parent or a judge in her decision.

Problems with Judicial Bypass

Is a judicial bypass a reasonable alternative for most young women?

The judicial bypass procedure is required to be speedy and to protect the young woman's privacy, but rarely achieves these goals in practice. In Ohio, the judicial bypass procedure can take up to 22 days, pushing many young women into riskier, more expensive, second trimester abortions.

In seeking judicial bypass, young women may also have to sacrifice their anonymity. In Minnesota, it is not unusual for as many as 23 people to learn about the young woman's pregnancy (and desire for an abortion) as she winds her way through the court system. In isolated and smaller communities, young women frequently encounter acquaintances and relatives while seeking judicial bypass.

> *"Young women who have used the judicial bypass procedure report that it was more traumatic than the actual abortion."*

Of 477 minors who sought judicial bypass of Massachusetts' two-parent consent requirement during a four-year period, all but nine were determined mature enough to make their own decision. Eight of these nine were granted the abortion as being in their best interest. Similarly, in a five-year period, Minnesota courts heard over 3,500 judicial bypass requests; six were withdrawn and nine denied.

In some states, judicial bypass is a time-consuming, costly and humiliating experience with little or no benefit to the teen. Young women who have used the judicial bypass procedure report that it was more traumatic than the actual abortion procedure. The typical teen reports that she was embarrassed and humiliated to have to explain her sexual life to an unfamiliar authority figure.

Is judicial bypass an option for all young women?

Significant numbers of young women do seek judicial bypass. Most of these teens, however, are from middle and upper class families. Minors who are poor, less educated, more wary of the court system or who live in rural areas are far less able or likely to seek a bypass. For those who do not live in counties where court hearings are held or who must consider absence from school or work, transportation and other expenses, judicial bypass may not be an option. In some counties, judges routinely deny all bypass applications, effectively eliminating this alternative.

In 1981, in Massachusetts, which requires consent of two parents, 25 percent of abortion patients under 18 used the bypass system. In Minnesota, where the law mandates that young women notify both parents, more than one-third of all teenagers seeking abortion in 1984 used the bypass system.

> *"Mandated parental involvement laws generally cause young women to delay abortion."*

In states that mandate the involvement of both parents, judicial bypass is frequently sought by the teen and one parent to avoid involving the other parent. In these cases, the second parent is typically absent, estranged or abusive. Approximately 25 percent of teens seeking bypass in Minnesota were accompanied by a parent.

Are there alternatives to the judicial bypass procedure?

Connecticut, Maine and Maryland have passed laws which attempt to diminish the negative aspects of these statutes by expanding the range of adults to whom a young woman may turn. The purpose of these laws is to ensure that the young woman gets support and information, the involvement of an adult is assured without limiting options to a parent or a judge.

In Maine, a 1989 consent law requires that a minor seeking an abortion must receive information and counseling from a health professional and must sign an informed consent form after this discussion. Alternatively, she may obtain consent for the abortion from an adult family member other than a parent or have the counseling requirement waived under certain conditions by a physician, professional counselor or judge.

The 1990 Connecticut law requires a physician or counselor to provide pregnancy information and counseling to young women under 18 before an abortion is performed. Maryland's 1991 law requires parental notification for those under 18, but allows a doctor to waive this requirement if it is not in the young woman's best interest.

The Impact of Involvement Laws

What effect have parental involvement laws had?

Mandated parental involvement laws generally cause young women to delay abortion either by creating a longer decision-making process, involving teens in conflict with parents, forcing teens to participate in lengthy court process or causing them to travel to a state without mandated parental involvement.

Teenagers, more than any other age group, tend to deny pregnancy and to delay abortion regardless of whether parental involvement is required. These laws increase the anxiety of pregnancy and lengthen delays. Later abortions are undesirable because they involve greater health risks than do earlier procedures and because they are more expensive.

Data from Massachusetts and Minnesota show that the ratio of late to early abortions increased by about 25 percent after implementation of parental consent and notification laws. In contrast, this ratio has declined nationwide for women not subject to parental involvement laws.

In a survey of Minnesota clinic patients, researchers found that women under 18 were 39 percent more likely than older women to delay abortion because they feared telling their parents or partner. In fact, 63 percent of minors having late abortions stated that they had delayed for this reason.

An unforeseen effect of the debate over mandated parental involvement, and restrictions on reproductive choice in general, is confusion about the basic nature of the procedure. A recent study of adolescent knowledge and attitudes about abortion found that many teens mistakenly believed abortion to be medically dangerous, widely illegal, emotionally traumatic and a cause of sterility. Most of these teens, however, also supported legal abortion as a woman's right.

Do parental consent laws reduce the number of pregnancies or abortions for teens?

Evidence suggests that they do not. Between 1980 and 1983, the Massachusetts law caused a third of young women seeking abortions to travel to nearby states where parental involvement was not required. Combining in-state and out-of-state abortions for teens reveals that the number of abortions for this group has not been significantly reduced since implementation of the law.

> *"[Minnesota's] parental notification requirement did not result in fewer pregnancies among teens."*

In Minneapolis, birthrates for 15-17 year olds increased 38 percent in the four years after implementation of the notification law. Prior to implementation, the birthrate for this age group had risen only 2 percent over nine years. The parental notification requirement did not result in fewer pregnancies among teens.

The authors of a recent study claim that Minnesota's statewide decline in teen abortion rates was due to the parental notification law. They do not explain, however, why abortion rates fell more for the population of teens (18- and 19-year-olds) unaffected by the law than for younger teens. During the same period, states without parental involvement laws also experienced declines in teen abortion rates which were as sharp as Minnesota's, indicating that other factors were involved in the abortion rate decline.

Laws Should Protect Unborn Children

by Mother Teresa

About the author: *Mother Teresa is the founder and mother superior of the Order of the Missionaries of Charity, headquartered in Calcutta, India. The order provides services to needy people around the world. Mother Teresa's following* amicus curiae *("friend of the court") brief was filed with the U.S. Supreme Court on February 14, 1994.*

I hope you will count it no presumption that I seek your leave to address you on behalf of the unborn child. Like that child I can be called an outsider. I am not an American citizen. My parents were Albanian. I was born before the First World War in a part of what was not yet, and is no longer, Yugoslavia. In many senses I know what it is like to be without a country. I also know what it is like to feel an adopted citizen of other lands. When I was still a young girl I travelled to India. I found my work among the poor and the sick of that nation, and I have lived there ever since.

Mothers and Children

Since 1950 I have worked with my many sisters from around the world as one of the Missionaries of Charity. Our congregation now has over 400 foundations in more than 100 countries, including the United States of America. We have almost 5,000 sisters. We care for those who are often treated as outsiders in their own communities by their own neighbors—the starving, the crippled, the impoverished, and the diseased, from the old woman with a brain tumor in Calcutta to the young man with AIDS in New York City. A special focus of our care is mothers and their children. This includes mothers who feel pressured to sacrifice their unborn children by want, neglect, despair, and philosophies and governmental policies which promote the dehumanization of inconvenient human life. And it includes the children themselves, innocent and utterly defenseless, who are at the mercy of those who would deny their humanity. So, in a

From Mother Teresa's amicus curiae brief filed with the U.S. Supreme Court, February 14, 1994, in the cases *Loce v. New Jersey* and *Krail v. New Jersey*.

sense, my sisters and those we serve are all outsiders together. At the same time, we are supremely conscious of the common bonds of humanity that unite us and transcend national boundaries.

In another sense no one in the world who prizes liberty and human rights can feel anything but a strong kinship with America. Yours is the one great nation in all of history which was founded on the precept of equal rights and respect for all humankind, for the poorest and weakest of us as well as the richest and strongest. As your Declaration of Independence put it in words which have never lost their power to stir the heart:

> We hold these truths to be self-evident: that all men are created equal; that they are endowed by their creator with certain inalienable rights; that among these are life, liberty, and the pursuit of happiness.

A nation founded on these principles holds a sacred trust: to stand as an example to the rest of the world, to climb ever higher in its practical realization of the ideals of human dignity, brotherhood, and mutual respect. It has been your constant efforts in fulfillment of that mission, far more than your size or your wealth or your military might, that have made America an inspiration to all mankind.

It must be recognized that your model was never one of realized perfection, but of ceaseless aspiration. From the outset, for example, America denied the African slave his freedom and human dignity. But in time

> *"Yours is the one great nation . . . which was founded on the precept of equal rights and respect for all humankind."*

you righted that wrong, albeit at an incalculable cost in human suffering and loss of life. Your impetus has almost always been toward a fuller, more all-embracing conception and assurance of the rights which your founding fathers recognized as inherent and God-given. Yours has ever been an inclusive, not an exclusive society. And your steps, though they may have paused or faltered now and then, have been pointed in the right direction and have trod the right path. The task has not always been an easy one, and each new generation has faced its own challenges and temptations. But, in a uniquely courageous and inspiring way, America has kept faith.

A Destructive Decision

Yet there has been one infinitely tragic and destructive departure from those American ideals in recent memory. It was this Court's own decision in 1973 [*Roe v. Wade*] to exclude the unborn child from the human family. You ruled that a mother, in consultation with her doctor, has broad discretion, guaranteed against infringement by the United States Constitution, to choose to destroy her unborn child. Your opinion stated that you did not need to "resolve the difficult question of when life begins." That question is inescapable. If the right to life is an inherent and inalienable right, it must surely obtain wherever human life exists. No one can deny that the unborn child is a distinct being, that it is human, and that it is alive. It is unjust, therefore, to deprive the unborn child of its fundamental right to life on the basis of its age, size, or condition of dependency. It was a sad infidelity to America's highest ideals when this Court said that it did not matter, or could not be determined, when the inalienable right to life began for a child in its mother's womb.

America needs no words from me to see how your decision in *Roe v. Wade* has deformed a great nation. The so-called right to abortion has pitted mothers against their children and women against men. It has sown violence and discord at the heart of the most intimate human relationships. It has aggravated the derogation of the father's role in an increasingly fatherless society. It has portrayed the greatest of gifts—a child—as a competitor, an intrusion, and an inconvenience. It has nominally accorded mothers unfettered dominion over the independent lives of their physically dependent sons and daughters. And, in granting this unconscionable power, it has exposed many women to unjust and selfish demands from their husbands or other sexual partners.

Human Rights Are for All

Human rights are not a privilege conferred by government. They are every human being's entitlement by virtue of his humanity. The right to life does not depend, and must not be declared to be contingent, on the pleasure of *anyone* else, not even a parent or a sovereign. The Constitutional Court of the Federal Republic of Germany recently ruled:

> The unborn child is entitled to its right to life independently of acceptance by its mother; this is an elementary and inalienable right which emanates from the dignity of the human being.

Americans may feel justly proud that Germany in 1993 was able to recognize the sanctity of human life. You must weep that your own government, at present, seems blind to this truth.

I have no new teaching for America. I seek only to recall you to faithfulness to what you once taught the world. Your nation was founded on the proposition—very old as a moral precept, but startling and innovative as a political insight—that human life is a gift of immeasurable worth, and that it deserves, always and everywhere, to be treated with the utmost dignity and respect.

> *"No one can deny that the unborn child is a distinct being, that it is human, and that it is alive."*

I urge the Court to take the opportunity presented by the petitions in these cases [against the state of New Jersey] to consider the fundamental question of when human life begins and to declare without equivocation the inalienable rights which it possesses.

The Supreme Court Erred in Reaffirming *Roe v. Wade*

by Antonin Scalia

About the author: Antonin Scalia has served as a U.S. Supreme Court justice since 1986 and is known for his conservative views on many issues. He was previously a U.S. Court of Appeals judge for the District of Columbia Circuit from 1982 to 1986.

My views on this matter are unchanged from those I set forth in my separate opinions in *Webster vs. Reproductive Health Services* and *Ohio vs. Akron Center for Reproductive Health*. The states may, if they wish, permit abortion on demand, but the Constitution does not *require* them to do so. The permissibility of abortion and the limitations upon it are to be resolved like most important questions in our democracy: by citizens trying to persuade one another and then voting. As the court acknowledges, "where reasonable people disagree, the government can adopt one position or the other." The court is correct in adding the qualification that this "assumes a state of affairs in which the choice does not intrude upon a protected liberty"—but the crucial part of that qualification is the penultimate word. A state's choice between two positions on which reasonable people can disagree is constitutional even when (as is often the case) it intrudes upon a "liberty" in the absolute sense. Laws against bigamy, for example—which entire societies of reasonable people disagree with—intrude upon men and women's liberty to marry and live with one another. But bigamy happens not to be a liberty specially "protected" by the Constitution.

Not a Protected Liberty

That is, quite simply, the issue in this case: not whether the power of a woman to abort her unborn child is a "liberty" in the absolute sense; or even whether it is a liberty of great importance to many women. Of course it is both.

From Antonin Scalia's dissenting opinion in the *Planned Parenthood of Southeast Pennsylvania v. Robert P. Casey*, June 29, 1992 (#112 S.Ct. 2791).

The issue is whether it is a liberty protected by the Constitution of the United States. I am sure it is not. I reach that conclusion not because of anything so exalted as my views concerning [what the Court terms] the "concept of existence, of meaning, of the universe and of the mystery of human life." Rather, I reach it for the same reason I reach the conclusion that bigamy is not constitutionally protected—because of two simple facts: (1) The Constitution says absolutely nothing about it, and (2) the long-standing traditions of American society have permitted it to be legally proscribed.

> *"The issue is whether [abortion] is a liberty protected by the Constitution of the United States."*

The court destroys the proposition, evidently meant to represent my position, that *liberty* includes [according to Scalia] "only those practices, defined at the most specific level, that were protected against government interference by other rules of law when the 14th Amendment was ratified." That is not, however, what [a 1989 opinion of Scalia's] says; it merely observes that, in defining *liberty*, we may not disregard a specific, "relevant tradition protecting or denying protection to the asserted right." But the court does not wish to be fettered by any such limitations on its preferences. The court's statement that it is "tempting" to acknowledge the authoritativeness of tradition in order to "cur[b] the discretion of federal judges" is of course rhetoric rather than reality; no government official is "tempted" to place restraints upon his own freedom of action, which is why [English historian] Lord Acton did not say "power tends to purify." The court's temptation is in the quite opposite and more natural direction—toward systematically eliminating checks upon its own power; and it succumbs.

Outrageous Arguments

Beyond that brief summary of the essence of my position, I will not swell the U.S. Reports [volumes of Court decisions] with repetition of what I have said before; and applying the rational basis test, I would uphold the Pennsylvania statute [restricting abortion] in its entirety. I must, however, respond to a few of the more outrageous arguments in [*Casey*'s joint] opinion, which it is beyond human nature to leave unanswered. I shall discuss each of them under a quotation from the court's opinion to which they pertain.

> The inescapable fact is that adjudication of substantive due process claims may call upon the court in interpreting the Constitution to exercise that same capacity which by tradition courts always have exercised: reasoned judgment.

Assuming that the question before us is to be resolved at such a level of philosophical abstraction in such isolation from the traditions of American society as by simply applying "reasoned judgment," I do not see how that could possibly have produced the answer the court arrived at in *Roe vs. Wade*. The opinion describes the methodology of *Roe* quite accurately as weighing against the woman's interest the state's "'important and legitimate interest in protecting the potentiality of human life.'" But "reasoned judgment" does not begin by begging the question as *Roe* and subsequent cases unquestionably did by assuming that what the state is protecting is the mere "potentiality of human life." The whole argument of abortion opponents is that what the court calls the fetus and what others call the unborn child *is a human life*. Thus, whatever answer *Roe* came up with after conducting its "balancing" is bound to be wrong, unless it is correct that the human fetus is in some critical sense merely potentially human. There is of course no way to determine that as a legal matter; it is in fact a value judgment. Some societies have considered newborn children not yet human or the incompetent elderly no longer so.

Roe Was Plainly Wrong

The authors of the joint opinion, of course, do not squarely contend that *Roe vs. Wade* was a *correct* application of "reasoned judgment"; merely that it must be followed, because of *stare decisis* [rule meaning "let the decision stand"]. But in their exhaustive discussion of all the factors that go into the determination of when *stare decisis* should be observed and when disregarded, they never mention "how wrong was the decision on its face?" Surely, if "[t]he court's power lies . . . in its legitimacy, a product of substance and perception," the "substance" part of the equation demands that plain error be acknowledged and eliminated. *Roe* was

> *"The right to abort, we are told, inheres in* liberty *because it is among 'a person's most basic decisions.'"*

plainly wrong—even on the court's methodology of "reasoned judgment" and even more so (of course) if the proper criteria of text and tradition are applied.

The emptiness of the "reasoned judgment" that produced *Roe* is displayed in plain view by the fact that after more than 19 years of effort by some of the brightest (and most determined) legal minds in the country, after more than 10 cases upholding abortion rights in this court and after dozens upon dozens of *amicus* briefs submitted in this and other cases, the best the court can do to explain how it is that the word *liberty must* be thought to include the right to destroy human fetuses is to rattle off a collection of adjectives that simply decorate a value judgment and conceal a political choice. The right to abort, we are told, inheres in *liberty* because it is among "a person's most basic decisions"; it involves a "most intimate and personal choic[e]"; it is "central to personal dignity and autonomy"; it "originate[s] within the zone of conscience and belief"; it is "too intimate and personal" for state interference; it reflects "intimate views" of a "deep, personal character"; it involves "intimate relationships" and notions of "personal autonomy and bodily integrity"; and it concerns a particularly "'important decisio[n].'" But it is obvious to anyone applying "reasoned judgment" that the same adjectives can be applied to many forms of conduct

The Abortion Controversy

that this court (including one of the justices in today's majority) has held are *not* entitled to constitutional protection—because, like abortion, they are forms of conduct that have long been criminalized in American society Those adjectives might be applied, for example, to homosexual sodomy, polygamy, adult incest and suicide, all of which are equally "intimate" and "deep[ly] personal" decisions involving "personal autonomy and bodily integrity" and all of which can constitutionally be proscribed because it is our unquestionable constitutional tradition that they are proscribable.

No Longer a Constitution

It is not reasoned judgment that supports the court's decision; only personal predilection. Justice Benjamin Curtis' warning is as timely today as it was 135 years ago [in *Dred Scott*]: "[W]hen a strict interpretation of the Constitution, according to the fixed rules which govern the interpretation of laws, is abandoned, and the theoretical opinions of individuals are allowed to control its meaning, we have no longer a Constitution; we are under the government of individual men, who for the time being have power to declare what the Constitution is, according to their own views of what it ought to mean."

Liberty finds no refuge in a jurisprudence of doubt.

One might have feared to encounter this august and sonorous phrase in an opinion defending the real *Roe vs. Wade*, rather than the revised version fabricated by the authors of the joint opinion. The shortcomings of *Roe* did not include lack of clarity: Virtually all regulation of abortion before the third trimester was invalid. But to come across this phrase in the joint opinion—which calls upon federal district judges to apply an "undue burden" standard as doubtful in application as it is unprincipled in origin—is really more than one should have to bear.

The joint opinion frankly concedes that the amorphous concept of "undue burden" has been inconsistently applied by the members of this court in the few brief years since that "test" was first explicitly propounded by Justice Sandra Day O'Connor in her dissent in *Akron I* [in 1983]. Because the three justices now wish to "set forth a standard of general application," the joint opinion announces that "it is important to clarify what is meant by an undue burden." I certainly agree with that, but I do not agree that the joint opinion succeeds in the announced endeavor. To the contrary, its efforts at clarification make clear only that the standard is inherently manipulable and will prove hopelessly unworkable in practice.

> *"It is not reasoned judgment that supports the court's decision; only personal predilection."*

The joint opinion explains that a state regulation imposes an "undue burden" if it "has the purpose or effect of placing a substantial obstacle in the path of a woman seeking an abortion of a nonviable fetus." An obstacle is "substantial," we are told, if it is "calculated[,] [not] to inform the woman's free choice, [but to] hinder it." This latter statement cannot possibly mean what it says. *Any* regulation of abortion that is intended to advance what the joint opinion concedes is the state's "substantial" interest in protecting unborn life will be "calculated [to] hinder" a decision to have an abortion. It thus seems more accurate to say that the joint opinion would uphold abortion regulations only if they do not *unduly* hinder the woman's decision. That, of course, brings us right back to square one: Defining an "undue burden" as an "undue hindrance" (or a "substantial obstacle") hardly "clarifies" the test. Consciously or not, the joint opinion's verbal shell game will conceal raw judicial policy choices concerning what is "appropriate" abortion legislation.

The ultimately standardless nature of the "undue burden" inquiry is a reflection of the underlying fact that the concept has no principled or coherent legal basis. As the chief justice [William Rehnquist] points out, *Roe*'s strict-scrutiny standard "at least had a recognized basis in constitutional law at the time *Roe* was decided," while "[t]he same cannot be said for the 'undue burden' standard. which is created largely out of whole cloth by the authors of the joint opinion." The joint opinion is flatly wrong in asserting that "our jurisprudence relating to all liberties save perhaps abortion has recognized" the permissibility of laws that do not impose an "undue burden." It argues that the abortion right is similar to other rights in that a law "not designed to strike at the right itself, [but which] has the incidental effect of making it more difficult or more expensive to [exercise the right,]" is not invalid. I agree, indeed I have forcefully urged, that a law of general applicability which places only an incidental burden on a fundamental right does not infringe that right, but that principle does not establish the quite different (and quite dangerous) proposition that a law which *directly* regulates a fundamental right will not be found to violate the Constitution unless it imposes an "undue burden."

Constitutional Rights at Risk

It is that, of course, which is at issue here: Pennsylvania has *consciously and directly* regulated conduct that our cases have held is constitutionally protected. The appropriate analogy, therefore, is that of a state law requiring purchasers of religious books to endure a 24-hour waiting period, or to pay a nominal additional tax of one cent. The joint opinion cannot possibly be correct in suggesting that we would uphold such legislation on the ground that it does not impose a "substantial obstacle" to the exercise of First Amendment rights. The "undue burden" standard is not at all the generally applicable principle the joint opinion pretends it to be; rather, it is a unique concept created specially for this case, to preserve some judicial foothold in this ill-gotten territory. In claiming otherwise, the three justices show their willingness to place all constitutional rights at risk in an effort to preserve what they deem the "central holding in *Roe*."

The Supreme Court's *Casey* Decision Should Not Be Obeyed

by Russell Hittinger

About the author: *Russell Hittinger teaches in the School of Philosophy at Catholic University in Washington, D.C. He is a member of the editorial advisory board of* First Things, *a monthly magazine covering issues of religion and public life.*

At the end of its 1992 term, the Supreme Court handed down its decision in *Planned Parenthood of S.E. Pennsylvania v. Casey*. And immediately it became clear that the implications of the decision reached far beyond the resolution of the case.

Despite twenty years of general success in electoral politics at the national level and twelve years of making judicial appointments—with five of nine Supreme Court justices having been named by Ronald Reagan and George Bush—and despite an open alliance with the pro-life movement, Republicans had failed to produce a Court willing to overturn *Roe v. Wade*. The three authors of the joint opinion in *Casey*—Justices Sandra Day O'Connor, David Souter, and Anthony Kennedy—relied on a substantive due process analysis as well as judicial consideration of social policy. . . .

The Fabric of the Constitution

In the aftermath of *Roe v. Wade*, it was possible to say that legal abortion was the result of an activist Court that took the already nebulous notion of privacy one step too far. Pro-life citizens, along with proponents of strict judicial discipline, refused to regard *Roe* as a permanent feature of our constitutional polity. For twenty years, there was reason to hope that judicial appointments would gradually produce a favorable chemistry and winning numbers on the Court. Indeed, the Court's case law after *Roe* strongly indicated a gradual chipping away

Excerpted from Russell Hittinger, "When the Court Should Not Be Obeyed," *First Things*, October 1993. Reprinted with permission.

of the abortion right. Only those who indulged their darkest suspicions had reason to believe that *Roe* (in its entirety) would be maintained for long. On the eve of *Casey*, both sides were gearing up to battle the issue in the legislative arena.

The *Casey* Court, however, insisted that the right to procure an abortion is a fundamental right guaranteed by the Fourteenth Amendment. The authors of the joint opinion made it clear that the right is recognized on its own merit, and has nothing immediately to do with the nebulous area of marital privacy. Those areas of the judge-

> *"Pro-life citizens . . . refused to regard* Roe *as a permanent feature of our constitutional polity."*

made abortion law that had provided occasion for chipping away at *Roe*—e.g., the scope of privacy, the trimester scheme [*Roe*'s framework regulating abortion during pregnancy], informed consent—were declared irrelevant to the "central holding" of *Roe*. If the rhetoric of the joint opinion is taken at face value, the abortion right cannot be denied without destroying the very fabric of the Constitution, the rule of law, and the legitimacy of the Court.

Therefore, the *Casey* decision forces us to ask unsettling questions. What does it mean for citizens to live in a polity in which the fundamental law of the Constitution requires them to cease and desist from conducting any serious business that touches upon the killing of the unborn? What does it mean for citizenship once the right to kill the unborn is equated with the franchise itself, and declared to be a more or less permanent feature of the law of the United States? What does it mean for a democratic republic if the people are declared legally incompetent to deal with an action that a large number of them regard as homicide?

The *Casey* decision has recklessly raised the political stakes on abortion. For the problem after *Casey* is not merely how to live in a culture that practices homicide as a form of birth control. Pro-life citizens were well aware that the culture had made this turn at least two decades ago. Moreover, the problem is not merely how to live in a political culture that would tolerate abortion. Most pro-life citizens understood that even if *Roe* were overturned, legislative abolition of all abortions was virtually impossible. The *Casey* decision recklessly raised the stakes by insisting that the abortion right is an unalterable feature of the fundamental law. . . .

Grounds for Upholding *Roe*

There is one issue in particular that needs to be addressed: why does the Court uphold *Roe v. Wade*? On what ground, and according to what principle, does it bind all of the legislatures of our polity to refrain from enacting laws that place an "undue burden" in the path of women seeking abortions?

The authors of the joint opinion aver that they uphold the "central holding" of

Roe on two grounds. First, the right to procure an abortion is justified on the ground of its intrinsic merit. Second, the right is justified in terms of the reliance of the people, especially women, on legal abortion.

The first path of analysis seeks to identify a fundamental right that ought to be placed beyond the processes of ordinary politics. As Justice William Brennan once declared: "It is the very purpose of a Constitution—and particularly of the Bill of Rights—to declare certain values transcendent, beyond the reach of temporary political majorities." So put, the substance of the abortion right represents a certain *debitum*—something owed in the order of justice to the woman.

The second path of analysis seeks to identify the contingent and evolving social and economic needs of citizens. Here, the right to an abortion is affirmed not because of its substantive merit in the moral order of things, nor because the Constitution mandates its protection, but rather because it is deemed to be in the interests of the common good. In effect, the Court ruled in *Casey* that, whether or not *Roe* was a mistaken application of constitutional law, the ruling has become woven into the fabric of the law—law, that is, insofar as it consists of customs, legal expectations, and that vast array of activities that rely upon settled rules.

These two paths of jurisprudence represent, as it were, the two lobes of the modern judicial brain. It is well known, of course, that they do not always communicate effectively, or even coherently, with one another. On the one hand, the Court wants to ar-

> *"The* Casey *decision recklessly raised the [political] stakes by insisting that the abortion right is an unalterable feature."*

ticulate and to defend certain individual rights against the pressure of political majorities; on the other hand, the Court wants to treat the right as something instrumentally necessary to social order. The former approach looks upon the right as something that transcends the political sphere, while the latter regards the right in the light of what would seem to be the very essence of the political: viz., in terms of policy issues related to the common good.

An Inherently Wicked Rule

While the tension between these two paths of jurisprudence is interesting in its own right, the problem becomes especially acute when the subject of abortion is brought into the picture. We cannot forget that *Roe* turned what used to be homicide at criminal law into a fundamental right at constitutional law. Hence, when the Court issues a command to the various branches and departments of government to cease and desist from legislating restrictions on abortion, the Court forbids citizens from making and applying criminal laws. This represents the most draconian limitation upon the legislative competence of the citizens.

In the matter of abortion, who is bound? We are. "We," that is, insofar as we are citizens who deliberate and act through democratic assemblies. The alleged right to abortion, therefore, renders the citizens themselves duty-bound to recognize the right of those who elect to kill the unborn. It is both false and useless to pretend that the moral issue is transacted in a merely private sphere, because the principle of the right binds all of the citizens as to what they may legitimately do *qua citizens* (that is, in making and enforcing laws, in formulating policies, and in conducting any public business that touches upon the alleged right). To use the language of *Casey*, citizens may not act through democratic assemblies to impose "undue burden(s)" upon the choice to have an abortion.

Given the two different paths of analysis, we can reasonably ask why we are duty-bound to obey this command of the Court. In terms of political morality, it makes a considerable difference which line of analysis generates the answer. On the first view, the limits upon our legislative and policy-making competencies are derived as implications of an inherent right of individuals to kill the unborn. On the second view, the limits are derived as implications of social needs. Here, we are duty-bound to operate according to the exigencies of the common good (as ascertained by the Court).

Even if the Court has no delegated authority to impose such a policy decision, it still makes a difference whether the rule is derived from the alleged merit of the right or from the purported needs of the common good. An inherently wicked rule can never be followed. At least for pro-life citizens, the notion that anyone has a fundamental right to kill the unborn is a rule that cannot be obeyed. In the moral order, no one can be obligated to respect that "right.". . .

Autonomy and Liberty

Not only the authors of the joint opinion, but also Justices John Paul Stevens and Harry Blackmun, in concurring opinions, range far and wide in the Bill of Rights, trying to pinpoint the precise nature and scope of this prodigious right. The joint opinion, for example, refers variously to woman's right of "autonomy" and "liberty" to make "intimate" decisions.

Justice Stevens found at least three distinct rights embraced by the liberty to abort fetuses: first, gender equality, as required by the Equal Protection clause; second, a general right of "conscience" to make "empowering decisions," presumably found in the First Amendment; and third, the right of the citizen, as against government, in respect to an establishment of religion. Justice Blackmun likewise referred to the Equal Protection clause and to the Establishment clause as textual places from which to build an argument against governmental interference in the decision to procure an abortion. Blackmun, however, took the argument one

> "**Roe** *turned what used to be homicide at criminal law into a fundamental right at constitutional law.*"

step further, by suggesting that restrictive abortion laws violate the Thirteenth Amendment right against involuntary servitude: "By restricting the right to terminate pregnancies, the State conscripts women's bodies into its service, forcing women to continue their pregnancies, suffer the pains of childbirth, and in most instances, provide years of maternal care."

> *"The notion that anyone has a fundamental right to kill the unborn is a rule that cannot be obeyed."*

Whether the right is placed under the rubric of "decisional autonomy" or "liberty," it is clear enough what the *Casey* Court wished to assert. The power of the state is limited in the area of abortion. The cause or principle of the limit is the individual's inherent right of autonomy.

According to the joint opinion, this right is as profound as it is extensive. We are given to understand that governmental interference in the matter of abortion constitutes nothing less than personicide. When the state outlaws abortion, or places "undue burdens" in the path of a woman seeking one, the state deprives the woman of a crucial self-defining decision, and robs her of those attributes of selfhood constituted by free choice. We are not surprised, then, that the justices would conclude that the "legitimacy" of both the judiciary and the rule of law requires the recognition of this right.

The Court has imposed a right of liberty that, by logic of analogy, and by consistency of application, would guarantee that a government of positive laws is morally impossible. Such a comprehensive right as the one announced in *Casey* implies that ordered liberty effected by the "compulsion of the state" necessarily violates the most solemn natural right of citizens to maintain the integrity, if not the very existence, of their persons. Read literally, and applied consistently, this right would give citizens an immunity from virtually all positive laws.

Once again, the key question is the principle or the reason for the limit. Looking only at this part of the *Casey* decision, the answer is clear. The judicially imposed right is not a mere creature of positive law. It is not a legislative enactment tolerating abortion. Nor is it a declaration of a want of power on the part of legislatures. Rather, the limit is due to the woman, according to the order of justice as understood by the due process clause of the Fourteenth Amendment. . . .

Public and Private Matters

If someone has a right, it means that others are duty-bound to do or not do something with respect to the claimant. It is important to understand that so long as we are not speaking in some loose or metaphorical sense about rights, a right does not bind its holder, but rather makes others duty-bound. For this reason, rights language can never be a merely private thing.

Moral conscience cannot be relieved by the legal fact that citizens also have a

125

not to kill their unborn children. Whether we elect to kill them or not, the principle stands undiminished and unqualified For the law recognizes a civil right of individuals to commit wrongful acts of homicide, and prohibits the citizens, working through democratic assemblies, from proscribing such acts. Put bluntly, but accurately, those who choose not to kill their own children are exercising the very same right as those who deliberately kill them.

What any of us does in a merely private capacity is irrelevant to the issue at hand. Had *Dred Scott* [an 1857 Supreme Court decision declaring that only states could prohibit slavery] been maintained, it would have been irrelevant to a Vermont farmer that he chose not to use slave labor, so long as the law required him to cease and desist from legislating or conducting any public business touching upon slavery.

Moreover, the abortion right seems to recognize a private franchise over matters of life and death. But such a power is exercised legitimately only in the light of a public end, and even then only according to public procedures and the most exacting standards of accountability. The power of lethal force does not belong to the individual citizen, except as it is recognized at common law in the case of self-defense. Neither the *Roe* nor *Casey* Courts made any pretense that this is what is at stake in the right to abortion. Rather, the woman is alleged to have a right to kill the unborn for private ends, without any public accountability or justification.

> *"The Court has imposed a right of liberty that . . . would guarantee that a government of positive laws is morally impossible."*

In fact, the abortion cases make it clear beyond any doubt that the reason and ground of the right consist in the woman's estimation of her private good. Of course, the Court could have argued that the right consists in the woman's liberty to effectuate some public good—such as population control. But, with respect to the abortion right, the "good" in question is essentially private. Indeed, the Court has repeatedly insisted not only that the right stands in sharp contrast to the public good represented by the pro-natalist policies of the state (and that, up to the point of viability, trumps the state's interests), but also that the right is to be exercised even against the express desires of the marital spouse.

Thus, the abortion right is nothing less than a purported right of individual citizens to use lethal force without even the charade of being deputized to do so, and without any of the constraints that the government ordinarily imposes upon itself when it kills persons. . . .

The Court's Justification

Once again, then, we return to the question of how and why we are bound to obey the Court's command in *Casey*. As the authors of the joint opinion say: "Consistent with other constitutional norms, legislatures may draw lines which appear arbitrary without the necessity of offering a justification." That is to say, were a legislature to make a determination in this area of abortion, all we need to know for purposes of law is that the legislature willed it. But the Court must give a constitutional justification. What is it?

The Court appears to be saying that we are bound because its ruling comports with the common good. Were the social facts to change—for instance, if most citizens no longer relied upon abortion as a method of contraception—then the holding could go the other way.

> *"Those who choose not to kill their own children are exercising the very same right as those who deliberately kill them."*

Therefore, despite all of the usual rhetoric about the Court defending rights against political majorities—such rhetoric being strewn throughout the joint opinion—the counter-majoritarian principle is reduced to the mere fact that a nonelected body imposed the rule in the light of what it deemed to be the perceptions of the "thoughtful part" of the nation. Moreover, despite all of the hand-wringing about the precedential force of judicial decisions, and about the importance of *stare decisis* [rule meaning "let the decision stand"], the joint opinion really has nothing immediately to do with the precedential standing of a body of legal opinion. After all, *Casey* explicitly overturns all of the previous case law regarding the trimester scheme, all of the previous case law regarding informed consent, all of common law regarding the interests and responsibilities of husbands. Chief Justice William Rehnquist observed that "one might inquire how the joint opinion can view the 'central holding' of *Roe* as so deeply rooted in our constitutional culture, when it so casually uproots and disposes of that same decision's trimester framework."

No, this is not a decision that respects precedent. Rather, it is a decision that respects the cultural and economic force of women and the impact of the decision upon their lives. While it is always prudent to respect the power of women, this is not necessarily the same thing as respect for precedent. So put, this second path of analysis seems to hold not only civil rights, but the precedent of the Court's own case law, hostage to what enlightened opinion regards as the common good, as defined by their social, economic, and lifestyle needs.

Not Bound to Obey

"Liberty," says the first sentence of the joint opinion, "finds no refuge in a jurisprudence of doubt." To paraphrase Jeremy Bentham, the Court set out in *Casey* to pluck the mask of mystery from the face of its abortion jurisprudence. But at the end of the day, the justices have created more doubt than existed under the regime of abortion imposed by *Roe*. On the one hand, they have made claims about the nature of the abortion right that go far beyond anything in *Roe* or in the post-*Roe* cases. Indeed, the right announced in *Casey* is more absolute and all-encompassing than any right heretofore recognized, even during the Court's most activist episodes. On the other hand, the legitimacy of the Court's command appears to depend neither upon the constitutional correctness of *Roe* nor upon the justices' philosophical ruminations about the nature of liberty. Rather, it depends upon the estimation of the Court about the culture's reliance on an ultimate method of contraception, and the justices' hunch about how much the Court's prestige would be diminished if it were to tell women that the Constitution provides no right to kill the unborn.

If the reason for obedience is the common good, rather than some intrinsic merit of the abortion right, then perhaps the crisis of conscience over the judge-made abortion law can be delayed. Even if the Court has acted *ultra vires* [transcending legal authority] in issuing the command, the substance of the command *could* be reconciled with conscience. That is, we could say that the Court has moved itself ahead of the legislative curve, and has imposed a statute of the sort that we would have had to live with anyway. The important point is that we are not bound to obey a rule that asserts the rightfulness of abortion. Nor are we committed to the notion that the right of abortion is an unalterable feature of the fundamental law (though we are left in the lurch as to how it might be altered).

But the Court does not give us a clear or consistent answer to the question of why we are bound. Under the most benign scenario, citizens must adjust themselves to a rule issued without due authority. This is problem enough. Yet Americans have been living under a kind of judicial oligarchy for decades. Under the worst scenario, citizens are bound to recognize as a matter of fundamental law (not mere statute) a right to commit wrongful homicide. For millions of citizens, this is intolerable. Though the moral sensibility of the citizenry be debauched, it is not so depraved that such citizens will be able to live with this situation for long.

> *"The Court appears to be saying that we are bound [to obey the Court] because its ruling comports with the common good."*

Abortion Should Be Restricted to the First Eight Weeks of Pregnancy

by Steven R. Hemler, Richard G. Wilkins, and Frank H. Fischer

About the authors: *Steven R. Hemler founded the Tri-Cities chapter of Tennessee Volunteers for Life in Kingsport. Richard G. Wilkins is a law professor at Brigham Young University in Provo, Utah. Frank H. Fischer is a physician at Children's Clinic in Kingsport.*

There are several lessons to be learned from Republican George Allen's stunning 1993 victory in the Virginia gubernatorial election, but one of the most important is how a conservative can handle the divisive abortion issue.

In 1989, the Republican gubernatorial candidate, Marshall Coleman, wavered in his pro-life position when confronted by a staunchly pro-choice opponent, Doug Wilder. Vacillation cost him precious support—without gaining him any votes from the other side—and he lost a very close election. The candidate this time, Mr. Allen, facing a radically pro-choice Democrat, Mary Sue Terry, took a moderate position on abortion, stuck to it, and won.

In addition to favoring parental rights and informed consent, Mr. Allen's position was that a woman should be allowed to have an abortion only until the point in pregnancy when there is medical evidence of a heartbeat and brain activity. While a position like Mr. Allen's is not satisfying as a long-term goal to those who oppose abortion for moral reasons, it has the advantage as a short-term goal of being acceptable to the majority of Americans.

Support for First-Trimester Limits

Polls consistently show that between 15 and 25 per cent of the public are on each extreme of the abortion issue. That leaves 50 to 70 per cent of Americans in the middle. In the end, this majority will play the decisive role in determining the outcome of the abortion controversy.

According to a recent Gallup survey, 73 per cent of Americans support a prohibition on abortion after the first trimester of pregnancy (about ten weeks after conception). This survey shows that 82 per cent of those who are strongly pro-life, as well as 82 per cent of those in the middle, would support such a proposal. More surprisingly, even 46 per cent of those identified as strongly pro-choice agree that abortion should be limited to the first trimester.

Other polls have consistently shown that, while a majority of Americans support a woman's right to choose an abortion in the early weeks of pregnancy, a majority also believe that at some point the government acquires the right to intervene to protect the life of the unborn child. But what should that point be?

Brain-Wave Activity

The universally accepted medical and legal definition of the end of life is the irreversible cessation of all functions of the brain, as measured by a flat electroencephalogram (EEG). Conversely, the presence of brain-wave activity is a "vital sign" of life. Brain-wave activity is consistently present by eight weeks after conception. (The heart has already been beating since three weeks after conception.) Thus the eight-week-old fetus is undeniably alive, according to the most widely accepted definition of life.

Furthermore, eight weeks is designated by scientists as the end of the embryonic period and the beginning of the fetal period. By then, every internal organ and external feature found in an adult human being has been established. The heart, kidneys, liver, stomach, and other organs are functioning, and all external bodily parts are formed.

> *"By [eight weeks], every internal organ and external feature found in an adult human being has been established."*

The educational impact of trying to accord legal protection to unborn children with both vital signs of life (heartbeat and brain-wave activity) should not be underestimated. The vast majority of Americans would undoubtedly be surprised to learn that the vital signs of life are present as early as eight weeks.

Furthermore, this proposal does not contradict the pro-life tenet that human life begins at conception. It merely establishes the most currently attainable point for beginning *legal* protection.

Of course, the Supreme Court would have to recognize that an eight-week limitation on access to abortion is constitutional. In its abortion decision *Planned Parenthood* v. *Casey*, the Court overturned *Roe* v. *Wade*'s "rigid trimester framework." Nevertheless, the Joint Opinion by Justices Sandra Day O'Connor, Anthony Kennedy, and David Souter reaffirmed *Roe*'s "central" holding that "the Constitution protects a woman's right to terminate her pregnancy in its early stages."

However, the Joint Opinion defined "early stages" of pregnancy as any point prior to fetal viability: "Viability marks the earliest point at which the State's interest in fetal life is constitutionally adequate to justify a legislative ban on nontherapeutic abortions." Viability is declared to be "the point at which the balance of interests tips" away from personal liberty and toward fetal life. However, fetal viability now occurs at 23 to 24 weeks' gestation. That is the end of the *sixth month* of pregnancy, an extreme definition of "early stages"— especially since the Joint Opinion said it was merely recognizing the "constitutional liberty of the woman to have *some* freedom to terminate her pregnancy" (emphasis added).

The Joint Opinion asserted that the Court "must justify the lines we draw. And there is no line other than viability which is more workable." A line drawn at eight weeks, however, could be seen as being precisely more workable than a line drawn at viability because it can be justified by applying to the beginning of legally protected life the same medical and legal criteria now used to define the end of legally protected life. Furthermore, with modern ultrasound technology, physicians can easily delineate this eight-week point.

No Undue Burden

Nor would this new line place an "undue burden" on a woman's ability to make an abortion decision; it would leave ample time for her to decide whether or not to abort. A woman can easily discover she is pregnant, using an over-the-counter pregnancy test, by two weeks after her first missed menstrual period, corresponding to the fourth week after conception. This would leave her at least a four-week window to secure an abortion.

The *Casey* Joint Opinion concluded that a change in constitutional principle is an appropriate response to "facts that the country could understand, or had come to understand already, but which the Court in an earlier day, as its own declarations disclosed, had not been able to perceive." Several facts regarding abortion apparently have not yet been "perceived" by the Court.

To begin with, over 70 per cent of Americans believe that abortion should *not* be permitted during the second and third trimesters. This is something that the country has "come to understand already."

Second, the Joint Opinion justified its result, in part, on the ground that abortion must be available "in the event that contraception should fail." This was premised on the assumption that "[a]bortion is customarily chosen as an unplanned response to the consequence of unplanned activity or the failure of conventional birth control."

> *"A line drawn at eight weeks . . . could be seen as being precisely more workable than a line drawn at viability."*

The available data, however, indicate that abortion has instead become a primary method of birth control. In 1978, 41 per cent of the women seeking an abortion in Utah reported that they had omitted their contraception or did not use contraception at all. By 1985, that number had risen to 66 per cent and by 1989 to 68 per cent. These statistics are typical. By providing unrestricted access to abortion throughout the first six months of pregnancy, *Roe* (and now *Casey*) discourage women and men from exercising sexual responsibility.

Clearly Inflicted Pain

Finally, it is certain that a fetus will—at some point long before birth—feel pain. The purposeful dismemberment generally involved in abortion would clearly inflict pain on a being with a functioning brain and central nervous system. Surely we are a compassionate enough society to seek to err on the side of the "little ones" (Latin meaning of "fetus"), by prohibiting abortion after the onset of brain-wave activity.

Public policy on abortion can only move in tandem with public sentiment. Public policy which reflects one extreme or the other in the current debate will only continue to polarize our society.

It is surpassingly important that we begin to move to some common ground—however uneasy—on this difficult issue. An eight-week limitation on abortion access represents just such a common ground. The time is now ripe to seize the initiative and lead our country to a creative response on this emotional issue.

The Pro-Life Movement Should Continue Advocating Restrictive Abortion Laws

by Kenneth D. Whitehead

About the author: *Kenneth D. Whitehead is a translator and writer in Falls Church, Virginia, and a former U.S. Department of Education assistant secretary for postsecondary education. He is the author of two books on the abortion issue,* Respectable Killing *and* The Agenda for the "Sexual Revolution."

In their usual crude, pragmatic way, the politicians seem to be arriving at a rough consensus on how to deal with the abortion issue, namely, abortion will continue to be legal, but for the most part the government will not pay for it. This seems to be the meaning of the October 1993 action taken by Congress reaffirming (in only slightly liberalized form) the Hyde Amendment, the perennial prohibition of federal funding for nearly all elective abortions under Medicaid. Even many normally proabortion legislators apparently decided a line had to be drawn at government funding of so controversial a procedure; even if they do not actually read their mail, apparently many of them have become aware of the volume of it against abortion.

A Legislative Compromise

With the re-enactment of the Hyde Amendment, the hard-line proabortion forces in Congress suddenly had to draw back in disarray and dismay. . . . They have clearly perceived that a line *has* been drawn by majorities in both houses of Congress. However, this majority is not doctrinaire: Some abortion funding has slipped through. Basically, though, the emerging consensus seems to be that the government will not use tax money for a procedure so many taxpayers find objectionable, if not abhorrent; meanwhile the procedure itself will remain legal, and at the moment nobody is really pushing to outlaw it. . . .

This rough legislative compromise pleases neither of the two sides that continue to be passionate on the subject of abortion. But almost all politicians are sick and tired of the subject, and hence are ready to put it to rest on almost any terms. Some conservative friends of the prolife movement show signs of being as sick and tired of the "insoluble" abortion issue as the politicians; they too are apparently prepared to see the issue "settled," however minimalist the terms of the settlement.

"Friendly Advice"

A case in point of the conservative "rush to settlement" is provided by Irving Kristol. In what he himself described as "friendly but pessimistic advice for pro-lifers" in a piece in the *Wall Street Journal*, he describes abortion as the principal answer of the "culture" to the consequences of today's accepted "sexually active" behavior (what used to be called "promiscuous" behavior). Kristol also says:

> It is one thing to deplore abortion, or to believe there is something inherently wrong, even sinful, about it. But it is quite another thing to demand that the secular authorities enforce a theologically defined "right to life" policy. This policy is politically unacceptable to the majority of the electorate, however ambivalent their feelings. It is also unenforceable as new abortifacients come on the market.

Kristol has packed many errors and misconceptions into a single paragraph. To begin with: Prescription drugs still must be licensed by the FDA [Food and Drug Administration], and it is not in the least unreasonable to hold that, for many cogent medical and moral reasons, no abortifacient should ever be licensed, regardless of whether such a ban can be completely "enforced." The kind of thinking that holds that we should provide people with the means to do "what they are going to do anyway" is the same sort of thinking that has already brought us to the moral nadir of supplying clean needles to drug addicts and condoms to "sexually active" teenagers.

More importantly, the right to life, an expression which Kristol unaccountably puts between quotation marks, is still assumed—and is supposed to be guaranteed—by the Fifth and Fourteenth Amendments to our Constitution and by our Declaration

> *"The emerging consensus seems to be that the government will not use tax money for a procedure so many taxpayers find objectionable."*

of Independence. These are the foundational documents of our polity; to place what they assume and guarantee between quotation marks is to signal a significant departure from the principles on which this country was founded. The practical political problem posed by legalized abortion under our system is that unborn children are excluded by simple definition from the equal protection of the laws—as slaves were so excluded until the passage of the Thirteenth Amendment. The principle of the right to life was not inconveniently dreamed up by some prolifers in order to gum up the political process; it is a fundamental principle we cannot give up simply by placing it within quotation marks.

Therefore, what may be "politically unacceptable" to a given "majority"—if it is a majority—is not the issue. Even though the position a majority takes at any given time may sometimes loom as a virtually insurmountable obstacle for those opposed to it, it is still of lesser moment than the truth about the issue.

> *"Unborn children are excluded by simple definition from the equal protection of the laws."*

Majority Opinion Must Be Challenged

If the right to life and the right to the equal protection of the laws are now to be denied to any class on account of mere majority opinion at a given time, in spite of what the Constitution and the Declaration of Independence specify, then our system has already been undermined in principle. Hence, whatever "majority opinions" happen to arise against our foundational principles must be challenged, and *changed*— no matter how long it takes.

Actually, the public opinion that currently tolerates abortion seems to be mired in ethical inconsistency. Many polls show that the majority thinks abortion is *needed* even when it is abstractly conceded to be *wrong*. Obviously, public opinion needs to be (further) educated, for we cannot operate a civilized society on the principle that what is seriously wrong should nevertheless be permitted.

According to *Roe v. Wade*, the unborn are defined as not enjoying the constitutional guarantees available to other Americans. This is the nub of the problem, for the humanity of the unborn is an established scientific fact. Kristol's reference to a "theologically defined 'right to life'. . . policy" is another one of his errors; actually there are two errors in his phrase, since upholding the right to life is in no way a mere policy but is rather a foundational constitutional principle—and a principle not based on any theological finding.

The words "embryo" and "fetus," like the words "baby," "adolescent," and "adult," do not describe some nonhuman being; rather they all describe a human being at a particular stage of development. To deny legal personhood to human beings who have not yet been born, as *Roe* does, is a purely arbitrary and semantic operation, exactly analogous to denying legal personhood to slaves, as the Dred Scott case did.

Nor is affirming the right to life of this as yet unborn human being an instance of "enforcing" a view that is somehow alien to the American system. Before 1966 all 50 states had laws prohibiting abortion except where considered medically necessary to save a mother's life (and in some states also to preserve her health). Between 1966 and 1972 a number of states liberalized their laws, mostly to allow abortions in accordance with certain so-called "indications" for abortion. Then *Roe* came along in 1973 and simply overturned all these state laws in one stroke, in what dissenting Justice Byron White called at the time "an exercise of raw judicial power."

People may take legal abortion for granted now. But *Roe* and the other decisions stemming from it are not carved in stone; they can be changed. Eliminating legal abortion does not represent some impossible dream; it merely means restoring what was in place a generation or so ago.

At the time our Declaration of Independence and Constitution were adopted, the scientific facts concerning human conception and gestation up to the time of birth were not completely known. Once they became known, it was—and is— eminently logical to apply the existing constitutional and legal rights and guarantees to human beings who have been conceived but not yet born. Instead, the opposite occurred. The "culture" was moving in a different direction—one coinciding with the development of new and more reliable means for performing abortions. The next thing we knew, we were saddled with the current massive carnage.

> *"To deny legal personhood to human beings who have not yet been born . . . is a purely arbitrary and semantic operation."*

What has now occurred with our society's deciding to reject many of the unborn members of the human family is a moral revolution in which we have now effectively put ourselves in charge of who is to live and who is to die. Not just the Ten Commandments but "nature and nature's God" have been put aside here; *we* are in charge now, and considering what "we" have shown ourselves to be capable of, nobody can be very sanguine about the future.

The Unborn Is Human

The unborn baby is a human being. As the journal *California Medicine* stated in a once-famous editorial way back at the dawn of the abortion era in 1970:

> In defiance of the long-held Western ethic of intrinsic and equal value for every human life regardless of its stage, condition, or status, abortion is becoming accepted by society. . . . Since the old ethic has not yet been fully displaced it has been necessary to separate the idea of abortion from the idea of killing, which continues to be socially abhorrent. The result has been a curious avoidance of the scientific fact, which everyone really knows, that human life begins at conception. . . . The very considerable semantic gymnastics which are required to rationalize abortion as anything but taking a human life would be ludicrous if they were not so often put forward under socially impeccable auspices.

The almost universal avoidance in our public discourse of discussion of "the scientific fact, which everybody really knows," namely, that a human being is killed by abortion, exemplifies the new and fundamental *dishonesty* legal abortion has brought to our public life. Where abortion as a political issue is concerned, we want to deny, semantically, that we are taking a life, although that is the reality. At the same time we understand perfectly well and act on the logic that if we can take life by abortion, we can take it for other reasons as well, and thus the field in which we consider ourselves allowed to take life legally very quickly becomes extended—as it is currently and rapidly being extended—to the terminally (and not so terminally) ill, the old, the retarded, the defective, and other specimens of Friedrich Nietzsche's "botched" and "bungled" or Adolf Hitler's "useless eaters"—and indeed, soon, if not already, to AIDS victims, in view of the astronomical medical costs associated with their extended care when their illness is "terminal" anyway.

> *"We have now effectively put ourselves in charge of who is to live and who is to die."*

The Decline of Society

None of this represents any hypothetical "slippery slope" argument. We are already on that slope and going down, as witness the nation's current inability to deal with the new phenomenon of "assisted suicide." It all started with legalized abortion; that was the point where we got on the slippery slope and started downhill toward a "killer society," as many warned at the time.

Kristol writes:

> In all the Western democracies (including Israel) a public policy has evolved that tolerates abortion while limiting it, regulating it, and discouraging it. It is safe to predict that this is where public policy in the U.S. will end up. And if in Israel the Orthodox—who utterly abhor abortion and do not themselves practice it—can live with such a compromise, there is no reason why our conservative Christians cannot do the same.

Living with a situation we can do nothing about may be one thing. No doubt the Orthodox are not numerous enough in Israel to affect "public policy"—just as prolifers in the U.S. have not yet been able to do much of anything about the fact of legal abortion. Therefore prolifers have to "live with" this current tragic situation, until they can succeed in doing something about it. But Kristol is evidently arguing for something very different from merely being obliged to live with a situation about which nothing can be done for the moment. He seems to be arguing for the *acceptance* of the current situation, however undesirable even he may think it is.

Much Can Be Done

But this is a counsel of despair. First, much *can* be done about the abortion situation, as Henry Hyde and his congressional allies have demonstrated in getting the Hyde Amendment re-enacted against all the odds and the predictions of the pundits. Other similar concrete prolife measures are also possible and doable, even in the present unfavorable climate. Secondly, abortion *must* be fought against on principle because it is wrong; we *cannot* leave our country in the hands of people willing to kill wantonly, meanwhile publicly lying about what they are really doing. One thing that continually motivated the anti-Communists in Eastern Europe and the former Soviet Union to bring down the rotten regimes there was the all-pervasive *dishonesty* of those regimes; we cannot give America over to the same kind of dishonesty, as represented by the proabortionists.

With all due respect, then, Irving Kristol is wrong. Legalized abortion is not something that any society can really tolerate or live with without losing its soul. It must be combated on principle, whatever the odds.

Let us not, however, single out Kristol. Over the past few years there has been a spate of articles and speeches by conservatives calling for a more pragmatic, less "absolutist" position on abortion. There is a strong trend among some of these conservatives to assume the existence of a "consensus" in the practical order in favor of a "compromise" on abortion.

> *"Legalized abortion . . . was the point where we got on the slippery slope and started downhill toward a 'killer society.'"*

Prolifers are now being given to understand that henceforth their cause can be championed in the political arena only through such measures as those which, in the words of a *National Review* editorial, "allow states to impose such clearly sensible requirements as parental, spousal, and informed consent. There are solid majorities for such an approach. . . . Republican policy should reflect that political reality," says the conservative journal, which continues to represent itself as basically prolife.

Politics vs. Principle

According to David Horowitz, writing in *National Review*, conservative support for the constitutional right to life would be fatal to the "majoritarian political ambitions" of conservatives. No doubt following the polls, he postulates a 30 percent minority out there determined to be proabortion in all circumstances, a 30 or 40 percent "center," highly ambivalent about the whole thing, and at most a 30 percent bloc believing in a right to life. Says Horowitz: "The arithmetic adds up to an insuperable political barrier." A majority "will defeat any political movement that organizes around the code word 'right to life.'" Curiously, Horowitz does not even raise the question of principle.

In another article in the same journal, William McGurn advocates doing away with the Republican Party platform plank calling for a constitutional amendment:

Taking into account the dramatic shifts in America's political, constitutional, and, yes, moral landscape, Republicans need to shift their position from support for a constitutional amendment outlawing all abortions to support for one asserting the constitutional prerogative of states in restricting abortion.

According to McGurn, holding out for an amendment outlawing all abortions "essentially guarantees there will be no restrictions at all." But this is not true, as proved, *inter alia*, by the Hyde Amendment vote. The prolife movement has continued to work, often successfully, for minor restrictions on abortion, even while continuing to aim at the principled goal of a constitutional amendment proscribing all abortions. A principal reason the prolife movement has been unable to be more successful is that we still remain under the thralldom of the courts, especially the Supreme Court, on the abortion issue. The courts keep rejecting what legislatures enact.

Prolife Strategy

Traditionally, in both law and morality, no one has the right "to choose" to take the life of another. But since our judges appear unable to understand law or morality on the matter of abortion, a maximalist constitutional amendment remains the best and perhaps only way they can be brought to their senses. Until then, nothing prevents prolifers from working on achieving all the interim measures which *National Review* and McGurn advocate. Indeed prolifers are precisely the ones who are doing this right now. Who else, indeed, is working so tirelessly in the various states even for such goals as these, heartbreakingly limited as they are?

But to disown the *ultimate* goal of prolifers currently working within the Republican Party by dropping or changing the platform language would be a catastrophic mistake for that party. Prolifers will not continue to work for or within a party that thinks it has to go to the trouble of expressly repudiating the clear goal of the vast majority of them—and the reason why many of them are working for the Republican Party in the first place. One recent poll showed that 58 percent of church-going Republican voters would *leave* the Republican Party if it abandoned its profamily and prolife positions.

The prolife demonstrators out there—e.g., in the proliferating Life Chains—

> *"Abortion must be fought against on principle because it is wrong."*

are not holding up signs calling for spousal or parental notification or for waiting periods before abortions (interim measures they are willing to work for because they are the best that can be realized at the moment); rather, their signs say "Abortion Kills Children." With abortion we are simply not dealing with a normal political issue. If the current arguments within the Republican Party for expediency manage to win out, that party may eventually come to be seen as having been *doomed* precisely by its inability to deal with this issue on a principled basis, just as the Whig Party in the last century was unable to deal with slavery on a principled basis.

And thus the kinds of arguments advanced by the conservative "friends" of the prolife movement such as Kristol and McGurn are really not too far removed from the arguments of the avowed enemies of the cause, who keep on impatiently insisting that the abortion issue must be "settled" and therefore prolifers are the ones who must compromise.

How can prolifers be expected to take seriously such "friendly" counsels as they are now getting from certain conservatives? With friends like these, we hardly need enemies.

Chapter 3

Should Women Have Greater Access to Abortion?

CURRENT CONTROVERSIES

Chapter Preface

Since its legalization in 1973, access to abortion has varied little for most women. In almost all cases, women have relied on doctors at either hospitals or abortion clinics to terminate their pregnancies surgically. Today, however, new developments may soon give women alternatives to traditional doctor-provided surgical abortions.

One of the most controversial of these developments is the RU 486 abortion pill, which aborts a fetus in the early weeks of pregnancy. In 1994, arrangements were made to begin RU 486 clinical trials in the United States. Another alternative that could also change traditional access to abortion is menstrual extraction, a technique introduced in the early 1970s that is increasingly sought by women. This procedure—in which the contents of a woman's uterus (which may include a fertilized egg) are suctioned out—has created controversy in part because it is often performed in private group settings by people who are not medical professionals and who use simple manual instruments.

While such alternatives have been condemned by groups and individuals who oppose abortion by any method, even some abortion-rights advocates, concerned with the health of women, have been critical of them. They question, for example, the need for and safety of RU 486 or menstrual extraction as a substitute for conventional abortion, which they argue is a simple and safe procedure. As women's studies professor Janice G. Raymond, a critic of RU 486, writes, "First-trimester suction abortion is one of the simplest of presently medicalized gynecological procedures."

Other advocates, however, argue that these alternatives enhance women's abortion rights by expanding access to abortion and by making women's abortion decisions more private. Regarding RU 486, abortion-rights pioneer Lawrence Lader contends, "RU 486's great advantages are effectiveness and safety. Above all, RU 486 puts women in control of their own bodies." The authors in this chapter debate such alternatives to traditional abortion and whether women should have greater access to abortion.

The RU 486 Abortion Pill Should Be Available to Women

by Allan Rosenfield

About the author: *Allan Rosenfield is the dean of, and a professor at, the Columbia University School of Public Health in New York City.*

Rarely has an important scientific advance been the subject of as much political, ideological, and social controversy as mifepristone (RU 486). The development of a safe and effective antiprogestin compound had been the goal of researchers in the field of reproductive biology for decades. The pioneering work of scientists at Roussel–UCLAF in France led to the approval of mifepristone by the French Ministry of Solidarity, Health, and Social Welfare in September 1988. The use of mifepristone, coupled with a prostaglandin [a hormone that causes the uterus to contract and expel its contents] and administered within 49 days of the last menstrual period, produces a complete abortion in approximately 95 percent of cases.

Greater Safety

Rémi Peyron et al., in [*The New England Journal of Medicine*, May 27, 1993], describe a new regimen of administration involving the supplementation of mifepristone with an oral prostaglandin, misoprostol, rather than the intramuscular or intravaginal prostaglandins that have been used previously. There are, as the authors suggest, several potential advantages to the use of an oral preparation to supplement mifepristone, including the possibility of greater safety with regard to cardiovascular complications and greater convenience of administration.

In addition to its use as an abortifacient, mifepristone has been reported to be effective as a postcoital medication, and it is being evaluated in the treatment of certain types of meningioma, recurrent breast cancer, Cushing's syndrome, and

From Allan Rosenfield, "Mifepristone (RU 486) in the United States: What Does the Future Hold?" *The New England Journal of Medicine* 328:1560-61 (1993). Copyright ©1993, Massachusetts Medical Society. All rights reserved.

glaucoma. Despite these potentially important medical uses, the drug is not available in the United States [as of May 1993], nor has Roussel submitted data to the Food and Drug Administration [FDA] for review. Instead, the drug has remained hostage to opponents of abortion, not on medical or scientific grounds but because of ideological and political issues.

The potential availability of a medical means to terminate an early pregnancy has been of tremendous interest to women's groups, to the medical profession, and to individual women throughout the country. The popularity of such a method is demonstrated by the large number of women in France, where mifepristone is available, who have chosen this method over first-trimester surgical curettage (a simple and relatively inexpensive procedure), despite a rather rigid protocol that requires four visits to one of the approved clinics that offer the drug.

> *"The drug has remained hostage to opponents of abortion . . . because of ideological and political issues."*

A Dramatic Advance

Many American women view access to a medical abortifacient to be taken privately as a dramatic advance for several reasons: harassment of patients outside abortion facilities has increased substantially, making a woman's visit to many of these facilities an emotional nightmare; 83 percent of U.S. counties do not have an abortion provider or facility; fewer and fewer physicians are willing to provide surgical termination of pregnancy, particularly in view of the harassment and increasingly violent protests by antiabortion groups (including the murder of Dr. David Gunn by an antiabortion activist); and few residency programs in obstetrics and gynecology routinely offer training in abortion procedures. In most programs such training is available only to residents who take specific steps to obtain it, either at their hospital or, often, at a planned-parenthood clinic or other freestanding facility. Abortion is the only important obstetrical or gynecologic procedure for which training is optional. Furthermore, board certification does not currently require that candidates demonstrate proficiency in this procedure.

As a result of the vocal opposition and threatening behavior of antiabortion groups in the United States, Roussel has been extremely restrictive in its marketing and distribution of mifepristone anywhere, and to date, it is available only in France, the United Kingdom, and Sweden. The company has been unwilling to provide supplies for clinical research conducted in the United States. Thus, a vocal minority has interrupted the normal progression of research on a new drug from the laboratory to clinical use.

The climate is changing, however, given the pro-choice position of the Clinton administration. This change has led to a reversal in the policies of Roussel and its parent company, Hoechst. The president of Roussel and Dr. David Kessler, the commissioner of the FDA, have discussed the submission of data on mifepristone for review by the agency. In April 1993, Kessler announced that Roussel had agreed to grant a license to a nonprofit U.S. organization, the Population Council, which, in turn, would select a U.S. manufacturer for mifepristone. The Population Council will sponsor an application to the FDA and manage a large clinical trial [scheduled for Fall 1994] in the United States. Roussel has also agreed to provide the FDA with its extensive toxicologic and chemical data on mifepristone.

There is every reason to believe that this review, once initiated, will proceed with some speed. Despite the fact that there has only been one clinical trial of mifepristone in the United States, it appears likely—given the extensive data already available from outside the country, including multicenter trials conducted by the World Health Organization—that approval will take place in a shorter time than usual, perhaps within two or three years from the start of the process.

One can expect opposition from some members of Congress to the review of this drug by the FDA, but clearly there are insufficient votes at present to pass any legislation aimed at preventing such a review (such legislation would be unprecedented). Under the Bush administration, administrative steps may have been taken to prevent the FDA review or at least to slow its progress. The opposite should be the case under the Clinton administration, and an expedited review can be expected.

Make RU 486 Available

In France, onerous regulations are in place concerning the use of mifepristone. These have been required by Roussel, apparently for political rather than scientific reasons. Mifepristone is available only in approved clinics, and each pill is labeled and treated almost like a narcotic. There are no medical reasons for such an approach. Once approved, the drug should be used primarily by obstetrician-gynecologists (and perhaps by family practitioners and nurse-midwives), since a pelvic examination should be carried out to check the uterine size before the drug is used. Furthermore, in a small number of women the abortion may be incomplete or excessive bleeding may take place, requiring a surgical intervention (suction curettage).

There is no reason, however, to restrict the drug's use to selected clinics; rather, it should be available in a private doctor's office, assuming that the physician has ready access to an operating room for surgical completion of abortion when necessary. The availability of mifepristone in a private doctor's office should substantially restrict the ability of antiabortion groups to harass patients, physicians, and clinic staff,

> *"There is no reason . . . to restrict the drug's use to selected clinics; rather, it should be available in a private doctor's office."*

since it will be much more difficult to target individual doctors' offices than to target the much more visible abortion clinics.

It is essential, however, that any physician who prescribes this drug provide careful and complete counseling about the surgical and medical methods of abortion and their expected side effects and potential complications. Some would argue that there should be a waiting area or examining room where a woman could remain for a few hours after the administration of the prostaglandin, because of the expected nausea, cramping (which can be moderately severe and may require pain medication), and bleeding. Providing such a waiting area could be a problem in some private offices. Others suggest that the mifepristone and misoprostol could be given to the women at the time of their first visit, with instructions to take the prostaglandin two days later.

Women's Needs

Even when mifepristone is prescribed at an abortion facility, in some women the abortion will be completed at home, rather than at the facility. But because of the availability of counseling, many women will choose to receive care in an abortion facility, particularly in areas where there is little if any harassment. For others, the privacy of a doctor's office will be preferred. Particular attention must be given to the inequities of access to any services for poor women, particularly poor minority women, and the possible negative consequences of delay in receiving care if bleeding complications occur after the administration of mifepristone and the prostaglandin.

The data presented by Peyron et al. on the use of misoprostol also provide a solution to a problem for the United States—namely, that no approved prostaglandin has been available. Misoprostol is marketed in the United States under the trade name Cytotec, for use in the treatment of gastrointestinal disease. The drug is inexpensive and is stored at room temperature. The French government approved the use of misoprostol as an adjunct to mifepristone for the termination of pregnancy. The process of reviewing misoprostol for use with mifepristone in the United States should be simplified greatly, since misoprostol has already been approved for other indications.

A medical means of terminating pregnancy would be an important advance in the provision of reproductive health services to women in the United States. The political and ideological opposition to abortion, which has resulted in the unwillingness of Roussel to study or market mifepristone in the United States, at least until now, has been described by [professors] David A. Grimes and Rebecca J. Cook as a "national disgrace." Perhaps this disgrace will finally pass, although clearly there will continue to be loud, and perhaps occasionally violent, opposition to the use of this agent.

A National Health Care Plan Should Include Abortion Services

by National Women's Law Center

About the author: *National Women's Law Center is a Washington, D.C., organization that works to advance and protect women's legal rights—particularly those of low-income women—in such areas as employment, education, reproductive rights and health, family support, and income security.*

Women's health needs cannot be met unless their reproductive health care is included. Reproductive health care is a critical component of the health care women need throughout their lifetime. It is often the first type of care a woman seeks, and for many the only form of primary care they receive. Women's reproductive health care includes pregnancy, delivery and post-natal care; contraception; infertility services; treatment for reproductive tract diseases; and abortion. Both women and their health care providers view these reproductive health services as part of a continuum. Therefore, to protect women's health, and respect women's choices, it is essential to cover the entire continuum, including abortion services, in a national health care plan.

Women's Health Requires Abortion Coverage

Current Industry Practice Includes Abortion Coverage. According to a large-scale study of private insurance coverage of reproductive health care services undertaken by the Alan Guttmacher Institute, 66% of large-group fee-for-service policies and 70% of HMOs [health maintenance organizations] routinely cover abortion services in their typical plans.

An informal survey conducted by the National Women's Law Center confirms these results. According to the survey, Blue Cross/Blue Shield policies in Arkansas, California, Illinois, Indiana, Kansas, Montana, Nevada, New York, Ohio, Oregon, Rhode Island, South Carolina, Virginia, Wisconsin, and

National Women's Law Center, "Abortion and National Health Care Reform," pp. 1-4, April 1994. Reprinted with permission.

Wyoming routinely provide coverage for abortion services.

National insurers such as Aetna, The Principal Financial Group, Employer's Health and Travelers all report that they commonly provide coverage for abortion services. According to a spokesman for Blue Cross of California, "This is not a new phenomenon. Private insurance has paid for abortion for quite a while."

> *"Abortion services . . . are as essential to women's health as family planning and prenatal care."*

To depart from current practices would deny millions of women access to an important health service which is routinely covered by private insurers. Taking away coverage of abortion services would cause health care reform to fail in its promise to provide Americans the same or better coverage than they have today.

Women Will Not Have the Same Full Coverage Afforded Men Unless Abortion Services Are Included in the Standard Benefits Package. Abortion services are linked to and inseparable from other reproductive health care, and are as essential to women's health as family planning and prenatal care. Moreover, abortion is one of the most common surgical procedures women undergo, and one of the safest. Indeed, access to early abortion is far safer than childbirth.

No health care reform plan proposes excluding from coverage any service essential to men's health, as abortion is to women's health. Without coverage of medically necessary or appropriate abortions, women's health needs simply will not receive the same coverage as men's.

Abortions Should Be Covered the Same Way as Any Other Health Service. Most health care plans cover services that are medically necessary or appropriate. The decision as to when an abortion is medically necessary or appropriate is best determined by health considerations, not political ones. Accordingly, abortion services that a woman and her doctor determine to be medically necessary or appropriate should be covered.

Endangering Women's Health

Health Reform Is an Opportunity to Ensure All Women Access to Basic Care. National health care reform will fall short unless it ensures access and coverage for all, and ends the two-tiered system of health care. This is the goal of the Health Security Act [President Bill Clinton's health care reform proposal], which folds Medicaid into the reformed system, eliminating the distinctions between those served by private and public insurance.

As with all abortion restrictions, failure to cover abortions will have the most devastating effects on low-income women. Required to pay the entire fee for services that are not included in a standard benefit package, poor women will be forced either to delay the procedure while they scrape together the funds—at great cost to their health and economic well-being—or to carry an unwanted pregnancy to term, compromising the child's health and well-being.

Failure to Cover Abortions Would Impose Serious Risks to Women's Health.
Terrorist activities by Operation Rescue and other anti-choice extremists have
already succeeded in vastly reducing the number of providers willing to perform abortions. As of early 1994, 83% of the counties in the United States have
no physician willing to provide abortion services. Moreover, in 1991 only 13%
of the nation's obstetrics and gynecology residency programs required training
in first-trimester abortions, and only 7% required second-trimester training,
compared to almost 25% that required both forms of training in 1985.

Excluding abortion coverage from a nationally mandated benefit package
would endanger women's lives and health by marginalizing the procedure and
further depleting the number of practitioners willing to provide the service.
Such a depletion will result in greater delays for women seeking to terminate
their pregnancies. There is a 30% increase in risk of major health complications
with each week after the eighth week of pregnancy, and the risk of death from
an abortion performed at 13 to 15 weeks is nine times greater than for an abortion performed at 8 weeks or earlier. According to the American Medical Association, restricting access to safer, earlier legal abortion will lead to increased
mortality and morbidity among women in the United States.

A Sound, Workable Public Policy

*A Strong Majority of Americans Favors Including Abortion in a Basic Benefit
Package Under the Medically Necessary or Appropriate Health Standard for
All Care.* A July 1993 public opinion survey conducted by Celinda Lake found
that 66% of those polled support coverage for abortions that are medically necessary or appropriate. Celinda Lake's research showed almost three-quarters
(72%) polled recognized that abortion is a very complex and personal issue,
with the decision best left to a woman and her doctor. They believe abortion is a
health issue, and should not be dictated by political considerations; the government should not try to judge who should get abortions and when.

Respondents overwhelmingly expressed the belief that increasing programs to
provide education and family planning
is more effective in limiting abortions
than excluding abortion coverage
from a basic benefit package.

The results of these polling efforts
make clear that Americans want a
health care system that responds to

> *"Restricting access to safer,
> earlier legal abortion will lead
> to increased mortality and
> morbidity among women."*

women's needs, including medically necessary or appropriate abortion services.

A Conscience Clause Allows Providers to Opt Out of Performing Abortions.
The federal government and most states have enacted "conscience clauses"
which allow health professionals to opt out of participating in medical procedures that are contrary to their religious beliefs or moral convictions. Thus, in-

dividual providers who are morally opposed to the procedure will not be required to perform abortions.

Including Abortion in the Benefit Package Is Consistent with Current Policy. Opponents of reproductive choice argue that abortions should not be covered because to do so would require employers and taxpayers who object to abortions to subsidize it with their tax dollars. They do not explain why women, as employees and taxpayers, should get less health care coverage than men. Nor do they refute the fact that it has never been acceptable national policy to permit individual citizens to refuse to pay taxes because they oppose some programs as a matter of conscience. Some, for example, oppose war on moral and religious grounds, but they may not legally withhold the portion of their taxes representing their contribution to the military budget. Inclusion of abortion services ensures that abortion is treated in the same manner as any other issue when a national standard is set.

Supplemental Insurance Is Discriminatory

Opponents of including abortion coverage in a guaranteed benefit package have suggested that abortion be treated as an "extra" for insurance coverage, requiring payment of an additional premium. This proposal is both discriminatory and unworkable. A rider option would require women to pre pay at an extra cost—for abortion coverage alone, when the need cannot be anticipated. This ill-advised approach will damage, not reform, women's health care.

> *"[Opponents] do not explain why women, as employees and taxpayers, should get less health care coverage than men."*

Offering supplemental coverage for abortion services also raises the issue of individual privacy. Such a scheme would require women affirmatively to assert that they wished to be covered for abortion services. For those who will continue to obtain their insurance through an employer, the confidentiality problem is particularly egregious. Under this scenario, a woman who opted to purchase a supplemental rider would be forced to disclose such a decision to her employer by indicating the level of payroll deduction for her insurance coverage.

Requiring that abortion coverage be offered as a separate rider sets a dangerous precedent. It opens the door to the exclusion of other services, such as contraception and voluntary sterilization which anti-choice advocates also oppose, and yet additional services which others may oppose, thus unraveling the fabric of a comprehensive benefits package.

Fiscally, a rider option for abortion services makes no sense. When the United States Office of Personnel Management added abortion coverage to the federal employees health benefit program, the results on premiums were cost neutral. The cost of optional riders would be arbitrary, unnecessary and unfair.

Women Should Have the Option of Menstrual Extraction

by Rebecca Chalker and Carol Downer

About the authors: *Rebecca Chalker and Carol Downer have been active leaders in the women's health movement for the past twenty years. Chalker is the author of* The Complete Cervical Cap Guide *and coeditor of* A New View of a Woman's Body. *Downer is a lawyer and the founding executive director of the Federation of Feminist Women's Health Centers. She helped pioneer the concept of vaginal and cervical self-examination as a key to self-empowerment.*

Menstrual extraction (ME) was developed as a technique to help women maintain control over their menstrual cycles, and hence, over their reproductive lives. On or about the day that a woman expects her menstrual period, the contents of the uterus are gently suctioned out, lightening and greatly shortening the expected period. If an egg has been fertilized within the preceding weeks, it will be suctioned out as well. Dealing as it does with normal bodily functions, ME is not a medical treatment—but a home health-care technique, similar in many ways to self-catheterization, at-home bladder instillations, and other health-maintenance routines.

Not "Self-Abortion"

The tabloids and the electronic media have labeled menstrual extraction "self-abortion" or "do-it-yourself abortion," but these terms are misleading. First of all, due to the location of the uterus, it is virtually impossible for a woman to do ME on herself. To do the procedure safely and correctly, a woman needs the help of one or more women who are trained and experienced in ME. In this sense, it is no more appropriate to label ME "self-abortion" than it is to call home birth "self-birth." Lorraine Rothman, one of the developers of ME, explains that the name *menstrual extraction* was chosen "because it is a very literal description of the process.". . .

In the last 20 years, perhaps 1,000 to 2,000 women in the United States have learned menstrual extraction by participating in small, close-knit groups based on friendship and a common goal of reclaiming control over their reproductive lives. These groups typically have from 5 to 10 members, and meet regularly— perhaps once a month or more often—to learn more about their bodies and their menstrual cycles, and to practice their skills. Groups that have been in existence for a long time may meet only occasionally, when one of the members chooses to have her period extracted.

The Safety of Menstrual Extraction

Trained practitioners—lay women, nurses, midwives, physicians assistants or other paramedics—have found menstrual extraction to be exceptionally safe. They maintain that because a smaller, more flexible cannula is used, because drugs are not routinely employed, and since conscientious practitioners have a commitment to be extremely careful and gentle, the risks of infection or perfo- ration are exceedingly low.

Long-time practitioners have found that the safety of menstrual extraction is dependent upon three factors:

- practicing sterile technique, that is, knowing how to disinfect the cannula [a plastic, strawlike instrument], the only instrument that enters the uterus, and accessory instruments.

- knowing the signs of a problem.

- having a backup plan, i.e., having a formal or informal arrangement with a doctor or clinic, and knowing how to deal with paramedics and emergency room personnel in the unlikely event of a medical emergency. . . .

While some doctors and family planning experts endorse menstrual extrac- tion, others have expressed concern that while it is quite possible for paramedics and trained lay practitioners to do them responsibly, ME and other home health-care techniques might be misused by young women who are des- perate and inexperienced, harming themselves in some way. But the scenario of young women harming themselves with menstrual extraction is based on a lack of understanding of exactly what ME entails.

> *"Trained practitioners . . . have found menstrual extraction to be exceptionally safe."*

While the ME technique is ele- gantly simple, and many women have demonstrated that it can be learned by virtually anyone with a commitment to acquire such knowl- edge and skills, it is not something one can just decide to do. Menstrual extrac- tion is a multistep process that requires considerable forethought, commitment, preparation, resourcefulness, and training over an extensive period of time. Acquiring information, becoming familiar with the reproductive anatomy, and assembling the equipment and learning to use it effectively are actually part of a months-long process. Realistically, there are enough stumbling blocks to discourage all but the most determined and resourceful women. . . .

Marianne's Menstrual Extraction

Marianne had her first menstrual extraction in 1986. She was not in a group at the time, but her friend Louise had been in one for several years. There was no abortion clinic in her town, so when she noticed signs of pregnancy, Marianne asked Louise if she knew where she could get an abortion. "Louise told me about a women's clinic in town a couple of hours away, but then asked me if I would consider having a menstrual extraction. At first I was a little skeptical, but after we talked for a while, I realized that my hesitation was based on things I had imagined that weren't true, and I decided to try it," Marianne says.

At the time, Marianne's period was about five days late. Louise called her group and they met at her house the next night. "We had a pretty long meeting before the procedure," Marianne remembers. "They showed me the equipment while they were testing it, and that made me feel more confident that things would go okay. Then we discussed the backup plan. If anything happened, we would call the clinic and someone would drive me there. I looked at my cervix with a light and mirror, which I had done before, and then Louise and two other members of the group felt my uterus. They thought it wasn't much enlarged, but that it felt softer than it normally would. Then I began to get a little excited that we were going to actually do it. Louise put the cannula at the entrance to my cervix, and then slowly pushed it into the uterus. I felt some mild cramping, which increased a little when the suction started. I was watching the cannula with a mirror and saw some blood coming into the tube. In just a couple of minutes we began to notice light-colored tissue mixed in with the blood. Ten minutes later, my cramps got stronger, but were not unbearable. After 15 more minutes, Louise suggested that we examine the tissue that had collected in the tube and jar. When we examined it, we saw a lot of chorionic villi and the sac, the membrane that contained the implantation. I felt relief, and all those things that women normally feel afterward, but I was also thrilled. I realized that I had complete control over my body, control I didn't have an hour ago, right there in my friend's living room! Needless to say, I joined the group."

> *"I realized that my hesitation was based on things I had imagined that weren't true, and I decided to try it."*

Whether the extraction lasts 20 minutes, an hour, or longer, the vast majority of procedures are completed without incident, although, as Marianne observes, "They are all interesting, and a little bit different in some way.

"Menstrual extraction will probably never be practiced by that many women," she adds. "Learning it is a very serious and demanding project. But I think that every woman who is pro-choice would want to know about its existence, and know that she and her friends could learn it if they suddenly found themselves without any other safe options.". . .

Legal Issues

Over the past 20 years, the excellent safety record of groups doing menstrual extraction has not presented the opportunity for a legal challenge, so its practice has remained in a gray area legally. Nevertheless, because of the potential for prosecution, many menstrual extraction groups have sought out attorneys and researched the laws of their states, in order to get a sense of the legal climate surrounding abortion and the use of home health-care techniques, and definitions of medical practice. This research has raised some intriguing legal issues.

"We see menstrual extraction as very different from abortion," says Rosalind, who was among the first wave of women who learned the technique in the early 1970s. "While it definitely has the potential for terminating a pregnancy, as it is practiced menstrual extraction is so much more than that. Women who practice ME operate in a mutually supportive and mutually consensual environment, with the common goal of maintaining reproductive control. If a woman is worried that her period won't come, she can get it. If she doesn't want her period, for a variety of reasons, she can get rid of it. The assumptions upon which menstrual extraction is based are quite different than those of abortion.". . .

A Small Risk

Even though menstrual extraction has been practiced safely for many years, its proponents recognize that they do run a small but irreducible risk of legal prosecution. If such a challenge is made, it is likely to result from someone's being injured—slightly or seriously—during an extraction. Prosecution will probably be made under current abortion laws, as well as under laws governing the practice of medicine.

Even though good legal arguments can be made that doing a menstrual extraction is not practicing medicine, and that legally, it is not an abortion, certain prosecutors may be anti-abortion and on the lookout for the opportunity to bring a suit. Even prosecutors who are pro-choice may believe that the technique is too dangerous to be practiced safely by lay people and feel compelled to take a case. Jurors may harbor such sentiments as well.

Because of the volatile atmosphere surrounding abortion and women's rights to control their own reproduction, menstrual extraction groups have increasingly sought counsel to help them research the laws of their specific states, to help them ascertain how they can work safely within those laws, and to assess, as far as possible, the chances of prosecution under existing laws.

More Doctors Should Perform Abortions

by Jane Doe

About the author: *Jane Doe is the pseudonym of a resident obstetrician/gynecologist whose practice includes performing abortions.*

I am an abortionist in training. When my residency in obstetrics and gynecology began three years ago I was asked if I was willing to learn to perform abortions. I said yes—but was amazed to find that 50 percent of my fellow residents had chosen *not* to be trained in this extremely common gynecologic procedure, one undergone by 1.5 million American women each year.

Abortion is the *only* procedure a medical student can choose not to observe. It is the *only* procedure that an ob-gyn resident can refuse to learn to do. Increasingly, residents do refuse, and go on refusing after they set up their practices. There has long been a disparity between doctors' voiced support for a women's right to choose and their willingness to actually provide abortions. In a 1985 survey of the members of the American College of Obstetricians and Gynecologists, 84 percent agreed that elective abortions should be performed, but a mere 34 percent said they performed them.

Antiabortion Sentiment

The situation has only gotten worse since 1985. That year, the number of ob-gyn residencies that routinely included training in abortion was 50 percent higher than it is now. Today, nearly 40 percent of residencies offer no abortion training at all. An antiabortion attitude is rife in medical schools across the country. My department chairman said to me, "I hate doing abortions. They are contrary to all else I do in my practice." He told me he had no objections to my writing this article as long as I made it clear I did not enjoy doing abortions. That is one of the reasons I am calling myself Dr. Jane Doe.

Luckily for my patients, I do not share the chairman's distaste for doing abortions. In fact, I find the procedure rather challenging, and it is rewarding to help

Jane Doe, "Why I Am an Abortionist," *Glamour*, October 1993. Reprinted with permission.

a woman making the difficult choice to end a pregnancy do so safely. I plan to be an ob-gyn who can provide competent and *comprehensive* care for my patients, from birth control to prenatal care to abortion.

My plans do not make me popular among my colleagues. In so many ways—from administrators, faculty and peers—doctors in training get the message that abortion is a sleazy and offensive procedure. We are encouraged to be excited about an upcoming vaginal hysterectomy ("It's going to be a good case—the uterus is practically falling out"), but this sort of scrub-sink talk is taboo when it comes to abortions. When we dictate the operation for hospital records we say, "And then the procedure was done in the standard fashion." This way even the transcription department is spared the details. A complication during a cesarean section is loudly discussed at the department's weekly morbidity-and-mortality meeting, but a difficult abortion is whispered about in the hallway.

The Abortionist Label

We also absorb the lesson that if we dare to include abortion in our ob-gyn practice, we will be marked as abortionists. A doctor who performs hysterectomies is not labeled a hysterectomist; she is not stripped of the dignity given to the term *physician*. But a doctor who does abortions—even if they are only a small part of her practice—is known as an abortionist. This label is supposed to be the kiss of death for any professional hopes she might have. Our teachers and fellow students suggest that our pregnant patients will flee in droves if they have to sit in the same waiting room as abortion patients, and vice versa. I don't believe this is true. How does one spot an abortion patient? Why do we assume a woman who doesn't want to be pregnant will be upset by a woman who does? But "everybody" knows that abortion patients and other patients can't mix. So if we insist on doing abortions we had better do them on the sly.

That is how most of us end up doing them. When *Roe* v. *Wade* [the Supreme Court decision legalizing abortion] became the law of the land in 1973, the majority of doctors and hospitals were not prepared to handle the new demand for abortions—or didn't want to, since the procedure, after so many years of being illegal, was still seen as disreputable. At the same time, feminist groups argued that freestanding clinics could offer cheaper abortions, with more caring doctors and counselors. And so such clinics were built, and still provide the majority of abortions. The clinic system perpetuates the abortion crisis. It isolates doctors who do abortions, and their patients, from the rest of the community; it puts a stigma on both. It is as if abortion is just barely legal: The procedure moved from the back alley into hygienic clinics but not into hospitals, and it did not become part of the routine care of women.

> *"It is rewarding to help a woman making the difficult choice to end a pregnancy do so safely."*

156

My residency's abortion-training program offers supervision through approximately 25 procedures. I want not just to perform abortions but also to teach others how to perform them, so I need more training than that. Abortions are blind procedures—they are done mostly by feel—and it is well documented that complications increase when novices are in charge. Therefore, I moonlight at an abortion clinic one Saturday a month. It is a three-hour drive each way. There is no registered nurse at the clinic and I am the only doctor present on these Saturdays, which means that when complications have arisen—once, I was unable to grasp part of the fetus with my forceps; another time a woman started hemorrhaging from her cervix—I have had only clinic staff (as experienced as they are) to turn to for advice. At our department retreat, I mentioned my concern that residents being trained in abortions needed more supervision. The response to my comment was silence, then, "Next on the agenda?" Translation: Abortions are not important. Abortions are not glamorous. Abortions are done in abortion clinics by abortionists.

> *"I want not just to perform abortions but also to teach others how to perform them."*

No wonder both the women who seek abortions and the doctors who provide them have become such easy targets of harassment.

Fear of Harassment

When I go to the abortion clinic these days I park a few blocks away and enter through a back door. For one thing, I'm tired of Bible Bob, a regular picketer, waving his plastic baby doll in my face. But more important, I'm now the mother of a one-year-old, which makes me more nervous than before about the risks of acting on my belief that abortion is a woman's right. When I read that abortion provider Dr. David Gunn had been fatally shot in Florida, I remembered that my medical license, which bears my home address, was hanging on a wall in the clinic. I've considered not telling the patients my name, but they are already frightened about having an abortion—this dreadful procedure that no doctor in their community will do. To be in the hands of a nameless person would be even more frightening and dehumanizing.

Still, I feel I must write this piece under a pseudonym. If I acknowledged publicly that I do abortions, I would not only risk more harassment and intimidation by antiabortionists but would also lose my mother as a friend and as a much-needed live-in baby-sitter. Before *Roe* v. *Wade* my mother was able to obtain a safe abortion because she already had five children and was a doctor's wife. About fifteen years ago she became a born-again Christian and now pickets abortion clinics while wearing a pink sweatshirt that reads "Protect the Rights of All Unborn Women." She is a wonderful person and, next to my husband, my best friend. I can tell her anything except that I am an abortionist.

It's time to reclaim those words—*abortion, abortionist*. Recently I noticed an advertisement in a medical journal that sought "a pro-choice physician part-time." The group that placed the ad wants to hire a doctor to do abortions, but it doesn't even feel free to use the word. Perhaps if *every* pro-choice ob-gyn called herself an abortionist, the label would lose its power to destroy one's career and family. The American College of Obstetrics and Gynecology could ask *all* of its members to become abortionists—to make pregnancy termination one of the services they offer to reproductive-aged women.

"The Lord's Work"

My generation—I am 32; *Roe* was handed down when I was 11—has not seen women dying from self-induced abortions, so it's hard for us to realize the urgency of keeping abortion legal and safe. We have adopted the attitude that *other* people can do the abortions. We have forgotten that although doctors call abortion an elective procedure, to many women it is a necessary and even emergency procedure. In John Irving's novel *The Cider House Rules*, the book that may best express my own feelings about abortion, one of the protagonists, Dr. Larch, runs an orphanage that is also an abortion clinic. Women arrive and choose either to end their pregnancies or to deliver an orphan. Of Dr. Larch the book says, "He was an obstetrician; he delivered babies into the world. His colleagues called this 'the Lord's work.' And he was an abortionist; he delivered mothers too. His colleagues called this 'the Devil's work,' but it was all the Lord's work to Wilbur Larch."

The RU 486 Abortion Pill Is Dangerous for Women

by Janice Raymond, Renate Klein, and Lynette Dumble

About the authors: *Janice Raymond is a professor of women's studies and medical ethics at the University of Massachusetts in Amherst. Renate Klein is a lecturer at the Deakin University School of Humanities in Geelong, Victoria, Australia. Lynette Dumble is a research fellow at the University of Melbourne Department of Surgery in Parkville, Victoria, Australia.*

Editor's note: Some of the quotes in this viewpoint refer to words and phrases used in an opposing article in the March/April 1993 issue of Ms. *magazine.*

It is vital that U.S. women understand that some international women's groups have been far more critical of chemical abortion than have their U.S. counterparts. The Sixth International Women and Health Meeting, held in the Philippines in 1990, issued a resolution opposing the introduction of RU 486/PG [prostaglandin], especially in "developing" countries, as did the Feminist International Network of Resistance to Reproductive and Genetic Engineering (FINRRAGE) Conference in Brazil.

Ensuring Safe Abortions

We are concerned that the amount of resources and energy spent on lobbying for the introduction of RU 486 may detract from the necessary fight to maintain (and expand) safe conventional abortion facilities. We believe that women's health activists must continue to put pressure on lawmakers and abortion providers to ensure that safe, low-tech abortion is increasingly made available to women. We already have abortion methods that can be performed *safely* by skilled (lay) practitioners. We do not need "a drug cocktail" fraught with unknown consequences for women's short- and long-term health. It is distressing that others do not recognize the dangers inherent in RU 486 abortion, and instead welcome it as a new "choice" for women, calling our analysis "seriously flawed" and "based on an incomplete understanding of the parameters of surgical abortion." Only now in the promotion of RU 486 is conventional abortion referred to as "surgical," a description that bears little resemblance to low-tech (manual) vacuum aspiration.

"A Drug Cocktail." To state that both "surgical" abortion and RU 486 abortion involve the widespread use of drugs misses the point. The former can be performed with minimal drug use—a local anesthetic—whereas the latter is a medication-dependent abortion consisting of a drug cocktail: RU 486 and PG.

> *"It is distressing that others do not recognize the dangers inherent in RU 486 abortion."*

Residual Effects. The antiprogesterone activity of RU 486 is not as localized as proponents claim. For example, it acts as an antiglucocorticosteroid blocker and can affect the central nervous system, and create unexpected and unnoted disturbances in metabolism. Evidence indicates that the drug's half-life is much greater than originally estimated; figures range from 10 to 14 days. The implications of this are serious, given possible adverse effects on a woman's future health, including infertility through exposure of immature eggs to RU 486.

Despite its "serious side effects," until 1983 the use of PG alone as an abortion method *was* suggested as a safe procedure. It was the European women's protests and resistance to PG that led to its gradual abandonment.

Heavy Bleeding. One should not trivialize the number of women who experience heavy bleeding with RU 486. To do so fails to address the implications this poses for women with fibroids, hypertension, or diabetes, as well as the large number of women with endemic anemia in "developing" countries. Heavy bleeding with conventional abortion usually occurs in a controlled setting, but the time and place of RU 486/PG–induced bleeding is *not* predictable. This can jeopardize a woman's life if she is unable to reach a medical center in time.

Complications. Citing heart attacks or strokes as "the only major complications" trivializes the consequences of RU 486/PG failure, which then involves a second conventional abortion procedure; and may require blood transfusion, which carries its own risk. Furthermore, to say that the one death and the cardiovascular accidents [among the 100,000 women who have had RU 486 abortions] could have been avoided "if established screening protocols had been followed" is incorrect. Screening procedures may have little value in predicting a fatal outcome, as evidenced by the death, following a PG–induced termination, of a 26-year-old woman who had no prior history of cardiac or neurological disorder as evidenced from her EKG and EEG.

RU 486 in Less Controlled Use

True, it is not possible to compare the death rate from conventional abortion (one per 200,000 in the U.S.) to that of present RU 486 figures (one per

100,000) because only 100,000 RU 486/PG abortions have been performed. But the crucial difference is that the vast majority of RU 486 abortions were performed under strict trial conditions, and accidents are more likely to happen in its less controlled general use.

Incomplete Abortions. To claim that a 3 percent failure rate in conventional abortions done by less skilled practitioners is not that different from the RU 486 rate of 4 to 6 percent misses the point. Conventional abortion *can* be made safe whereas, because of the nature of these drugs once they have entered a woman's body, the risks of chemical abortion defy control.

Medical Supervision. To receive the PG, it is mandatory to visit a center that has resuscitation equipment and medication. Given the virtual nonexistence of such centers in many rural areas, as well as in the "developing" world, it will be very troublesome, if not impossible, for many women to return not just once, but importantly yet another time to make sure (often with ultrasound) that the embryo has been completely expelled. This is *very* different from conventional abortion where the checkup can be done by a paramedic, and few women need postabortion treatment at high-tech clinics.

Early Termination. We consider the timing of RU 486 [used in the first seven weeks of pregnancy] one of its major drawbacks, for the following reasons: Teenage pregnancies, in particular, often go undetected until well into the first trimester. Because up to 30 percent of fertilized eggs are sponta-

> *"Accidents are more likely to happen in its less controlled general use."*

neously aborted, large numbers of women may be unnecessarily exposed to RU 486/PG drugs. And finally, given the "ease" of RU 486/PG administration *for medical personnel*—and its disputable "ease" for women—it is not too far-fetched to imagine a future where it would be the only available abortion method as a result of legislation or the lack of skilled personnel to perform conventional abortions. This would reduce choice for women whose pregnancies are further advanced, and would play right into the hands of the antiabortion movement, surely a serious and unintentional consequence of RU 486 advocacy!

In the "Developing" World. We have never claimed that all currently available abortion services are satisfactory, but to suggest that under less than ideal conditions RU 486 could "save lives" is unrealistic. The fact that 50 to 60 percent of women suffer some complication during RU 486/PG abortion in well-controlled trials in predominantly industrialized countries makes us fear that many more women will be seriously damaged under less than "ideal" conditions. And women deserve better than a second-rate solution.

As to the use of Cytotec [a prostaglandin], a number of studies have documented that half of the women who took it had incomplete abortions. Apart from the disastrous consequences for women from the continuation of unwanted pregnancies, uterine infections, or other health hazards, there is also the risk of severe fetal malformation.

Privacy & Control. Given that in France the majority of abortions are performed under general anesthetic, RU 486 may indeed be seen as "more natural." But would women consider it superior to safe, compassionate, conventional abortion by skilled abortion providers? Second, it is wrong to say that a woman would emerge from the bathroom at the clinic, "her abortion completed," and leave the clinic "within 10 to 15 minutes after the abortion just as she would for nonanesthetized, early-termination suction procedures." The bleeding induced by RU 486/PG does not necessarily mean that the embryo has been expelled. Even if it has, tissue may remain in the endometrium and the vagina, causing infection and bleeding and possibly requiring a conventional abortion procedure.

Summary. We disagree with the statement that "RU 486 appears to provide a safe and effective abortion alternative." We do agree, however, that it "could prove to be less successful among women with fewer resources and poorer health." Abortion is one of the simplest of presently medicalized gynecological procedures, requiring less expertise, training, and skill than attending births. Trained paramedics in "Third World" countries perform abortions safely and competently. Why then cannot trained laywomen do abortions safely and competently in Western contexts? Rather than advocating for one more dubious reproductive technology such as RU 486/PG, feminists should be fighting for demedicalizing conventional abortion methods, and doctors and family planning groups should be joining suit.

A National Health Care Plan Should Not Include Subsidized Abortion

by David R. Carlin

About the author: *David R. Carlin is a former member of the Rhode Island Senate and was a 1992 Democratic candidate for the U.S. House of Representatives. He is an associate professor of sociology at the Community College of Rhode Island in Warwick.*

As a life-long Democrat, I am both proud and ashamed of President Clinton's national health care proposal. I am proud that a Democratic president has taken the lead in bringing health insurance to all Americans, but I am ashamed that Clinton's proposal includes abortion coverage, thereby making all Americans, even the most ardent and conscientious prolifers, collaborators in the evil of abortion.

The President's plan would implicate government in the provision of abortion in two ways, one direct, the other indirect: a) directly, by having taxpayers pay for abortion coverage for the unemployed and underemployed; b) indirectly, by requiring employers to pay 80 percent of the cost of insurance plans for their employees, plans that would in most cases include abortion coverage.

What follows are considerations I think the prolife party should bear in mind when campaigning against the President's abortion proposal—or against any other abortion proposal that in the course of deliberation may get substituted for the President's.

Clinton's Choice

1. *Clinton's political dilemma.* Politically speaking, President Clinton had little choice but to include abortion coverage. Had he refused to do so, he would have pleased his enemies while outraging his friends; but there is no political percentage in such a strategy. This would not have turned his prolife enemies

David R. Carlin, "Paying for Abortion," *America*, November 20, 1993. Reprinted by permission of the author.

into friends, since they would still have plenty of reasons for disliking Clinton (his repeal of the "gag rule" [an executive order imposed by then President George Bush declaring that federally funded family planning clinics could not discuss abortion services with patients], his appointment of Ruth Bader Ginsburg to the Supreme Court, etc.). But it would certainly have turned a good many of his friends into enemies, since the sexual liberation party would have regarded

> *"Politically speaking, President Clinton had little choice but to include abortion coverage."*

this as a betrayal of the prochoice cause. Clinton would have put himself in the same position with the left wing of the Democratic Party that George Bush put himself in with the right wing of the Republican Party a few years back when he reneged on his "Read my lips: no new taxes!" pledge. When Mr. Bush agreed to a tax increase he won polite applause from liberals, who nonetheless would never dream of voting for him, while provoking conservative true believers to write him off as a Benedict Arnold. To exclude abortion coverage from the health care plan would have been equally suicidal for Clinton.

But the President has made it plain that although he will support the agenda of the sexual liberation party—abortion, gay rights, condoms in schools and other morally elevating programs of this ilk—he will not go to the wall for it. Consider his track record. He soon gave up the fight on gays in the military. He proposed dropping the Hyde Amendment, which prohibits Medicaid funding for almost all abortions, yet he twisted no Congressional arms, and the amendment was once again adopted (though in a slightly modified form). True, he withstood a certain amount of flak in order to stay with the Joycelyn Elders appointment as Surgeon-General, but in that case it was the Congressional Black Caucus he was afraid of, not the sex lib caucus.

No Strong Fight

Clinton's message to the sexual liberation party and their fellow travelers seems to be this: "Look, I'll do what I can to promote your agenda. I'll sign executive orders. I'll make appointments to high office. I'll submit legislation and sign bills passed by Congress. But it's up to you to get the bills passed. My fund of political capital is very small. I can afford to spend it on essential items only. I can't spend any of it on Bosnian Muslims, and I can't spend much of it on you either."

What this means with regard to abortion coverage in the national health plan is that the President will defend it when asked but will not strenuously fight for it. Further, my guess is that he would prefer seeing the abortion component of the measure killed sooner rather than later. For the longer it remains an issue, the greater the chance that the prolife forces will enter into alliances with those who oppose his plan for other reasons. From Clinton's point of view it would be best to get the prolife party out of the game early, and that can only be done if they win an early victory.

2. *Is the issue inconsequential?* Those prochoice people who at least faintly understand why many of their fellow Americans oppose abortion are nonetheless puzzled that prolifers should also oppose public funding of abortion. "You wish abortion were illegal," they say, "and we can respect that though we disagree with you, but since it is legal, why should the poor be denied a right that everyone else possesses? Isn't your attitude discriminatory? And since a disproportionate number of the poor are racial minorities, doesn't your attitude smack of racism?" This is a particularly striking instance of the failure of the prochoice party to grasp the idea behind the prolife movement.

At the same time it must be admitted that many prolifers hold a view resembling this. For them the one and only issue is *Roe v. Wade*. As they see it, the great goal of the prolife movement is to reverse this erroneous decision, hence the question of who pays for abortion is a relatively minor issue. On the whole they would prefer that someone other than the taxpayer put up the money, but compared with the constitutional question, the funding question is small potatoes. If Clinton wants his national health care plan to include abortion— well, that's regrettable, but really it's not that big a deal. It's not worth a life-or-death fight. Let's save our energies for the thing that really counts: the ultimate reversal of *Roe*.

> *"[Clinton] would prefer seeing the abortion component of the measure killed sooner rather than later."*

Nothing, it seems to me, could be further from a correct view. There is all the difference in the world between permitting evil and causing it. It was bad enough, for instance, that the Constitution permitted slavery prior to passage of the 13th Amendment; it would have been considerably worse had the United States Government subsidized the purchase of slaves. Nor would the evil have been mitigated if the subsidies went only to the poor, with the proslavery party justifying this practice in these terms: "We respect your opposition to slavery, but since holding slaves is a constitutional right, why should the poor white farmer be denied the power to exercise that right? To refuse government subsidies for poor customers at the slave market is a clear case of discrimination."

Roe was indeed a dreadful decision. Government support for abortion is *Roe*-plus-one, and is therefore worse than *Roe* all by itself.

Taxpayer Funds

3. *Is it simply a question of taxes?* In its objection to public funding for abortion, members of the prolife party frequently say something like this: "You have no right to use my tax money to pay for something I consider to be homicide." This argument has great rhetorical merit—especially in a society that, rather perversely, has decided that the status of taxpayer is more fundamentally im-

portant than the status of citizen. But it has one significant disadvantage: It suggests that the individual's tax money is the issue.

Let's suppose someone on the prochoice side were to respond by saying: "You know, the antichoice people have a point. Why should they be compelled to pay for something they find morally objectionable? So let's give a prorated tax rebate to everyone who has conscientious scruples about paying for abortion. Then their consciences will be clear, and they'll have nothing to complain about."

Now let's suppose there were to be 200,000 abortions per year paid for by taxpayer funds, and let's suppose each abortion cost $500. This would add up to $100 million. Since the population of the United States is 250 million, this comes to 40 cents per person. Thus an average rebate of 40 cents per person per year would, on this logic, silence the prolife objectors.

Or some boxes could be placed on the tax form, and when you check one of them, that portion of your tax that would otherwise have gone to abortion will go instead, for example, to AIDS or cancer research, to providing shelters for the homeless, to scholarships for inner-city youth, to campaign finance reform.

But, of course, all this is beside the point. Even if it could be shown that not a single prolife penny went to abortion, the prolife party would still have a right to be outraged that the U.S. Government, acting in the name of all of us, is subsidizing abortion. Keep in mind: Not all taxpayers are citizens (some are aliens, some are corporations, etc.), and not all citizens are taxpayers (some are too poor to pay taxes). Government funding of abortion is offensive to prolife persons in their essential capacity as citizens, not in their incidental capacity as taxpayers. It makes them unwilling partners in a collective crime.

Violating Essential Values

4. *Conscientious objections.* When told that prolifers object to supporting a practice that they consider to be gravely immoral, prochoicers commonly respond that this kind of thing is a normal occurrence in a democratic society. Why, they themselves oppose many a government policy! But as long as the policy was arrived at by democratic procedures, they have no choice but to endure it until such time as they can win enough votes to change the policy. Accordingly, if the prolife party does not like public subsidies for abortion, let them win elections and then eliminate the subsidies. But in the meantime they will simply have

"Government support for abortion is Roe-plus-one, and is therefore worse than Roe all by itself."

to put up with the situation. They will have to recognize that they have come out on the short end of a democratic contest.

But not all objections to government policy are created equal. Some come from the deepest or most central parts of our personality, arising because the government policy in question violates the essential values upon which we have staked our lives. Those essential values having been outraged, we feel we have been violated at the core of our being. At the opposite end of the spectrum are objections of an incidental sort, which insult our personality hardly at all, and certainly not at its core. And, of course, in between the extremes are objections with varying degrees of intensity. Objections to abortion felt by the typical prolifer lie toward the more intense end of the spectrum. Public subsidies for abortion are experienced by them as an attack on their central values, a violation of the core of their personalities.

> *"Government funding of abortion is offensive to prolife persons in their essential capacity as citizens."*

Of course, the mere fact that some citizens experience intense objections to a certain policy is not a sufficient reason to abstain from the policy. If it were, then every individual who happens to feel strongly about something would have a veto on any public policy. But when tens of millions feel strongly about something—and feel strongly not on a whim but for carefully thought-out religious and philosophical reasons that have a long tradition behind them—then a civilized society overrides their convictions only for the most compelling reasons. Such reasons may, of course, exist: For instance, to save the nation, a government may have to disregard the wishes of a large pacifist minority and go to war against the enemy at its gates.

No Compelling Reasons

The question, then, is this: Does the U.S. Government have a compelling reason for disregarding the principled and deeply felt convictions of America's tens of millions of committed prolifers? Without question, the answer is No. Clearly the safety of the republic is not at stake. Nor is the national well-being jeopardized if a certain number of reluctantly pregnant women find themselves in a situation in which they a) have to pay for their own abortions, b) have to find someone else (for instance, a boyfriend) to pay for them, c) have to find a clinic that provides free abortions in needy cases, or d) decide for financial reasons not to have abortions.

Any society, but especially a liberal democracy, requires that a great percentage of its citizens be persons who take moral values seriously. Of course, society can put up with a certain number of downright criminals and an even larger number of pure egoists whose pursuit of self-interest is sufficiently rational to make them tolerable (though perhaps not admirable) neighbors. But these immoralists and amoralists are "free riders," parasites who live off the moral capital provided by those citizens who take morality seriously and try, in their stumbling and imperfect ways, to live up to its demands. Committed prolifers are almost never immoralists or amoralists. They fall into the category of the morally earnest (as do many of the committed prochoicers); they add to society's moral capital. Now America's moral endowment is not so ample at the moment that we can afford to tell these morally earnest prolifers to "take a hike" or "drop dead" on the abortion subsidy question. If those who are running the nation at present cannot agree with the prolife party, they should at least have enough appreciation of this prolife group's social value not to enact a public policy that grossly insults them.

Who Wins and Loses?

5. *Consciences in conflict.* It might be objected that there is a zero-sum game going on here. Let us grant—these objectors will say—that it will be an outrage to the prolife party for the government to subsidize abortion, but to refuse to subsidize abortion would be an equal outrage to the prochoice party. Either way, someone is bound to be outraged. The prolife people are not, as they imagine, privileged in their potentially outraged status. The prolife party feels it is a great injustice to subsidize abortion, but the prochoice party feels it is a great injustice not to. This is a game that will have a winner and a loser. It is just a question of who wins and who loses.

There are two answers to this objection. One is an empirical answer; namely, that it is doubtful that many pro-

> *"Objections to abortion felt by the typical prolifer lie toward the more intense end of the spectrum."*

choice people actually do consider it a great injustice not to have tax subsidies for abortion. Without question, they feel that a *prohibition* of abortion would be terribly unjust, and this is a feeling the prolife party will have to deal with if it ever gets in a position to enact significant restrictions on abortion. But prohibiting abortion is one thing; permitting it while refusing to pay for it is something else. A good deal of evidence will be needed before we conclude that a refusal to subsidize abortion causes as much moral anguish among prochoicers as a decision to subsidize it will cause among prolifers.

But waiving the empirical question, we may rest our case on an old principle of moral reasoning: Negative precepts take precedence over positive. "Thou shalt not" takes precedence over "thou shalt." The Good Samaritan did a praiseworthy thing when he took the robbery victim to the inn, true; but it would have been wrong of him to embezzle money in order to pay the innkeeper, even if the result of his abstention from embezzlement would have been that the robbery victim was left uncared for. We are obliged to refrain from committing crimes even though such abstinence will inhibit our capacity to perform charitable deeds.

Prolifers believe that a program of government subsidies and mandated private sector subsidies for abortion compels them to participate in the violation of a negative precept of morality, and not just any negative precept but a very serious one: *Do not commit unwarranted homicide.* Prochoicers on the other hand believe that the failure to subsidize abortion bars society from complying with a positive precept: *Help needy people to pay for their abortions*. Even granting for the sake of discussion that there exists such a positive precept, still there is no moral equivalence between the two. The burden placed on the prolife conscience is far heavier than that placed on the prochoice conscience.

I should acknowledge, however, that the distinction between the relative obligatoriness of negative and positive precepts of the moral law is unlikely to cut any ice with the typical prochoice person. For this distinction is rooted in an ancient tradition of moral thought, a tradition derived on the one hand from the Bible, on the other from the Stoic conception of natural law. Prochoicers generally stand outside this tradition. If they did not, it is highly unlikely they would be in favor of abortion on demand in the first place; for unrestricted abortion is plainly incompatible with the tradition. To the ears of these prochoicers, talk about the distinction between negative and positive precepts, and the priority of the former to the latter, is meaningless.

For that matter, talk about the moral law itself is largely meaningless to them. Prochoicers speak quite a lot about *morality* and the *moral autonomy* of women confronting reproductive decisions, but the meaning they attach to the terms "moral" and "morality" is radically different from the meaning given these words in the biblical-Stoic tradition. Some prochoicers hold that the morality of an action is determined by its net consequences. Others hold that it is a function of the sincerity and good intentions of the person choosing it. Still others that it is morally good if the actor thinks it is good. Most hold a combination of two or three of these views. But almost none would hold that the morality of a deed is determined by its conformity or nonconformity to a transcendental moral law.

Better to Have No Health Program

6. *We have not yet begun to fight*. Suppose the prolife party loses its fight to keep abortion coverage out of the national health care plan? Should we then, despite our reservations about abortion, support the plan, or at least not oppose it? By no means. Government-promoted abortion is an injustice of such monumental proportions that it would be better to have no national health program at all than to have one that includes this feature.

> *"Any society . . . requires that a great percentage of its citizens be persons who take moral values seriously."*

But suppose, despite our efforts, that the plan—abortion and all—becomes law. Should we retire gracefully from the field, conceding that abortion coverage will henceforth be a perpetual feature of America's health care program? Not at all. If after 20 years we have not yet given up on our attempts to modify and even to reverse *Roe v. Wade*, we certainly should not give up on the issue of public subsidy for abortion. For, in fact, this is worse than *Roe*, which required us as a nation to do no more than tolerate abortion. That is bad enough. This new proposal would require us to promote and pay for it.

If the abortion proposal becomes law, it will be the most intolerable act to pass Congress since the Fugitive Slave Act of 1850, which obliged the free states to assist slaveholders in capturing and returning runaway slaves. It had been bad enough that the Constitution protected the institution of slavery and required the rest of the nation to tolerate it. This new law was worse still, since it made the rest of the nation actual collaborators in the evil of slavery. It was a way of rubbing the antislavery person's nose in it. Similarly, the proposal for including abortion coverage in national health care is a way of rubbing the prolifer's nose in it. It is a way of requiting all Americans, not just prochoicers, to become partners in promoting this peculiar institution of the late 20th century.

Of the Fugitive Slave Act, Ralph Waldo Emerson said in disgust: "This filthy enactment was made in the 19th century, by people who could read and write." Just change "19th" to "20th" and you have an appropriate evaluation of government-subsidized abortion. Civilized human beings do not retire gracefully from the field when "filthy enactments" are the order of the day.

Women Should Not Choose Menstrual Extraction

by Louise Tyrer

About the author: *Louise Tyrer, a physician and medical writer, is the medical director of the Association of Reproductive Health Professionals in Washington, D.C. Tyrer previously served for sixteen years as vice president for medical affairs at Planned Parenthood Federation of America.*

With abortion debates escalating, "self-help" menstrual extraction (M.E.) has been promoted as a way for women to exercise full control over their reproductive options. While all women should be actively involved in all matters related to their healthcare, the health dangers and political risks associated with this unsupervised medical procedure far outweigh any possible conveniences or advantages in a society in which legal abortion is still an option.

Every woman should be free to choose whether or not to undergo "self-help" M.E., be it to minimize monthly cramps or to terminate a suspected pregnancy. However, women deserve the opportunity to make a fully informed decision which must include the case against menstrual extraction.

Health Risks

Menstrual extraction refers to removing, by suction, the contents of a woman's uterus, which may be the lining that builds up prior to menstruation as well as the products of conception. This entails the insertion of a small, flexible, blunt-tipped cannula into the uterus and attaching it to a vacuum source, generally a hand-held syringe. Most lay women who perform this procedure for other women will only do so within 50 days of the onset of the last menstrual period, in an attempt to avoid initiating an abortion in a woman whose pregnancy is so far advanced it cannot be completed with the equipment utilized. Some lay providers will perform it for women with late periods without establishing that the woman is in fact pregnant. In all cases, M.E. can pose serious health risks.

Louise Tyrer, "The Case Against Menstrual Extraction," *On the Issues*, Spring 1993. Reprinted with permission.

Infection. Every time a woman's uterus is invaded, as it is when a cannula is inserted into the uterus during monthly menstrual extractions, the chance of pelvic infection becomes greater. Any degree of pelvic infection can increase a woman's chance of subsequent ectopic (tubal) pregnancy, or lead to infertility.

Hidden symptoms. Heavy menstrual flow, which sometimes leads to a desire for repeated menstrual extractions, may be an indication of cancer of the lining of the uterus, as may intermenstrual bleeding. Women with such symptoms need to be examined by specially trained physicians to evaluate, diagnose, and manage their condition.

Pregnancy. For a woman who is pregnant, the risks associated with M.E. as a "self-help" abortion technique are particularly great. First of all, pregnancy tests alone are not always accurate. If a woman thinks she may be pregnant, a pelvic examination and sometimes ultrasonography are necessary to establish the certainty of a suspected pregnancy, and to identify whether the pregnancy is a normal uterine implantation, or is an ectopic pregnancy. Furthermore, some women continue to have periodic bleeding with pregnancy and a woman may be unknowingly 12 or more weeks pregnant before she suspects that she is so. Since "self-help" M.E. is performed by a non-medical person unqualified to determine the site and duration of the pregnancy or perform a complete medical examination, the risk of complications—such as the inability to complete the abortion, uterine perforation, hemorrhage and/ or infection—would be significantly increased.

Pre-existing pelvic conditions. Sometimes women unknowingly have a pelvic pathology such as uterine fibroid tumors, a double uterus, ovarian cysts, or cervical scarring. When a woman is pregnant, each of these conditions can increase the likelihood of an incomplete abortion, or complicate the performance of the procedure. A pelvic evaluation by a specially trained health professional is essential to determining the appropriate procedures and techniques to terminate pregnancy safely in these situations.

Puncturing the uterus. Improper use of surgical equipment can occur in "self-help" M.E. and may result in uterine perforation. This risk is lessened when the procedure is performed by an experienced clinician.

> *"For a woman who is pregnant, the risks associated with M.E. as a 'self-help' abortion technique are particularly great."*

Incomplete abortion. The more complex the abortion procedure, the less chance of hemorrhage, infection, or both. Health professionals experienced in performing abortions are more capable of determining whether the products of conception have been fully removed. They can send the specimen to a pathology laboratory when indicated in order to establish whether a woman's pregnancy is ectopic, which is a life-threatening condition.

Post-abortion infection. Health professionals are trained and better equipped to minimize the risk of infection, as well as diagnose and treat possible infections that may occur after abortion. Carefully sterilized instruments, "no-touch" techniques, and minimal insertions of instruments into the uterus are necessary to reduce risk. A "self-help" procedure, however, may require multiple insertions of the suction cannula to finish the abortion procedure. Furthermore,

> *"Women must not be lulled into thinking that menstrual extraction will provide a safety net should abortion again be made illegal."*

trained health professionals are better able to identify abnormal cervical and vaginal discharge, which may require antibiotic treatments, as well as administer antibiotics at the time of abortion to minimize the risk of post-abortion infection. "Self-help" M.E. groups are not able to do so.

AIDS. The emergence of AIDS and Hepatitis B pose an ever greater need to minimize possibilities of infection during the abortion procedure. This requires the wearing of clothes, gloves, and plastic eye and face masks to protect the operator and patient from any potential contamination with blood and other bodily fluids, such as vaginal secretions. Abortion tissue requires the utmost care in analysis. Furthermore, all instruments must be decontaminated and sterilized, and all disposables must be properly bagged and handled by designated collection centers. Even the slightest break in skin, e.g., a torn hangnail, can be an entry point for the fatal HIV virus. It is reasonable to assume that women seeking abortion care and providers alike will want to be in a medical-care environment that can assure the minimum risk.

Consistency and continuity of care. The woman who obtains an abortion from a licensed and specially trained health professional is assured of more consistent quality of care, as well as 24-hour access to experienced physicians who have surgical capabilities for the rare—but sometimes serious—complications that may occur with any abortion.

Political Risks

It is unfortunate that current laws and harassment by antichoice bigots have created a climate in which physicians are discouraged from providing abortion services. However, "self-help" menstrual extraction is *not* the answer.

As a resident physician in ob/gyn [obstetrics/gynecology] prior to the legalization of abortion, I saw too many women die from every manner of complication or become reproductive cripples for the rest of their lives as a result of illegal abortion. We cannot, we must not, go back to those dark days, nor should women ever need to rely on less than the most informed, technically advanced and individually sensitive reproductive healthcare services—including elective abortion.

For the benefit of the health of women in the U.S., we need to expand our energies to ensure that abortion remains a legal, available and accessible option for all women. In this light, "self-help" menstrual extraction must be seen not only as a potential health risk, but also as a counterproductive political tactic. Women must not be lulled into thinking that menstrual extraction will provide a safety net should abortion again be made illegal. I say we can *Never* go back.

I envision that a more useful way to ensure women full control over their reproductive health is to take two courses of action. First, we need to change the dynamics of the politics in this country so that medical providers and women seeking abortion can feel comfortable in providing and receiving high quality abortion care. Bill Clinton's ruling to overturn the "gag rule" is an important step in this direction.

Specialists Are Needed

Second, we need to expand the pool of adequately trained abortion providers to include licensed, non-physician reproductive healthcare specialists as well as certified nurse midwives, nurse practitioners, and physician's assistants. These health professionals, many of whom are women, are already grounded in the anatomy and physiology of women's reproductive systems. Unlike "self-help" menstrual extraction providers, this cadre of specially trained health professionals can recognize in advance when a patient has a pelvic pathology and make sure that she receives specialized physician care. Furthermore, they are experienced in working as members of teams, including physicians, who are experienced in handling the sometimes life-threatening emergencies that can occur with abortion.

> *"'Self-help' menstrual extraction . . . cannot be considered either safe or empowering."*

Not only has this innovative approach to women's reproductive healthcare been endorsed by organizations such as the American College of Obstetricians and Gynecologists, the National Abortion Federation, the Association of Reproductive Health Professionals and Planned Parenthood Federation of America, it has been proven successful: A report by NAF found that women undergoing early abortion by trained non-physician health professionals experienced no increased risk than had the procedure been performed by a medical doctor.

"Self-help" menstrual extraction—no matter how many anecdotal reports of individual experience are put forward—cannot be considered either safe or empowering. Women deserve, and must demand, the best healthcare available, including abortion training for non-physician health professionals. Furthermore, women must unite to ensure that safe and legal abortion is always an option. We can never forget how many women lost their lives before the right to choose became the law of the land.

Abortion Vaccines Should Not Be Available

by Lawrence F. Roberge

About the author: *Lawrence F. Roberge is a biotechnology consultant in Ludlow, Massachusetts. Roberge advises on business, regulatory, patent, and technical issues for biotech, medical, and pharmaceutical companies and entrepreneurs.*

Recent developments by Dr. Vernon C. Stevens at Ohio State University and by Dr. G. P. Talwar at the National Institute of Immunology, New Delhi, India, have brought closer the dawn of a new form of abortion.

Since the 1970s, under support from the World Health Organization (WHO), research has been directed at immunologically blocking conception or the immunological termination of a pregnancy. One key target has been the hormone, human Chorionic Gonadotropin (hCG). This hormone created by the developing embryo signals the maintenance of the corpus luteum which provides progesterone and estrogen to maintain the vascularization of the uterine endometrium during the first few months of pregnancy.

Death of the Embryo

Should hCG levels drop in the first critical six to ten weeks, the uterine vascularization would break down, resulting in the death of the developing embryo while the uterine endometrium sloughs off the uterine wall. . . .

Early studies to develop a vaccine against hCG were hampered by immunogenic cross-reactivity with [other hormones]. . . . The last 35 amino acid sequence of hCG . . . , now referred to as the hCG beta peptide fragment, has served as the focal immunogen in the development of an hCG vaccine. Further versions have included linking the hCG beta peptide fragment to various carrier molecules (for example, tetanus or diphtheria toxoids) to enhance immune responses to the hCG peptide.

Recent research has begun to reap results at various facilities across the

From Lawrence F. Roberge, "An Abortifacient Vaccine: The Latest Anti-Life Menace," *The Wanderer*, December 23, 1993. Reprinted by permission of the author.

globe. Phase II studies for the Stevens vaccine are still in progress, but Talwar's group reports that early Phase II studies indicate that sexually active women sustained high antibody titers [concentrations] to hCG and were prevented from getting pregnant. No major side effects were reported in either the Phase I or early Phase II trials The high levels of antibodies acted to remove hCG molecules from the blood. This would cause any developing embryo to fail implantation (nidation) and pass out during menstruation. As no disruption of the ovulatory cycle or menstrual cycle was reported, it could be presumed that the embryo passed from the fallopian tube into the uterus and never achieved complete endometrial implantation. . . .

Talwar's and Stevens' work suggests that this vaccine could last beyond the initial six months that Phase I studies describe. Further improvements in the vaccine, including those based on monkey trials which used delayed release biodegradable microspheres to achieve active immunization lasting two years, indicate that a long-lasting hCG vaccine is now within reach for human use. Talwar has stated that he has been contacted by pharmaceutical firms from Korea, Indonesia, France, and Holland, but not yet from the United States.

In Conflict with Church Teaching

As recent events have demonstrated, the marketing and distribution of an abortifacient medical product (such as RU 486) outside of the United States can still eventually be brought here under the miasma of political rhetoric, and with the assistance of nonprofit groups like The Population Council. With social and political organizations promoting a pro-abortion agenda, any device that offers simplicity of use, longevity of effect, and little evidence of side effects becomes an attractive product to promote in the United States. The hCG vaccine is such a device. With rapidly advancing vaccine technology, the hCG vaccine could become easily accessible in the next few years; and with improvements, could attain a five-year efficacy life span between booster vaccinations.

Furthermore, ready acceptance in developing countries, Europe, Japan, and the Pacific rim nations, would add further political/social pressure to allow acceptance within the United States under the guise of contraceptive choice and population control.

"[The vaccine] would cause any developing embryo to fail implantation . . . and pass out during menstruation."

Several points must be addressed with regards to hCG vaccine use. First, clearly this vaccine induces an abortion of a developing embryo each month (when such an embryo is conceived). Whereas Talwar's studies demonstrate that menstrual and ovulatory cycles were maintained and regular, it then becomes easy to understand that hCG vaccines cause one abortion per ovulatory cycle (if the woman is sexually active); ergo, 12 ovulation cycles per year, 12 abortions per year. This clearly conflicts with biblical and [Catholic]

Church teaching on the sanctity of life and God's condemnation of abortion.

Second, although hCG titer studies have lasted less than one year, no large-scale and long-term (five years or more) studies have been conducted. No studies have addressed the possibility that if the immune system is repeatedly exposed to the immunogen (hCG), then the subject could eventually become "immunologically sterile." That is, a subject would be fertile for having and regularly producing healthy oocytes [eggs], capable of having the oocyte fertilized and travel through the fallopian tubes, but because the immune system attacks the hCG blood levels . . . , the developing embryo/life will never come to term/birth. Should later hCG vaccine recipients develop this problem, I wonder if WHO funding would be directed to address this situation. . . .

> *"The hCG vaccine could become easily accessible in the next few years."*

Third, this vaccine would become an abused tool to "control conception." In developing countries, forced sterilization and abortion have been considered or actively used as policies to achieve reductions in population growth. Applications of hCG vaccines could be applied either by force or coercion (withholding employment, voting rights, or health care to women who refuse hCG booster vaccinations).

Within the United States, this vaccine could become abused as well. Instead of handing sexually active adolescents condoms and other contraceptives, hCG vaccines could be a parental/societal response to adolescents who refuse sexual abstinence. Furthermore, the application of the hCG vaccine could become the answer to deal with other reproductively related societal problems. An hCG vaccine could be court mandated to prevent child-abusing women from having any more children which they might later mistreat. Some individuals like [U.S. surgeon general] Dr. Joycelyn Elders have suggested that birth control could be the answer to poverty, crime, and other social problems; it could be proposed that further welfare support would become dependent on young mothers' suppressing further births by using the hCG vaccine.

An Appropriate Response

Clearly the hCG vaccine is nearing complete development. With its absence of major side effects, convenience of use, and guarantee of zero pregnancies, the hCG vaccine will appear attractive to a world market desperately searching for "more effective methods" of birth control.

The hCG vaccine's method of action is clearly abortifacient. As the hCG vaccine enters into the final vaccine testing phases and eventual marketing, it must be up to the Church as a whole not to be lulled into complacency by world-market acceptance, but rather to develop an appropriate response to this "abortion vaccine."

Chapter 4

Should Protesters Target Abortion Clinics?

Deadly Protest: An Overview

by Laurie Goodstein

About the author: *Laurie Goodstein is a* Washington Post *staff writer.*

The only doctor who still admits to performing abortions in Mississippi wore an Army combat helmet and bulletproof vest as federal marshals drove him past a knot of protesters to his clinic in Gulfport in early August 1994.

Two weeks before, 128 miles away, a Florida physician and his civilian escort were shot to death in a pickup truck outside a Pensacola abortion clinic. Many antiabortion leaders have condemned the bloodshed and denounced Paul Hill, arrested minutes after the shooting, as a lone, sick extremist.

But there is a sizable faction among the antiabortion movement's activists—the "rescuers" who use civil disobedience to disrupt clinic business—who have applauded Hill as a righteous defender of babies. Most leaders of the Mississippi protests still stand by the petition that 32 of them signed in 1993 at Hill's request declaring that murdering abortion providers is "justifiable homicide." They call their new campaign "No Place to Hide."

Theological Justifications

They have spent the 18 months since the first assassination of a doctor outside a Pensacola abortion clinic forging ethical and theological justifications for killing in the name of saving babies. Promoters of this doctrine include fundamentalist Christian preachers, lay leaders of antiabortion "ministries" and several Catholic priests, one of whom was suspended by his archbishop. They cite the Bible, the Holocaust, the fight to end slavery and the theory of "just war."

"Any force that is justifiable to protect born children is also justifiable to protect unborn children," says Cathy Ramey, associate director of Advocates for Life Ministries in Portland, Ore., one of the few women among the 32 signers of Hill's petition. "It's dishonest for somebody to say that they care about unborn children and then in the same breath condemn Paul Hill for having shot the abortionist."

Donald Spitz, spokesman for Operation Rescue Chesapeake, says, "If there was a sniper in the schoolyard sniping off children one by one and the only way you could stop him was by stopping that sniper you would stop that sniper."

This position has become a subject of heated debate among antiabortion activists in meetings, churches and newsletters. And now the debate has split the ranks of the activists in Operation Rescue, which until recently could mobilize thousands to risk arrest for blockading clinics.

"No Place to Hide"

A new group called the American Coalition of Life Activists (ACLA), with members in nine states, is mounting the "No Place to Hide" protests. Organizers say their goal is to expose doctors performing abortions until neighbors, relatives and other patients pressure the physicians to quit.

They not only refuse to condemn but speak warmly of Hill—who faces two counts of murder and was indicted Aug. 12, 1994, by a Tallahassee grand jury for allegedly violating the new federal clinic-protection law—as well as two other activists who have been con-victed in previous shootings. Yet they have asked every demonstrator participating in the protests against Mississippi physician Joseph Booker to sign a "nonviolence" pledge in language that is itself something of an incitement.

> *"The increasing visibility of this more militant antiabortion faction is both painful and infuriating to the leaders of mainstream groups."*

It begins, "I will not engage in, plan or recruit for any acts of violence toward the child killer."

Believers in "justifiable homicide" cite moral absolutes and "truth" to explain their position. If the fetus is a child, just not yet born, then doctors who perform abortions are "serial child killers," they say, in a theme repeated in interviews with a dozen activists around the country. Killing a doctor who performs abortions thus becomes an act of defense.

No Prohibition Against Killing

The approach varies, but the logic does not. Michael Bray, a Bowie, Md., pastor who served four years for bombing clinics in the Washington, D.C., area and has written a book called *A Time to Kill*, says, "There is no prohibition in the Bible against killing."

The ancient Hebrew word translated as "kill" in the Sixth Commandment—"Thou shalt not kill"—does not refer to self-defense, Bray argues.

Says the Rev. David Trosch, the suspended Catholic priest in Mobile, Ala.: "It took World War II to stop the slaughter of millions of innocent people."

All of these activists say they would not themselves kill a doctor. They say they are either too important to the cause, too committed to their families or too smart to publicly proclaim their intentions. Before the murders in Pensacola, Paul Hill assured several friends that he would not himself resort to violence either.

Infuriating the Mainstream

The increasing visibility of this more militant antiabortion faction is both painful and infuriating to the leaders of mainstream groups that have relied on organizing and lobbying since *Roe v. Wade* legalized abortion in 1973. The National Right to Life Committee, with 3,000 local chapters, prohibits its staff and board members from even picketing or blockading clinics because such actions could be illegal.

Mainstream antiabortion leaders have denounced shooting doctors in equally absolute terms. "The shooting itself bears too much resemblance to abortion," says the Rev. Frank Pavone, founder of Priests United for Life. "It is violence and it buys into the same mentality that death can be a solution. And that's precisely what we reject."

Cardinal John J. O'Connor, a staunch abortion opponent, recently wrote in his column in *Catholic New York:* "If anyone has an urge to kill an abortionist, let him kill me, instead. That's about as clearly as I can renounce such madness."

A Philosophical Quandary

But some mainstream antiabortion leaders privately voice fears that they have arrived at a philosophical quandary: If they agree that fetuses are children, why isn't it right to resort to the most desperate measures—even violence—to save them? Instead, they argue strategy: that killing one doctor will not stop others, and that violence alienates potential supporters and provokes government repression. They talk of the need to reach the women who choose abortion. But they admit that such reasoning fails to convince extremists prone to think in absolutes.

"There's been some frustration on our part, because I think our side has not come up with a clear, concise response," says Frederica Mathewes-Green, director of communications for the National Women's Coalition for Life. "All our explanations for why this is wrong are not meeting perhaps the real need for what is going on, which is that people have reached an explosive level of frustration."

On the other side, prominent abortion rights leaders have accused antiabortion leaders of bearing some responsibility for the bloodshed.

"The inflammatory rhetoric and concepts such as 'murderer' and 'baby killer' create the conditions for extremist individuals to feel justified in taking violent actions," says Kate Michelman, president of the National Abortion and Reproductive Rights Action League.

"Insiders describe an antiabortion movement in disarray."

Cardinal O'Connor retorts that this is like saying author Harriet Beecher

Stowe caused the Civil War. O'Connor wrote that just as Abraham Lincoln credited Stowe's *Uncle Tom's Cabin* for calling attention to the injustice of slavery, "One day this great country of ours, and perhaps even a president, will thank pro-life leaders for raising the consciousness of so many about treating unborn human babies as non-persons."

A Movement in Disarray

Insiders describe an antiabortion movement in disarray, with five branches that sometimes cooperate but often fail to work together: the "politicals" who work on electoral strategies; the "culturals" who teach about the value of life; the "crisis-pregnancy workers" who minister to women; the "religious" who hold prayer vigils; and the "rescuers" who rely on civil disobedience to disrupt clinic business.

Leaders in the political and cultural branches say that those now endorsing deadly force originated in the "rescuers" faction, first mobilized when Randall Terry began his highly visible Operation Rescue campaigns in the 1980s. Among Terry's slogans: "If abortion is killing, act like it is."

Terry has left Operation Rescue and now travels the speaking circuit railing against homosexuals and President Clinton. The Rev. Flip Benham, the new director of what is now called Operation Rescue National, announced at a Chicago summit meeting of antiabortion activists in April 1994 that anyone who believes in deadly force could not participate in his group's activities. That move prompted the creation of the more militant ACLA.

Proponents of "justifiable homicide" defy characterization by class, profession or educational background. But all describe themselves as Christians committed to a literal interpretation of the Bible.

Spitz dabbled in Eastern religions in San Francisco's Haight Ashbury district before becoming a born-again street preacher in New York's Times Square. Bray, a Baptist seminary graduate, began as a youth minister who tried to wrest young people from cults. Trosch was a small businessman, never married, who at 46 entered the priesthood.

Desperate Frustration

What they share is a desperate frustration with legal tactics and a biting disdain for their more moderate colleagues in the cause.

"There is no pro-life movement," Spitz says. "The pro-life movement is getting its butt kicked. They can't even go out and picket in front of an abortion mill because it's a federal penalty. If they want to do that for 20 more years and have 50 million more dead babies, that's all they're going to get."

Protesters Should Target Abortion Clinics

by Randall A. Terry

About the author: *Randall A. Terry has been involved in pro-life work since the early 1980s when he founded the New York–based Project Life, an educational and activist group that launched both the Crisis Pregnancy Center for women who want to keep their children and the House of Life, a home for unwed mothers. Terry is best known as the founder of Operation Rescue, which in 1986 began the pro-life abortion clinic sit-ins that would for several years involve thousands of abortion protesters in cities across the nation.*

We're all familiar with the Battle of Jericho. (See Joshua 6 in the Bible.) God promised that He would fight for the Israelites, but that He would fight *where their bodies* (and swords) went! God would defeat their enemies, but He would do it as the Israelites faced the enemy.

The Israelite army marched around Jericho for seven days in silence. They were undoubtedly beseeching God at that time for victory on the seventh day. At the appointed moment, they gave a shout, and the walls of the city fell down. But they still had to go in and *physically possess* the land before victory was complete.

Can you imagine the walls falling, and the jubilant army jumping up and down, saying, "Great job, God! We can see everything now! Okay, God, go get 'em! Finish the battle! Kill 'em, God! Strike them with a lightning bolt! Open the earth and swallow them! Defeat the enemy, God! We beseech You, O, Lord. . . ."

Praying, but Not Acting

As ridiculous as it sounds, that is exactly what many Christians are saying today. They are concerned about abortion and the future of America, and they are praying, but that's all. They are praying, but not acting, and little happens. The abortion mills stay open. The abortionists go on killing.

I am not downplaying the importance of prayer. We *must* beseech God for His help and blessing, for without His intervention we cannot win. He is the "master of breakthrough," who can break through the walls of the enemy. But after we pray and the "spiritual walls" come down, we must do what the Israelites did—occupy enemy territory.

God brought victory when a portion of the Israelites went in and faced the enemy, on the enemy's turf. If we would see God bring victory against abortion, a portion of the church must bodily confront the abortionists head-on.

Gaining Political Clout

The pro-life movement lacks political clout. Most politicians do not take us seriously. Why? Because our actions betray our words. Christians and non-Christians alike who are adamantly against abortion refer to abortion as murder, *but we do not act like it's murder.* Our cries of "murder!" go unheard because our actions are so far removed from our rhetoric.

If a child you love was about to have his arms and legs ripped off, and you could intervene to save him, what would you do? Would you write your Congressman saying, "My little friend is about to be killed, and I ask you to introduce legislation as soon as possible that would prevent such atrocities" ?

> *"[We] must prove to Congress that we believe abortion is murder by acting like it's murder."*

No! You would do whatever you could to physically intervene and save the life of that child! That is the *appropriate response* to murder.

Well, children we love *are* having their arms and legs torn off, but our response has been grossly inadequate. I am not undermining the validity of writing our Congressmen. I'm saying that many in our ranks must prove to Congress that we believe abortion is murder by *acting* like it's murder. Then laws to stop this holocaust could be passed.

Up until now, the pro-life movement has been like the boy who cried, "Wolf!" We lack credibility. Politicians know how someone *should* respond to murder.

When government officials see people peacefully blockading abortion mills, they begin to take them seriously. When a politician sees good, decent citizens risking arrest and prosecution, he knows they mean business. The strength of their convictions forces him to consider the reasons for their actions and the merits of their arguments.

Creating Social Tension

Even a brief overview of American history will prove that political change usually results from social tension. The birth of America, the end of slavery, women's voting rights, the labor movement, the repeal of the Eighteenth Amendment (which outlawed alcohol), the civil rights movement, the anti–Vietnam War movement, the sexual revolution, the homosexual rights movement, and the feminist movement all testify to one truth: *Whether for good or bad, political change comes after a group of Americans bring enough tension in the nation and pressure on the politicians that the laws are changed.*

Somebody put it this way: Politicians see the light after they feel the heat!

The most famous act of "civil disobedience" in American history was the drafting and signing of the Declaration of Independence. That celebrated day and document were clearly illegal, calling for treason against the British crown.

> *"The peaceful, nonviolent, non-retaliatory* suffering *of the black civil rights activists . . . helped win the hearts of millions."*

The "social tension" created on July 4, 1776, and more importantly, the war that followed, resulted in the establishment of possibly the greatest nation ever on earth, except for ancient Israel. No doubt the loyalists, some of them Christians, refused to side with the founding fathers on the grounds that it was a rebellion. I'm glad the revolutionaries won!

Susan B. Anthony and the Suffragette Movement, which secured the right for women to vote, was a street level activist movement. When Susan B. Anthony went to voting booths *demanding* the right to vote, she was arrested and sent to jail. But her actions forced social tension and a national debate on the issue of women's voting rights.

The women won. But had Susan B. Anthony not been overt in her demands, had she not created social and political tension, had she only written letters to her Congressmen, women *still* might not have the right to vote.

The Civil Rights Movement

The best example of changing the course of the nation was the black civil rights movement in the late fifties and early sixties, particularly under the leadership of Dr. Martin Luther King, Jr.

By enlisting the black church leadership, and then mobilizing thousands of churchgoers, the civil rights leaders were able to direct people in actions that produced social tension, then political change.

If blacks were forbidden to eat at a given lunch counter, they were trained to sit peacefully at the counter until arrested. If they were forbidden to exercise their First Amendment right to free speech and peaceful assembly, they gathered anyway. If they were told to ride in the back of the bus, they rode in the front. If they were not allowed to register to vote, they went to the registrar and demanded to be registered.

Wherever the boil of segregation existed, they would insert the lance of confrontation, so all the world could see the sickening truth.

While some radical groups were inciting violence in the mid to late sixties, the main leadership of the civil rights movement believed in *nonviolence* of word, deed, and heart. Who can forget the sight of water cannons and dogs being turned on defenseless people, including children?

Remember the brutal beatings the Alabama State Police gave the marchers who dared cross the Edmund Pettus Bridge going out of Selma [during the 1965 march to demand voting rights for African Americans]? Those trained in the nonviolent ethic remained true to their vision despite opposition and retaliation.

The peaceful, nonviolent, non-retaliatory *suffering* of the black civil rights activists, many of them Christians, helped win the hearts of millions, and was the catalyst to the Civil Rights Act of 1964, and the Voting Rights Act of 1965. Blacks, willing to suffer and risk arrest in order to stand for what was right, created a tension in the nation that forced politicians to take action.

While the injustice blacks faced was intolerable, can segregation be as bad as murder? Isn't this slaughter of the innocent a far darker evil than segregation ever could be? Isn't the decapitation of millions of defenseless children more barbaric than the sufferings blacks endured?

Why haven't we confronted this bloodshed with a fraction of the sacrifice that blacks made? Because we are afraid, selfish, and blind to the vested interest we have in ending this holocaust.

Pushing the Right Button

The ultimate legal victory for the children will be an amendment to the Constitution, outlawing abortion. Overturning *Roe vs. Wade* would be a step in the right direction, but that would only restore individual states' rights regarding abortion laws. Liberal states like New York, California, and others would become havens where the killing would continue.

We need a paramount Human Life Amendment to bring about a national change. That means we must have a political victory. Pro-lifers have been seeking political victory without success for many years. We have obviously been pushing the wrong buttons.

The winning button—the soft underbelly of the government—has not been pushed. Our founding fathers recognized that soft underbelly when they said the government derives "its just powers from the consent of the governed." When large numbers no longer consent, the government loses its power to govern.

What politicians fear most is social unrest and upheaval. When unrest occurs in small numbers, it can be put down by force. But when unrest and upheaval begin to incorporate hundreds and thousands of people, government officials pay attention. Ultimately, they *desire* to give in to the demands of the disgruntled, so that tranquility can be restored to the realm and they can get on with the business of governing a sleeping nation.

> *"The ultimate legal victory for the children will be an amendment to the Constitution, outlawing abortion."*

Victory over abortion is possible. All we need is for a remnant of the church to repent and rise up and say, "No more dead children! We are not going to let you kill innocent babies anymore!" With the prayers and blessing of others in the church, in harmony with other avenues of pro-life action, we would see the tide begin to turn.

Victory in Numbers

When I wrote most of my book *Operation Rescue*, I was in jail in Binghamton, New York. Why? Because we did rescue missions in very small numbers and I was the only one with multiple arrests and convictions. Hence, I sat in jail for a few days.

> *"No more dead children! We are not going to let you kill innocent babies anymore!"*

But the entire Binghamton jail system, which can hold about 200 people, is almost full now. Over 20,000 professing evangelicals and probably three times as many Catholics live in the Binghamton area. Only two abortion mills mar our community. That's 80,000 Roman Catholics and evangelicals against two death camps.

If three percent of that group, just 2,400 people, agreed to do multiple sit-ins at the local death camp, what do you think would happen? Probably nothing would happen to us, and we would likely keep the abortion mills from doing their bloody work. Children and mothers would be rescued, and virtually no one would go to jail. We would totally *clog the system.*

The police, the district attorney, the courts, and the jails are not prepared or designed to deal with such huge numbers. And that uprising would only consist of *three percent* of the religious community.

The Only Way to Win

Now imagine people blocking abortion clinics all across the country. Imagine politicians reading in the *New York Times* and *Washington Post* that scores, hundreds, or even thousands of decent, tax-paying citizens in New York City, Washington, D.C., St. Louis, Chicago, Philadelphia, and *your town* were demanding an end to the killing.

Envision pastors and priests in jail together for a few days. Imagine the evening news finally beginning to reveal the true horror of abortion because our sacrificial actions *demand* a fair hearing. Think what stirring speeches would be made on the House and Senate floor by politicians who used to be pro-abortion, but who have seen the light—after they felt the heat!

Imagine the political bandwagon forming to amend the Constitution and restore peace, tranquility, and unity to the country. Hear the President eulogizing those courageous Americans who have been willing to risk personal liberty for the justice due their fellow human beings. And see, once and for all, the end of this legalized bloodshed by means of a Constitutional amendment.

I confess, it will take the hand of God for this to happen, but His hand has moved before when others stood in the gap, and attempted what seemed impossible. Why couldn't it happen now? The war can be won, and this is what it will take.

Rescue missions are *not* simply one part of this battle. The truth is *victory cannot be had without them.*

Without rescues, children continue to die, and mothers continue to be maimed. Without rescues, our obedience to God is incomplete, and His full blessing will continue to be absent. Without them, the political machine will continue to ignore us. Without rescues, our rhetoric is shallow and meaningless. Without righteous, peaceful uprising that demands an end to the killing, America is racing toward divine judgment.

Who will stand in the gap? Who will rise up? Who will the courageous "three percent" be? In a conventional war, the government can draft conscripts to fight. No draft exists in the church. Each one must pray and count the cost himself.

Pro-Life Activists Must Protest Nonviolently

by Joseph Scheidler

About the author: *Joseph Scheidler is widely regarded as the father of the pro-life activist movement. His 1985 book,* Closed: 99 Ways to Stop Abortion, *is a detailed manual for targeting and nonviolently closing down abortion clinics. The following viewpoint is chapter 81 of the 1993 edition of* Closed.

By violence here we mean a direct, physical attack on some type of facility or the personnel who work there.

There is a small faction within the pro-life movement—just as there is within any movement—who, from time to time, talk about the advisability of stopping abortion by force. We have even heard some who discuss the possibility of the abortion conflict escalating into a "shooting war."

Most of this is just talk. The fact remains, however, that there have been incidents of violence against both pro-life facilities and abortion clinics and offices. Generally, this violence has taken the form of damage to property, although there was also a kidnapping of an abortionist and his wife, and in 1993, the shooting death of an itinerant abortionist in Pensacola, Florida, Dr. David Gunn.

A Target of Violence

This author has been struck, spit on, pushed, and received innumerable death threats, warnings, insults, and crank calls; he has had his sight damaged, tires slashed, office windows cut with glass-cutters and broken with rocks, and his office painted with roofing tar. Nearly all pro-life activist leaders can cite a similar list of malicious acts. Some pro-life offices have been fire bombed. Pro-life pickets and counselors have had buckets of water thrown on them, have had cars driven toward them at high speeds, have been struck by these cars and with clubs by clinic guards. We have almost all been subjected to a variety of insults and injuries. Few of these incidents ever get reported, since many police departments are reluctant to acknowledge that they happened. There have been very

Excerpted from Joseph Scheidler, *Closed: 99 Ways to Stop Abortion*. Rockford, IL: Tan Publishers, 1993. Reprinted with permission of the publisher.

few arrests of abortionists made, and even fewer guilty verdicts handed down.

On the other hand, there are a growing number of highly publicized incidents of what appears to be pro-life violence against abortionists and their clinics. The kidnapping of abortionist Hector Zevallos in August 1982 by the so-called "Army of God" was an isolated and unusual incident, allegedly the responsibility of a few zealous anti-abortionists acting independently of any larger group. Zevallos and his wife were released unharmed after eight days, and one of the men implicated in the "conspiracy and attempt to interfere with interstate commerce" was sentenced to thirty years in jail, with twelve more years added to the sentence later.

> *"This author has been struck, spit on, pushed, and received innumerable death threats, warnings, insults, and crank calls."*

Another anti-abortionist, admittedly acting alone, was jostled after he entered a New York abortion clinic, spilled gasoline on the property, and set the clinic ablaze. The only one who suffered injury was the anti-abortionist. The building housing the clinic was damaged. In 1984 there was a rash of attacks on abortion clinics, mostly on the East Coast, in Texas, and in Washington State. In these and other cases, the aim seems to have been to curtail abortion by putting the facility out of commission, at least temporarily.

A Commitment to Nonviolence

It should be pointed out that the abortionists, in presenting what they believe to be cases of pro-life violence, often lack evidence that the attack was made by pro-life people. And they lump together all kinds of "terrorist tactics" such as telephone calls, pickets, and peaceful sit-ins, in an effort to present a sinister picture of what is in fact non-violent pro-life activism.

All of the activist pro-lifers the Pro-Life Action League works with concur with the League's position against violence and its program of *non-violent direct action*. We take our commitment to non-violence seriously, believing that violence on our part would be counterproductive. It is the abortionists who are engaged in routine violence against unborn children (dismemberment, salt poisoning, strangulation) and their mothers (hemorrhage, scarring, infection, sterility). The use of violence could damage the reputation of pro-life activists, while undermining traditional non-violent methods. The use of violence might reinforce the erroneous belief that the end justifies the means, and that evil can be overcome by evil.

Violence Does Not Work

Besides, the use of violence probably would not work in the long run. The destruction of an abortion clinic is a temporary solution. New quarters can be found. Putting an abortionist out of commission for a while, as in the 1982 Zevallos kidnapping, did not stop abortions. While we might respect the zeal that would prompt such activities, we do not condone or recommend them.

We have corresponded with Peter Burkin, who was implicated in an abortion clinic firebombing in New York. Several of us have visited Don Benny Anderson, who has been sentenced to a federal penitentiary in connection with the 1982 Zevallos kidnapping. We are also in touch with Joseph Grace, implicated in a case of damage to an abortion clinic in Norfolk, Virginia, and have visited with Curtis Beseda, implicated in a clinic fire in Everett, Washington. All four men are dedicated to the belief that unborn children's most basic right—the right to life—is being violated by abortion and that daring actions are needed to awaken Americans to the terrible reality of abortion. But most pro-lifers would say that all four, if guilty, went too far.

What lasting advantage is there to show for the actions they were accused of? Zevallos went back to Hope Clinic to do more abortions; the damaged clinics have reopened or have sent their clients elsewhere. Was the effect these actions had on the image of a movement that condemns violence helpful? While we understand the feelings of anger, outrage, and frustration that likely prompted these and similar actions, we advise pro-lifers not to resort to violent tactics, but to save lives and stop abortions through non-violent, direct action.

Direct Action Is Key

Direct action, and even civil disobedience, have an important part to play in winning the pro-life battle. But violence, we believe, does not.

We must point out for the sake of proper perspective, however, that no amount of damage to real estate can equal the violence of taking a single human life. Civilized societies rate the loss of life as far more serious than property damage. But today, in our society, punishment is meted out to those who damage property while those who destroy life are rewarded. It is a sign of the deterioration of our values that much of the national media concentrates on damaged buildings, with pictures of charred real estate, while refusing to present pictures of the human victims who are heartlessly and systematically dismembered and painfully killed inside that real estate.

Pro-lifers are rarely allowed to show on network television the victims of abortion—the real violence of the abortion debate. Yet we have had to watch ad nauseam pictures of damaged buildings carefully panned on America's TV screens, while being directly or indirectly accused of causing the damage.

But we will not play the abortionists' violent game. We plan to win without resorting to violence.

The shooting death of Dr. Gunn, while allegedly committed by a man new to the movement, only served to bring on a rash of restrictive bills, speed up legislation aimed at curtailing totally non-violent pro-life activity and gave the pro-abortionists a "martyr." It made it momentarily more difficult to convince the man-on-the-street that pro-lifers had an undisputed claim to the high moral ground.

Violent Protest Is Justified

by Frank Morriss

About the author: *Frank Morriss, a teacher at the Colorado Catholic Academy, is the author of* The Conservative Imperative *and* The Divine Epic *and has, since 1950, been a columnist for several Roman Catholic journals.*

Any moral, or even humanly decent, society would consider the illustration in *Newsweek* (Feb. 11, 1993) obscene. It showed an unborn baby and pointed out its various parts that might be harvested (or to be more honest, cannibalized) for treatment of various diseases. Brain cells can help experimental surgery to treat Parkinson's disease, neurons "might treat" spinal-cord injuries and multiple sclerosis, pancreatic cells "reduced patients' need for insulin," liver cells "helped one boy" with Hunter's syndrome, stem cells "might treat" sickle-cell anemia and other disorders.

It might have been a chart such as once hung in old-fashioned butcher shops showing areas of animals from which choice and less-choice cuts came for the kitchen. The caption to the *Newsweek* illustration betrays just what the attitude of the secularized, pagan society of today is toward unborn life—"The Sum of Its Parts." If there is any doubt about what the article's intention might be, words of its headline should make it clear— ". . . saving a life is a moral imperative, yet we restrict the use of aborted fetuses." The headline goes on to call "the ethical landscape" of this issue a "minefield."

In Perspective

I cite this as important in thinking about the tragedy in Pensacola, Florida, in which an abortionist "doctor" was slain. The slaying may have deepened or widened the tragedy, but it did not of course create it. The tragedy was there, created by the mentality of the *Newsweek* illustration and by the pragmatic, sociological jurisprudence that has taken over control of our judiciary since the natural law legal philosophy was scuttled by [liberal Supreme Court justice] Oliver Wendell Holmes, Jr., and his ilk. [Natural, or true, law was an 18th- and 19th-century legal philosophy that held certain human rights to be God-given and hence unassailable by the state.]

Frank Morriss, "How Protect the Unborn When the Law Permits Their Execution?" *The Wanderer*, March 25, 1993. Reprinted with permission of *The Wanderer*.

If the tragedy might be measured by blood, then that of the slain abortionist contributed a drop in what are streams of innocent blood flowing into America's sewers from its abortion abattoirs. For the first time, the blood of the guilty joined the rivers of it from the victims.

This makes some of the words coming from some on both sides rather meaningless, or at least not to the true issue. Much of the disavowal from the pro-life side and the indignation from the pro-death side implies that innocent and guilty life are equal. They

> *"The force of the state should defend all innocent life."*

are, of course, ontologically and in the possession of human rights. But if that ends the matter, then deadly war may not be fought, the state may not execute, and no one can mount deadly defense in behalf of innocent life, either one's own or that of one's neighbor—and I take to be our neighbor any and all who face aggressive and malevolent evil that we might stop.

This, incidentally, shows how pacifist or even the "seamless garment" ideas can muddy the ethical and logical waters concerning a vital issue. It also dignifies the "legalization" of what is morally and ethically perverse in essence. . . .

True Law and Morality

The force of the state should defend all innocent life. The right of true law exists only on one side—that which labels all slaying of the innocent murder to one degree or another, and the overt intention to slay such life never defensible. That this intention to slay the innocent is present in the case of abortion is undeniable. (The claim that some do not recognize abortion as the deliberate killing of an innocent human is inadmissible, for subjective opinion does not determine the moral or natural law reality.)

What, then, is the moral situation when the state refuses to protect some innocent life, and in fact gives mandate for its murder? Is all protection removed from that life? If, by some miracle, the unborn targets of abortionists were able to mount some defense by force against their attackers, some way to slay the "doctor" before he slayed them, could they be condemned for doing so? Alas, that cannot be expected to happen. The next question is, can someone who might act with such force on their behalf be accused of murder, as the abortionists certainly can be on the level of true law and morality? The same civil law that "legalizes" abortion cannot be cited when it judges deadly defense murder. It has lost its authority in this question. What that means in regard to actual cases of force on behalf of the unborn on the part of individuals or combinations of them, I leave to others. But I have no doubt that this is the real heart of the question about events in Pensacola.

It becomes, perhaps, clearer when we consider what actually happened. An abortionist left his car and was headed to the "clinic." There weapons of death aimed at the unborn, and them alone, awaited him. Within minutes—or certainly within an hour or two—he would have been using them to kill innocent life. No police were on hand to stop him. Indeed, were they there, representing the state or federal government, they would have instead facilitated his progress. All of this is certain fact.

What then is the moral, natural law quality of what was done by one who acted, almost certainly, with the intention of preventing what that abortionist clearly intended to do, as he had been doing in the past and would have continued to do had he been able? That is the question to be considered, and not whether the end justifies the means (it does not), or whether one must adopt a "seamless garment" attitude about all taking of life.

Nor does it deal with the real issue by saying or believing that what happened in Florida was a tactical blow to pro-life efforts, or thinking it might discredit those efforts. All such questions are important, but they must not determine our thought toward the central issue—what authority exists in defending innocent life for which no police (I mean state or judicial) defense is afforded? Does all authority in their defense vanish? If it does not, where does it exist?

If we are going to concede that all deadly force against aggressive evil is itself evil, then we must pretend we are helpless against any aggressive evil. That, of course, is the pacifist position. But, then, such pacifism is error, not truth. Some pro-lifers hastening to present "clean hands" in regard to what happened in Florida have, unfortunately, taken a pacifist stance. And of course the enemies bent on the "right" to take innocent life would be glad to have pacifism prevail on one side—the pro-life side—but not on theirs. Indeed, that is the hypocritical stand of all aggressors.

> *"Let it be said honestly and openly, the moral aggressors at Pensacola were the abortionists and their agents."*

Let it be said honestly and openly, the moral aggressors at Pensacola were the abortionists and their agents, encouraged by pseudo-law that in the case of the unborn countenances and authorizes deadly aggression, identical to that for which we executed Nazis after the Nuremberg trials.

Historical Precedents

Most historians would give their sympathy, if not their outright approval, to Charlotte Corday, who slew "the Toad," Marat [a leader of the French Revolution], in his bathtub. She felt, with reason, that he had betrayed the true Revolution and led it into a swamp of blood. She added his blood to that swamp. I know of no one who mourned the passing of the agitator Marat.

The fictional "Scarlet Pimpernel" [from the similarly entitled 1934 novel about the French Revolution by Baroness Emmuska Orczy] did not, at least ordinarily, resort to killing to rescue royalists from the guillotine. But I doubt if any reader or viewer of the exploits of this English "rescuer" would have complained had he killed a few Jacobins and their agents in order to save some helpless persons being hauled to the place of execution, where the ground was so blood-soaked that, it is said, horses reared back in terror at the smell.

I suggest that what happened in Florida had, at the very least, the coloration of Corday's assassination and the Pimpernel's refusal to accept French revolutionary "law" as the final determination—certainly not a moral determination.

Indeed, the traditional ethical teachings based on the natural law can be cited more precisely to the case in Florida than to the two events in Revolutionary France, one historical, the other fictional.

It should be realized that it is certain that good morality cannot allow the killing of the unborn to continue, and that there will be those of good and informed conscience who will act in one way or another to bring it to an end, whether that can be accomplished by ordinary "legal" means or not. The question then becomes what actions can a true and valid conscience indicate.

Restricting Protesters Violates Their Constitutional Rights

by *Commonweal*

About the author: Commonweal *is a biweekly Roman Catholic publication that reviews public affairs, religion, literature, and the arts.*

Violence is anathema to all but fringe elements of the prolife movement. Still, in the aftermath of Dr. David Gunn's senseless murder outside an abortion clinic in Florida [in March 1993], some prochoice groups are eager to link mainstream anti-abortion sentiment to the actions of extremists. The perils of such a strategy are exemplified in the Freedom of Access to Clinic Entrances Act now before Congress. [The FACE bill was passed May 12, 1994, and signed into law by President Clinton two weeks later.] The bill's disregard for constitutional guarantees of free speech and assembly should make every pro-choice civil libertarian blush.

Hardball Politics

This is crude, hardball politics, but it is not without its own sad irony. Civil suits brought by abortion clinics and others that asked and got confiscatory damages have effectively bankrupted groups such as Operation Rescue. We have never applauded Operation Rescue's methods of protest, but in destroying whatever organizational structure might have impeded the lawless actions of some individuals, has this prochoice strategy really been wise? To now further intimidate or even disenfranchise anti-abortion protesters engaged in peaceful civil disobedience will surely marginalize such people even more. Isn't the result likely to be more anarchy, not any movement toward the resolution of this tortuous issue? Can any of us afford that?

At some point, all those engaged in this dispute must recognize that the struggle over abortion should not require the unconditional surrender of either side.

As prochoice groups and their friends in Congress move to absolutize the right to abortion through the Access and Freedom of Choice acts, and by lifting the ban on federal funding for abortions, they should keep in mind the mixed consequences of their previous successes. At the same time, radical anti-abortion activists must recognize that each act of violence or harassment only adds to the persuasiveness of the case made by those who say that any restriction of abortion represents an "undue burden" placed on women exercising what our highest court says is a constitutional right.

Dangers to Liberty

The Freedom of Access bill highlights the dangers to liberty courted by the unrestrained political ambition the abortion question generates. The bill, designed to make the "obstruction" of clinic entrances a federal felony, is worded so broadly yet aimed so specifically at anti-abortion protesters as to threaten the repression of even peaceful protest. Indeed, since the vast majority of demonstrations are peaceful, it is hard to imagine what legitimate remedies such a law provides to those seeking abortion. Surely blockading clinics, like blockading the entrances to nuclear power plants or even military bases, is already a violation of local and state laws. Should there be a law making peaceful civil disobedience at the entrance to a military base a federal felony? Or, as this law proposes for those confronted by anti-abortion protesters, should soldiers or sailors be entitled to civil damages for "emotional distress" caused by antimilitary protesters? (The parallel here is legal, not moral or emotional.)

> *"All those engaged in this dispute must recognize that the struggle over abortion should not require the unconditional surrender of either side."*

Suffice it to say, the statute, which punishes anti-abortion obstruction of clinics but specifically exempts any obstruction by those involved in a labor dispute, is unconstitutional on its face. Such "content-based" prohibitions are a denial of First Amendment rights, since they outlaw only those acts that are the expression of an identifiable point of view. "Whoever, with intent to prevent or discourage any person from obtaining reproductive health services. . . ." is the kind of thinking the Freedom of Access bill punishes. If a demonstrator's intent is to prevent or discourage a parsimonious boss from entering the clinic, that's not a federal concern. Opposition to abortion is what this law is meant to curb.

The bill's criminal and civil penalties, up to three years in jail for previous offenders and treble damages for those experiencing pain and suffering, are further efforts to "chill" political speech. Doubtless the distress of women entering clinics confronted by anti-abortion protesters is real. But all our freedoms ultimately rest upon the First Amendment; it must not be held hostage even to the anguish of women seeking "reproductive services." The Access bill is precisely targeted; it renders the First Amendment null and void for those who oppose abortion.

More broadly, the Clinton administration's apparent determination to expand access to abortion is more than a political mistake; it is a tragedy. Americans as a people are irrevocably divided on this question. Although the murder of Dr. Gunn has undoubtedly diminished the perceived moral stature of the prolife movement, neither abortion absolutists nor abolitionists can claim anything like a popular majority. The Democrats in Congress seem intent on pushing back what few restrictions now apply to abortion. Many Americans, however, think the Court erroneous in its discovery of an ostensible "right" to abortion, and find current U.S. abortion practice a moral travesty at least partly analogous to the nation's long denial of constitutional protections to blacks.

Indeed, with each passing year the much-remarked-upon parallel between *Roe v. Wade* (1973) and the notorious *Dred Scott* decision (1857) becomes more poignant. In *Dred Scott*, the Supreme Court managed to find no legal protection for "Negroes" in the Constitution, and further astounded its critics by ruling that no territory or new state could prohibit slavery even if it voted to do so. As Abraham Lincoln, the most eloquent and steadfast opponent of *Dred Scott*, characterized the moral and political bankruptcy of the Court's decision: "That if any *one* man, choose to enslave *another*, no *third* man shall be allowed to object."

Lincoln was not an abolitionist. Slavery, he recognized, was a historical fact that mere reason or moral exhortation could not miraculously untangle or uproot. But in *Dred Scott*'s expansion of the "rights" of slaveholders Lincoln recognized a logic both inimical to self-government and false to this nation's historical promise of equality, and the protection of life and liberty, for all. He pledged to resist the decision peaceably but resolutely.

Similarly, in a country as vast and varied as this, no question as morally complex and socially divisive as abortion can be resolved by an edict from Washington. Unilateral federal decisions ignore the deeply held convictions of too many citizens. "When he invites any people willing to have slavery, to establish it," Lincoln said of anyone who embraced *Dred Scott*, "he is blowing out the moral lights around us." People of good will might rightly fear that 1.5 million abortions a year, whether the practice is guaranteed by the highest court or the highest legislature, is no less a darkening of the human spirit.

Terroristic Clinic Protest Must Be Opposed

by Barbara Radford and Gina Shaw

About the authors: *Barbara Radford is executive director of the Washington, D.C.–based National Abortion Federation (NAF), a professional forum for abortion service providers and others committed to making abortion safe and accessible. Gina Shaw is a member of NAF.*

After March 10, 1993, it seems that any discussion of antiabortion violence must begin with the same grim set of facts. On that sunny morning in Pensacola, Florida, Dr. David Gunn was shot in the back and killed as he tried to enter Pensacola Medical Services, where he was medical director. His murderer, Michael Frederick Griffin, cried "Don't kill any more babies," as he fired.

What led to the murder of David Gunn, and to the growing violence of the extremist wing of the antiabortion movement? Antiabortion groups' first response to the *Roe* [*v Wade*, 1973] decision was not to start shooting doctors, burning down clinics, or assaulting patients. It took years for this violence to be planned and grow, until in the first half of 1993, the National Abortion Federation (NAF) recorded 1.8 million dollars' worth of damage from arsons, bombings, and vandalism at facilities that provide abortions.

A Political and Social Perspective: The Early 1980s

In the mid-1970s, the newly opened clinics that provided abortions across the country fielded the occasional harassment call and the odd piece of hate mail. On Saturdays, they might find a Catholic church group saying the rosary outside their doors. Not a typical way to come to work, but something one could get used to. In Washington, groups like the National Right to Life Committee were doing what political groups do—lobbying, marching, and writing letters.

Violence against abortion providers in the late 1970s and early 1980s was not unheard of; in the 7 years 1977–1983, there were a total of 21 acts of arson and bombings of facilities that provided abortions. However, in 1984, the picture changed dramatically. In one violent and terrifying year, there were 18 bombings and 6 acts of arson directed against abortion providers in the United States. This literal "explosion" of actual violence was accompanied by an increase in threats of violence; from 1977 to 1983, only 4 death threats were reported to NAF, whereas in 1984 alone, NAF recorded 23 death threats.

Sociologist Dallas Blanchard provides an interesting interpretation of this sudden burst of violence in his book *Religious Violence and Abortion: The Gideon Project*. He theorizes that the radical right, which had claimed the credit for Ronald Reagan's election in 1980, was disheartened when the President's public support for their antiabortion agenda failed to produce

> *"The rhetoric of the antiabortion leaders has a chillingly clear purpose: to dehumanize abortion providers."*

any tangible results, such as a Human Life Amendment [a proposed Constitutional amendment outlawing abortion] or a Supreme Court decision overturning *Roe v Wade*. "Our point is not to cast Reagan as leading a 'call to violence,'" Blanchard says, "but to cite the effects of Reagan's failure to issue a call *against* violence in the context of the ideological struggle that intensified after the 1984 election." Blanchard explains, "When rising expectations are met with a reduced perception that goals are being realized, then an 'intolerable gap' between goals and perceived success exists, producing a sense of political deprivation. Under these conditions, more radical efforts toward the enactment of social goals tend to emerge."

This theory also accounts for the brief drop in antiabortion violence from 1988 through 1990, followed by a sharp rise in 1992 and into 1993. The election of George Bush seemed to many in both camps to solidify the hold of the radical right on the judicial process, and although a Human Life Amendment no longer seemed possible, *Roe* appeared to hang by a thread that would easily be cut by one of Bush's Supreme Court appointments. When the court refused to overturn *Roe* outright with either the *Webster* [1989] or *Casey* [1992] decision, once again, the far right experienced an "intolerable gap" between their goals, their expectations, and their perceived success.

When Is Terrorism Not Terrorism?

Whether or not he achieved any of the political goals of the antiabortion movement, Ronald Reagan's inaction to stop the ongoing violence against abortion providers was viewed by many as an implicit endorsement of their tactics. In 1985, Reagan's FBI director, William Webster, refused to categorize arsons and bombings at abortion facilities as "terrorist" acts—thus keeping the FBI out of the investigations and leaving them up to the smaller, overburdened Bureau of Alcohol, Tobacco, and Firearms. The FBI manual defines terrorism as "the unlawful use of force or violence against persons or property to intimidate or coerce the government, the civilian population or any segment thereof in furtherance of political or social objectives." It would be difficult to find a definition that is more perfectly suited to the attacks on clinics, but the Reagan administration turned a blind eye as antiabortion zealots became more bold.

The Roots of a Burgeoning Movement

For antiabortion extremists in the climate of the early 1980s, the journey from political dissent to organized force and violence lacked only one thing—a guide. The gap was filled, and the militant antiabortion movement given its marching orders, by the teachings of a former Catholic seminarian named Joseph Scheidler. The extremist antiabortion groups have multiplied exponentially in recent years—indeed, they can be recited almost like a biblical genealogy: "Joe Scheidler begat Houston PLAN [Pro-Life Action Network], which begat Operation Rescue and Rescue America, which begat the Missionaries to the Preborn and Operation Rescue National, which begat. . . ."

With this organizational proliferation in the late 1980s and early 1990s, attention turned away from Scheidler and focused upon his more mediagenic heirs, such as Randall Terry. Nonetheless, it is with Joseph Scheidler that the idea of militant effort to end abortion began, and it is back to Joseph Scheidler that the origins of many of the more radical groups can be traced.

Budding antiabortion zealots learned their activist lessons from a book by Scheidler that is well known to both clinic blockaders and abortion providers, *Closed: 99 Ways to Stop Abortion*. Each of the book's 99 chapters is a step-by-step guide to

> *"When abortion becomes 'murder,' then the killing of an abortionist becomes justifiable homicide."*

one form of activist behavior or another. The chapter on "sit-ins" is the early blueprint for the now-familiar clinic blockades; another chapter describes the use of private detectives to track patients, a tactic now used to stalk physicians and clinic staffs as well as their clients. Indeed, many antichoice activists have become virtual private detectives themselves in their quest for personal information about abortion providers.

The book's publication in 1985 followed hard on the heels of the violence of 1984, and Scheidler immediately set about planting seeds of local grassroots activism with his "Year of Pain and Fear," in which he crisscrossed the country leading militant activities directed against clinics. Early Pro-Life Action League conferences were the first appearances of activists who would later go on to lead other groups, such as Randall Terry of Operation Rescue and Don Treshman of Rescue America. Scheidler's book and his lessons in terror tactics have thus been passed along to a new generation of zealots.

A lesson learned by Scheidler, Terry, and their compatriots as the extremist wing of their movement grew was the potency of language. The rhetoric of the antiabortion leaders has a chillingly clear purpose: to dehumanize abortion providers and to instruct their followers to regard providers as demons, evil butchers worthy of contempt at least and extermination at worst. Clinics are "abortion mills" or "abortuaries"; physicians who provide abortions are "baby butchers"; and volunteer escorts who help patients avoid harassment outside clinics are "deathscorts."

A Violent Worldview

In this violent worldview, believers may—and should—ask God to cause the death of anyone involved in providing abortion services. Milwaukee's Missionaries to the Preborn routinely pray for the deaths of physicians who perform abortions. A recent issue of the *Life Advocate*, a magazine that brings together the voices of the most extreme players in the antiabortion movement, includes a self-satisfied tale from a Chattanooga "pro-life" leader [T. Snowdon] of how such "imprecatory prayer" had afflicted two clinic directors with cancer. One died of the disease.

How great a leap is it from praying for death or destruction, to taking action to bring about that death or destruction? *Washington Post* columnist Richard Cohen summed up the power of this rhetoric by invoking British writer George Orwell [author of *1984*, a novel about a totalitarian society that destroys privacy and distorts truth]. "Orwell might have noted how the debasement of language can so simplify complex matters that violence is either committed or condoned," Cohen wrote. "When abortion becomes 'murder,' then the killing of an abortionist becomes justifiable homicide. First you kill the language and then you kill the person."

Words are not their only weapons. Despite repeated avowals of nonviolence, the leaders and troops of Operation Rescue and related groups have clear ties to perpetrators of violence, and the rhetoric of hatred motivates both the blockader and the bomber.

When a bombing, arson, or assault occurs at a clinic, Operation Rescue and related groups take to the airwaves to declare two things: 1) we had nothing to do with it, because our followers are nonviolent, but 2) we understand the motivations of the arsonist/bomber/vandal, and we cannot condemn his/her actions because they sought to save babies. Despite insistence by the better-known radical antiabortion groups that they are unconnected with acts of violence, some clear correlations emerge.

Michael Griffin, Dr. Gunn's murderer, had been taken under the wing of John Burt, regional director in Pensacola for Rescue America, a national group that traces its origins to a Joseph Scheidler Pro-Life Action Network conference in Houston in the mid-1980s. Burt was also tied to a 1988 attempted ar-

> *"The leaders and troops of Operation Rescue and related groups have clear ties to perpetrators of violence."*

son at Pensacola's Ladies Center; he guided perpetrator John Brockhoeft, who would later be convicted of several arsons in Ohio, to his target. Several other examples are available.

The implication is clear: in many cases, very little separates the clinic blockader from the clinic bomber. Not all those who blockade clinics bomb them; but many of those who have been convicted of violent assaults have been involved with blockades and other militant group efforts. Those who are not bombers or arsonists themselves, such as high-profile group leaders like Randall Terry of Operation Rescue and Joseph Foreman of Missionaries to the Preborn, often serve as public apologists for those who commit acts of violence.

> *"Those who are not bombers or arsonists themselves, such as high-profile group leaders . . . , often serve as public apologists for those who commit acts of violence."*

Who are the followers of the antiabortion militants? Blockading a clinic, vandalizing it, threatening its physicians, and bombing it are all points on a continuum of violence, and the people on this continuum differ more in degree than in nature. This theory is supported in the writings of two observers of the antiabortion activists, sociologist Blanchard and journalist Alissa Rubin. In a May 16, 1993, *Washington Post* article, "In God They Trespass," Rubin examines a group of Operation Rescue members she met in Baton Rouge, at a nationally organized attack on Louisiana clinics. She paints a picture of people on the fringes of society. ". . . Those who become full-time members of Operation Rescue are virtual nomads, moving from city to city, schooling their children at home," Rubin writes. "Many Operation Rescue members are drifters, financially and socially. . . . Many have escaped a past of drinking or drugs and come from severely dysfunctional families. Being born-again as Christians is often an attempt to bring order to their lives."

Blanchard's observations of those convicted of acts of extreme violence show parallels with Rubin's description of the blockaders in Baton Rouge. Both Rubin and Blanchard note that their subjects are "religiously ardent," and Blanchard adds that "[a]ll are dualists, viewing the world in clear-cut black and white." It is easy to imagine such a person, a converted "rescuer" or "missionary," listening day in and day out to the violent rhetoric of the group's leaders, and drawing the simple conclusion that violence "in defense of the unborn" is justified.

The Effects of the Violence

The effects of the epidemic of antiabortion violence and harassment are perhaps more easily understood than are its causes. Wide-ranging attacks on abortion providers have a profound effect on the staff of targeted facilities, their patients, and the families of both groups. The surge of violence has also affected the staff and patients at facilities that have not been direct victims of violence, but who perceive themselves as a potential "next target." There are also larger social consequences, including reduced availability and access to abortion services and increased costs for abortion and contraceptive services where they are available.

The shooting of Dr. Gunn was but the most devastating in the latest surge of violence and threats against providers that began in early 1992 and escalated with the inauguration of the first actively pro-choice president this country has ever had. The year 1992 rivaled 1984 in violent attacks, with 1 bombing, 16 arsons, and 13 attempted arsons or bombings. In the first 5 months of 1993, 5 abortion providers were victims of arson—all but one instance of which caused extensive damage. The midsummer months and the Christmas season are known for particularly sharp spurts of violence. [On July 29, 1994, Paul Hill, an excommunicated Presbyterian minister, shot and killed Dr. John Britton and his escort, James Barret—and wounded Britton's wife, June—as the three drove up to Britton's abortion clinic in Pensacola, Florida.] One fact is clear: the cost of damages is likely to reach an unprecedented level, quite probably well over $2 million. Although this cost is nothing compared with the loss of Dr. Gunn's life, it is nevertheless a grave crisis for providers who seek to provide affordable health care services.

> *"Blockading a clinic, vandalizing it, threatening its physicians, and bombing it are all points on a continuum of violence."*

Providers of abortion services frequently comment that "we learn how to normalize the abnormal." The staffs of facilities that provide abortions learn to live with bricks through their windows, threats toward them and their children, and gauntlets of jeering picketers and blockaders surrounding their cars as they come to work. The NAF statistics on violence and disruption at clinics, although the most comprehensive in the nation, are assumed to be an underestimation because, as the horrifying becomes the commonplace, many occurrences just aren't reported. Death threats, in particular, are often undercounted because of their very pervasiveness. Working on the front lines of what has been described as "the new civil war" takes its toll. From bulletproof vests to electrified fences, bomb-threat drills, floodlights, and elaborate security systems, the simple act of providing health care becomes one requiring the most extensive precautions and protections. . . .

Effects on Clients and on the Accessibility of Abortion Care

The Feminist Women's Health Center in Redding, California, is a perennial target of violence. It has been nearly destroyed by arson three times in as many years, and media accounts of the ongoing violence and harassment there have familiarized area residents with the situation.

According to Penny Bertsch, Director of Clinic Services for this clinic and three other affiliates in California, the violence has had a profound effect on patients. She explained at a recent meeting of NAF that women will choose to drive 2 hours out of their way, to the clinic in Chico, out of fear of more violent attacks at the Redding clinic.

Although fear of personal injury is a factor, particularly for women in areas where violence is most pervasive, the real fear expressed by most patients is that of harassment and invasion of privacy. Even a small picket line provokes nervous questions from patients: "Does this mean my picture will be on television?" In Milwaukee, the answer is often yes. Camera operators for a local religious television station often film a patient's face, then pan to a closeup of her license plate, then return to a shot of her entering the clinic. This footage is aired on an evening television program.

Mississippi has a law that requires a 24-hour waiting period after a woman's first office visit before she can obtain an abortion. Local activists have taken full advantage of this law, scribbling down license numbers during the woman's first visit and using friends in the department of motor vehicles to find out addresses, names of relatives, and employers. Many women have returned home to find the picketers from the clinic at their door, haranguing them, their families, their parents, and their neighbors. The tactic has received the most publicity in Mississippi, but it has been used elsewhere as well.

There is no evidence that militant antiabortion activism has stopped women from having abortions. Nonetheless, it has caused untold trauma, unnecessary and unconscionable health risks, and the loss of personal integrity and privacy for hundreds of thousands of women.

Fewer Abortion Providers

Examining the situation in a broader perspective, the statistics speak for themselves. Only 17% of US counties have an abortion provider. Two larger states, North and South Dakota, have only one provider. Only 12% of obstetrics-gynecology residency training programs teach abortion technique as a regular part of the residency rotation. By no means can the extremists in the antiabortion movement take all the credit for this crisis, although they would like to. Nonetheless, the cumulative effect of years of violence has no doubt taken its toll, and some physicians have stopped performing abortions because of the climate. . . .

> *"The greatest victory of the antiabortion extremists . . . is their ability to transform acts of violence and viciousness into 'just another part of the political debate.'"*

[But] the greatest victory of the antiabortion extremists in their campaign of terror is their ability to transform acts of violence and viciousness into "just another part of the political debate." When David Gunn was murdered, news articles and broadcast programs bent over backwards to permit "equal time" to those who condoned and made possible his murder. It even seemed fashionable to write of similarities in the lives of the doctor and his killer—"two men much alike" wrote the *New York Times*. Other victims of murder are not cavalierly compared to their killer, as if this makes victims somehow responsible for their own deaths.

The press and the public must recognize the fundamental difference between legally expressing dissent in a free society, and engaging in terrorist behavior. This is the underlying problem that must be addressed before we can put a stop to antiabortion violence.

A Backlash, Maybe?

There is hope for such a reaction, as communities begin to turn against the reactionaries in their midst. In Missoula, Montana, when the Blue Mountain Clinic was burned to the ground by an arsonist in March 1993, donations and support were overwhelming. Neighbors and patients sent financial contributions, area businesses offered loans of space, equipment, and resources, and other physicians resettled the clinic's various services in their offices until it could rebuild. One area physician called the clinic's director and told her that this was his call to action; he wanted to start providing abortions for free at the Blue Mountain Clinic as soon as they reopened.

Violence and terror operate well in darkness and secrecy; they do not do well when exposed to the light. It is a positive step that national polls reveal a wave of public revulsion at the behavior of the militant antiabortion groups. This revulsion must now be channeled into positive community action, with all pro-choice citizens ensuring that their own communities, their own clinics, and their own physicians are not targeted for violence and intimidation. The purveyors of violence win only as long as people shake their heads, say "Isn't that terrible?" and keep walking without a backward glance. From Pensacola to Missoula to Milwaukee, the responsibility for ending this epidemic lies with each one of us. It is important to know the causes of the disease, and to understand its effects. We must all be the cure.

The Pro-Life Movement Should Condemn Violent Protest

by *Glamour*

About the author: Glamour *is a monthly magazine covering women's issues.*

Though *Glamour* has always supported abortion rights, and will continue to do so, we recognize that there are deeply felt differences of opinion on this issue. In our democracy, voices from all sides are entitled to be heard—but the right to free speech is not the right to coerce. We function as a society by tolerating differences and expressing our beliefs without interfering with the rights of others. Responsible activists on both sides of the abortion debate have always known that. Yet pro-life extremists no longer feel bound by these rules. Instead of peaceful protest, their tactics now reek of outright terrorism. In the past 15 years, they have bombed or torched 117 clinics and vandalized another 457. They have drilled holes in clinic walls and poured in noxious chemicals. In the first quarter of this year [1993], three clinics were destroyed by arsonists.

Targeting Doctors

The most dangerous tactic of all, however, is the targeting of doctors who provide abortions. They have received death threats and been pictured on "wanted" posters that listed their names, addresses and phone numbers. Last March [1993], only days after a speech in which Randall Terry, head of Operation Rescue, declared, "We've found that the weak link is the doctor," the growing violence reached its obvious crescendo: Dr. David Gunn of Pensacola, Florida, who had been featured on a wanted poster, was shot to death by Michael F. Griffin, a pro-life demonstrator.

To say that this was the random act of a madman, as some pro-life leaders have done, is to deny the realities of the abortion conflict in America. Extremists are seeking to dominate the antiabortion movement, and while advocates of

Editorial (written by Lorraine Dusky) in *Glamour*, August 1993. Reprinted with permission.

choice are alarmed, we suspect that many pro-life women are too—as they should be, since what is at stake is not just the credibility of their movement but its future.

So far, not enough of the mainstream pro-life leadership has chosen to try to stop the violence. For example, the National Right to Life Committee (NRLC), the largest pro-life organization in the United States, has not put much distance between itself and the extremists. After the murder, Wanda Franz, Ph.D., president of NRLC, said that the organization "condemns the violence against abortionist Dr. David Gunn, as NRLC condemns the violence of abortion that has killed 30 million unborn children in the last 20 years." She went on to deem it "false and offensive to suggest, as some pro-abortion groups have done, that speaking in favor of the right to life somehow causes violence. Such a suggestion is like blaming the civil rights movement—and all those who courageously spoke in favor of the rights of African Americans—for rioting or deaths that were a part of that era."

Agreed: *Speaking* in favor of the right to life does not cause violence—but then no one said it did. The murder of a doctor—and its failure to provoke clear condemnation from enough of the pro-life mainstream—may indeed encourage future violence.

Just as important, Dr. Franz's comparison of the civil rights struggle with pro-life activism is not an honest one. Civil rights protesters practiced a philosophy of nonviolence: *They* were not the ones who brought out the dogs and hoses; they were not the

> *"To say that [Gunn's murder] was the random act of a madman . . . is to deny the realities of the abortion conflict in America."*

ones who killed people. In Florida, an antiabortion protester was not killed; he *did* the killing. In other incidents, extremists have not been terrorized; they have done the terrorizing. By seeking to link violent extremists with this country's most nonviolent protesters, Dr. Franz seems to be dignifying the pro-life movement's fringe rather than sincerely condemning its actions.

The Extremists Take Over

The NRLC may come to regret that choice. Until the Gunn murder, the extremists operated, if not in the shadows, at least in the background. But now there's reason to think that they feel entitled to take the lead. In March [1993], Randall Terry told the *Los Angeles Times* that the antiabortion movement has failed. "We're taking the gloves off," he said. "We are not going to tolerate cowardice and compromise in our camp. . . . We want to change the face and most important principles of the pro-life movement—God is, and he has spoken."

But God has not spoken to all of us in the same way, or every pro-life supporter would belong to a version of Operation Rescue. Instead, some have chosen to pursue distinctly nonviolent, yet effective, methods of protest. The National Conference of Catholic Bishops (NCCB), for example, recently spearheaded a letter-writing campaign against the proposed Freedom of Choice Act (FOCA), which would guarantee a legal right to abortion. The campaign has generated between three and four million cards, and seems to have had an effect. "I think the cards have influenced some people," says Sarah Pines, spokeswoman for the National Abortion Rights Action League, "though it remains to be seen if they actually change anyone's vote."

The NCCB was one of several major pro-life groups to condemn Dr. Gunn's murder unequivocally (Americans United for Life, which sponsors most of the pro-life litigation in this country, and Texans United for Life were others). "The violence of killing in the name of pro-life makes a mockery of the pro-life cause," said Helen M. Alvare, spokeswoman for the NCCB. "It is not enough to say 'We sympathize with Mr. Griffin's motivations, but disagree with his actions.' . . . We call on all in the pro-life movement to condemn such violence in no uncertain terms." *Village Voice* columnist Nat Hentoff, a liberal pro-life activist, put it this way: "There are those who say they are pro-life but are not. They are only against abortion. But life means life."

> *"The violence of killing in the name of pro-life makes a mockery of the pro-life cause."*

Unless dissent over abortion is to descend into increased violence and death, the extremists must be actively opposed by *many* such voices. Responsible, committed opponents of abortion cannot avert their eyes from what is being done in the name of "pro-life." History is filled with tales of terrorism committed and wars fought in the name of God. It must not happen here.

Clinic Protest Deprives Women of Their Rights

by *Revolutionary Worker*

About the author: Revolutionary Worker *is a weekly newspaper published by the Revolutionary Communist Party in Chicago, Illinois.*

On March 10, 1993, in front of an abortion clinic in Pensacola, Florida, Dr. David Gunn was murdered in cold blood by an anti-abortion demonstrator. This shooting has sharpened up what the anti-abortion movement is all about. The fanatic antiabortion crusades have nothing to do with "saving lives" or fetuses. The real political and ideological program of the anti-abortion movement has to do with controlling women and enforcing all the oppressive social relations that keep women down.

The murder of Dr. Gunn reflects the sharpening battle over abortion in this country. On the one hand you have doctors, clinic personnel and pro-choice activists who are willing to take enormous personal risks in order to give women the right to choose. And on the other hand, you have anti-abortion activists who promote the BIG LIE that "fetuses are babies" and use reactionary violence to take away abortion rights and tighten the chains of women's oppression.

He Believed in Choice

Dr. Gunn was targeted by the anti-abortion movement because he believed women should have a choice. He started off delivering babies. He went to Alabama because it had the highest infant mortality rate in the nation and he wanted to help turn this around. Then an abortion clinic asked for his help because no other doctors would perform abortions in this rural, southern area. Susan Hill, executive director of the Women's Health Network, which operates eight clinics including the Columbus, Georgia, clinic where Dr. Gunn worked, recalled: "Dr. Gunn was a laid-back '60s kind of guy who didn't like the politics of medicine. He wanted to help." Gunn started out doing abortions once a week, but before long he was making the circuit of six clinics, driving 1,000

"The Anti-Women Crusaders," *Revolutionary Worker*, March 29, 1993. Reprinted by permission. This article has been retitled and subheadings have been added by Greenhaven editors.

miles a week.

Anti-abortion groups put Dr. Gunn's picture on "wanted posters" with his name, address and work schedule. He received late night phone calls and mail that contained death threats. In order to protect himself he carried three guns in his car. But all this only made him even more committed to a woman's right to choose. On January 22, 1993, he celebrated the anniversary of the Supreme Court *Roe v. Wade* decision that legalized abortion by blasting Tom Petty and the Heartbreakers' "I

> *"Dr. Gunn was targeted by the anti-abortion movement because he believed that women should have a choice."*

Won't Back Down" from speakers at the clinic in Montgomery, Alabama, where he worked.

On the other hand, there was the man who put an end to Dr. Gunn's life. Michael Griffin is a fundamentalist Christian who had joined "Rescue America." This anti-abortion group is led by former Ku Klux Klan member John Burt. Burt has said he can't be held responsible for what Griffin did. But he admits, "I am the general who sends out the order to the troops."

Perhaps one of the most revealing things about Griffin—and the whole movement he is part of—is his relationship to his wife. In 1991 Patricia Griffin filed a divorce action which portrayed her husband as a violent man who physically abused her. But later, after being "counseled" by people in "Rescue America," she withdrew her request for a divorce. John Burt told reporters, "It seemed like the marriage was improving. We just pointed out to her that God hates divorce. She was talking about getting her tubes untied so they could have another child." It's clear here what Griffin and "Rescue America's" views are of women's role in society: That they should be controlled by men and kept "in their place" as dutiful and subservient wives, breeders and child rearers. . . .

Specter of Civil War

The anti-abortion movement and its whole anti-woman program has always promoted reactionary violence. Publicly, organizations like Operation Rescue say they don't support the murder of Dr. Gunn or things like clinic bombings. But it's clear what their real position is when they repeatedly imply that Dr. Gunn deserved to die and immediately started raising money to support Michael Griffin. More generally, "debating" the pros and cons of using bombs and guns in the anti-abortion movement has frequently served as a cover for calls for reactionary violence. And there has been open talk in the anti-abortion movement about the "civil war" aspect of the battle around abortion.

A "Pro-Life Manifesto" released in 1988 by a major Christian publisher said:

> Armed aggression is a very tempting route to take. Open and tangible results would be seen, and even if it meant defeat—and it would—at least we could go down with our guns blazing. The cause for which we would be sacrificing

ourselves would be lost, but at least we would get attention. Abortion would still go on, and there would be stringent and severe punishment for those who attempted to advocate the pro-life position. There would be martyrs on both sides and little would be accomplished beyond that.

If armed aggression were the answer, it would have to be done on a large scale, and more than a few abortion clinics would have to be destroyed. To succeed, it would require the destruction of all hospitals or clinics that performed abortions. Heroes who would lay down their life for the cause would have to come forth. Armies would need to be organized. Companies producing abortifacients would have to be bombed and their employees terrorized. In short, we would have to be willing to plunge ourselves into civil war.

Leaders in the anti-abortion movement have frequently sent messages to their "flock" that reactionary violence against clinics, doctors, staff and patients is justified. For instance Joseph Scheidler, Executive Director of the Pro Life Action League and author of *Closed: 99 Ways to Stop Abortion*, a handbook of ways to harass and attack abortion clinics, told his followers: "While we disagree with burning down abortion clinics, we see that destruction as trivial, as compared with the human destruction that goes on routinely inside these places. . . . I do understand the emotions that might prompt one to violence. . . ."

Anti-Woman Program

"If women can get abortions, then how can we control them any more?"
A male anti-abortion demonstrator, when asked by the press to explain why he was picketing a women's clinic

The anti-abortion movement clearly sees its mission as enforcing the repressive social relations that keep women down. For these reactionaries, support for "traditional family values" has always been a code word for (among other things) keeping women subordinate and stifled by their role as wives and mothers. One anti-abortion project, called "Women Exploited by Abortion," tries to "neutralize the word 'choice'" by focusing on the so-called "scars" that abortion leaves on women. They claim abortion is linked to promiscuity, divorce, suicide, eating disorders, and child abuse. It's clear what their real worry is here: that legalized abortion increases the independence and control women have in their lives.

> *"The anti-abortion movement clearly sees its mission as enforcing the repressive social relations that keep women down."*

A look at one group of abortion clinic bombers, the "Gideon Project," illustrates the anti-woman politics of the anti-abortion movement.

On December 25, 1984, bombs exploded at three clinics that provided abortions in Pensacola, Florida. No one was hurt, but there was a half million dollars' worth of damage. Leaders in the anti-abortion movement immediately voiced support for these bombings. The Rev. David Shofner of the West Pensacola Baptist Church said "bombing was not God's way." But he then went on to say, "Bombings and fire will certainly stop it [abortion]. . . Picketing doesn't." John Burt from "Rescue America" added, "If there is an element of our society that does that, and no one is hurt, I'm glad the killing [abortions] has stopped."

The "Gideon Project"

This kind of support for clinic bombings gave rise to the "Gideon Project." This group was made up of two young couples who took as their model the biblical story of Gideon, an intensely faithful religious character who served God by destroying the shrine of the false god Baal. Under cover of night, these Gideon crusaders bombed a number of abortion clinics. Two people were later convicted of conspiracy and two others were convicted of conspiracy to build a bomb and three counts of making a bomb and of damaging a building with a bomb.

Through church groups these Gideon crusaders had viewed anti-abortion movies and read all kinds of anti-abortion pamphlets. They became convinced of the unscientific and wrong lie that fetuses are babies, and this was part of what led them to create the "Gideon Project." But it was also their more general reactionary views, especially on women, that led them to carry out these bombings.

One of these clinic bombers told government authorities that his "motivation was love for God, my country, my family." And a major feature of these people was their view of women as subordinate, passive, and primarily designed for child-rearing. One "Gideon Project" member said his favorite song was "I've Never Been to Me," a top-forty, "easy-listening" tune that told the story of a woman who had lived an exciting life but felt lost because she had never had a baby.

"It's clear what their real worry is here: that legalized abortion increases the independence and control women have in their lives."

The two male clinic bombers called themselves "knights" and wore T-shirts printed with the motto "Protectors of the Code." This "code of chivalry" portrayed women as "damsels in distress" and men as "knights in shining armor." One of the women in the group, when asked about her role in the bombing, said, "Women are not allowed. . . . It's white knights. We're not allowed. We're the damsels in distress." Meanwhile one of the other bombers, a man, emphasized that the women couldn't actually carry out the bombings, but the men could—they had to provide strength and support because they were the "knights of the Round Table." As part of their defense, the attorney for one of the woman bombers said that his client had merely "believed St. Paul when he said, 'Submit unto your husband as unto the Lord.'"

This is only one example of the completely backward and reactionary views toward women in the anti-abortion movement. And this movement and its politics of "God, Patriotism, and Family" have consistently been not only supported, but LED by major figures in the government—both Republican and Democrat.

The question of who controls the reproductive functions of women is KEY to the overall status of women in society and to the workings of society itself. And the ruling class not only tolerates, but leads and encourages the anti-abortion movement because it is in their class interests to restrict and control women's reproduction.

> *"The question of who controls the reproductive functions of women is KEY to the overall status of women in society."*

Throughout history one of the main ways oppressive societies have established control over women is by controlling women's reproduction. Capitalist society has developed and enforced rules and customs to control women's sexuality and reproduction and dictate when, where and with whom a woman can or cannot bear a child. In this way, patriarchal society is able to define "women's place" in society and set limits on what they can do. This is what the anti-abortion movement is all about.

Chapter 5

Should Aborted Fetuses Be Used for Medical Research?

The Ethics of Fetal Tissue Research and Transplantation: An Overview

by Kenneth L. Woodward, Mary Hager, and Daniel Glick

About the authors: *Kenneth L. Woodward is a senior writer for* Newsweek*; he writes on bioethical and social issues. Mary Hager and Daniel Glick are* Newsweek *correspondents at the magazine's domestic bureau in Washington, D.C.*

There are 1.5 million induced abortions every year. What's to be done with the remains? Bury them in a landfill or donate them to medical research, where organs and tissues may produce some good for others? The answer seems obvious. Or is it?

Science does not advance in a moral vacuum. Time and again it intrudes on the concerns of conscience. Consider: in 1973 a team of Finnish and American scientists decapitated a dozen human fetuses, each aborted live through hysterotomy [caesarean section], and kept the heads alive artificially for study. The ghoulish experiment—partially funded by the National Institutes of Health—was designed to measure fetal metabolism. At about the same time, another research team kept a batch of aborted fetuses alive in saline solution in order to find out if they could absorb oxygen. One fetus survived for nearly a day.

Moral Questions

When word of these experiments reached the public, the outcry was such that NIH halted all federally funded fetal research except that which directly benefited the fetus. [The fetal research ban was lifted by President Clinton in 1993.] But now that the NIH is free to fund research using aborted human tissue for transplantation, the public—no less than politicians, physicians and science researchers—still faces profound moral questions. What limits, if any, should be observed when experimenting with human fetuses? Does a mother who aborts her fetus have the moral right to then donate that fetus to science—or have any say at all about the disposition of the body? Will the opportunity to donate their fetuses to research that might help others influence more women to elect abortion?

Now factor in the profit motive. Why not allow fetuses to be sold, like blood, or imported from poorer countries? Should society allow the stockpiling of spare fetal parts for non-

> *"Science does not advance in a moral vacuum."*

medical purposes, such as replacement therapy for sagging cheeks and aging stomach muscles? Will fetal research lead to a bioengineering industry that, in turn, will require more and more fetuses as raw material for pharmaceutical and other products? Could there—should there—be a futures market in precious fetal organs? Who will police ethics guidelines—and who will punish violators?

No one denies the pertinence of such questions. Difficult in their own right, they also illuminate the confounding ambiguity that still haunts the issue of abortion. It's been 20 years since the U.S. Supreme Court's decision in *Roe v. Wade*. In legalizing abortion, the court ruled that the fetus has no constitutional right to protection by the law. Legally, the fetus is now a nothing. And yet, as public-policy analyst Andrew Kimbrell argues in his book, *The Human Body Shop*, the fetus is clearly a growing *human* organism; a *human* nothing. That is why it is so highly prized as a source for tissue and organ transplantation. And that is also why, Kimbrell believes, the morality of using fetal materials is too important to leave to scientists alone.

Proposed Regulations

Many ethicists who specialize in biomedical issues believe that fetal research and transplantation can, and should, be regulated. Indeed, much of the legislation considered by Congress is based on the recommendations issued by an NIH ethics advisory panel in 1988. In essence, the panel suggested a series of procedural guidelines aimed at erecting a wall of separation between the scientific use of fetal remains and the means—induced abortion—by which they are obtained. In its report, which passed 17-4, the panel insisted that abortion counselors should not even discuss the donation of fetuses to science until *after* clients have decided to undergo an abortion. In other words, pregnant women should not allow the possible scientific benefit to others to influence their decision whether to abort or carry their child. Similarly, physicians should not alter the means or methods of abortion in order to produce better specimens for subsequent experiment. In short, women should not be morally or physically coerced into providing fetal tissue for scientific or therapeutic purposes. Both decisions—to abort and to donate—should be hers alone and made independently of each other.

In addition, once a woman chooses to abort her fetus, the panel urged that she not be permitted to designate the beneficiary of the aborted tissue. This regulation would thus prevent women from conceiving and aborting in order to provide fetal tissue for transplantation for an ailing relative or friend. Further, in keeping with laws in some states, the proposed guidelines would disallow the sale of fetal tissue or organs for transplantation, in an effort to prevent both physicians and women, here or abroad, from seeking abortions for profit. But they would permit payment of reasonable fees to companies and other third parties for the retrieval, preparation and storage of fetal materials. Finally, the panel declared that at all stages everyone involved in fetal research and transplantation should "accord human fetal tissue the same respect accorded other cadaveric human tissues entitled to respect." That's a curious rule that only a committee could love. Cadavers were once human beings and hence worthy of respect. But fetuses, what were they? In life, nothing. In death, deserving a modicum of care.

Far from Agreement

Even though the panel achieved an ethical majority, the testimony they heard made clear that Americans are far from agreement on the morality of fetal-tissue transplantation. In general, representatives of the diabetes and other advocacy associations judged the ethics of using fetal tissue solely by the hoped-for end of finding cures. They make a powerful case: extract

> *"Americans are far from agreement on the morality of fetal-tissue transplantation."*

some good from tragedy by easing those who are suffering. The medical researchers themselves, while welcoming procedural guidelines, bristled at the notion that their intentions could be regarded as anything other than altruistic. Just as predictably, pro-life spokespersons maintained that intentionally aborted fetuses should not be "harvested" for medical research.

The majority of the panelists concluded that, regardless of how one judges the morality of abortion, researchers in fetal transplantation "could be ethically isolated" from physicians who do abortions. But in a vigorous minority report, moral theologian James T. Burtchaell of Notre Dame University and James Bopp Jr., an attorney for the National Right to Life Committee, challenged this conclusion. On the contrary, they argued, both procedures are so intertwined—materially, financially and technologically—that "a symbiotic relationship between the abortion industry and fetal-tissue transplantation therapy" cannot be avoided. Further, they wrote, everyone involved in an elective abortion—especially the mother—is morally disqualified from deciding how the fetal remains should be disposed of, "as the man who has killed his wife is morally disqualified from acting as her executor." In this respect, they insisted, the donation of aborted fetal tissue is ethically different from the choice facing the guardian of an accident victim whose organs are suitable for transplant.

There are some pro-choice feminists, too, who nonetheless worry about the implications of fetal research. In the worst-case scenarios, they see the specter of dehumanized women, whose bodies have become fetal factories. "The role of women in fetal-tissue research is, after all, to provide the raw material," says Janice Raymond, a professor of Women's Studies and Medical Ethics at the University of Massachusetts. "One primary effect of fetal-tissue research and transplants," Raymond writes in *On the Issues*, a liberal women's quarterly, "has been to turn women into fetal-tissue containers; mere material environments for the fetus."

Enforcement Problems

Even with the adoption of the panel's guidelines, Raymond and other critics doubt that they can be enforced or properly policed. Though long on ethical procedures, the panel had no advice on corresponding penalties. Just as physicians could and did do abortions when they were illegal, so could they privately arrange to have fetal tissue supplied to relatives of the donor. Laws proposed by Congress, however, criminalize the sale of fetal tissue across state lines; state laws will have to do the rest. But the NIH itself has no power to police free-standing abortion clinics in order to ensure that counselors do not advocate abortions for the sake of science, or use abortion methods that are medically riskier for women in order to obtain better fetal specimens.

Yet without some sort of ethical standards, fetal-tissue transplantation threatens to become an unsupervised private industry. In many ways it already is. Kimbrell charges that at least a half dozen companies supply fetal tissues to clients and estimates annual sales of several million dollars. "A fetal-tissue transplant industry," warns economist Emanuel Throne, coauthor of a report for Congress's Office of Technology Assessment, "could dwarf the present organ-transplant industry."

Worse, argues Kimbrell, there currently are few legal barriers to prevent private firms and hospitals from using fetal transplantation for cosmetic and other nonmedical purposes. For example, he cites researchers in Canada who have found that injections from fetal tissue accelerate the healing of muscles in animals. What works for animals could help humans as well. The next step, he suggests, could be the use of fetal injections to enhance—like steroids—the ability of athletes, thus raising the specter of Olympic competitors running on "baby power."

> *"A fetal tissue transplant industry . . . could dwarf the present organ-transplant industry."*

Although such scenarios may seem farfetched, even ethicists who support fetal-tissue research warn that the research and medical communities need to take action to keep emerging biotechnologies in check. Unlike drugs or medical devices, which are regulated by the Food and Drug Administration, fetal-tissue transplantation is a surgical procedure that can be regulated only by each hospital's research ethics committees. "These committees have institutional loyalties and a heavy medical membership," observes Arthur Caplan of the Center for Biomedical Ethics at the University of Minnesota, "and may not always be able to give independent assessments." Bioethicist LeRoy Walters of Georgetown University thinks the only practical solution is for the federal government to fund a fetal-tissue bank to keep "research and transplantation carefully insulated against commercialization."

Clearly, society should foster research to alleviate human suffering. Just as clearly, it must also protect itself against the callous use of human material, even in its early stages of development. Even though human fetuses have been thrust into a legal limbo, they still elicit feelings of protection and respect. The question society still has not resolved is: how much?

Fetal Tissue Research Will Benefit Medical Science

by Sharon Begley, Mary Hager, Daniel Glick, and Jennifer Foote

About the authors: *Sharon Begley is a senior writer with* Newsweek *magazine who writes on medical and social issues. Mary Hager and Daniel Glick are correspondents for* Newsweek *in Washington, D.C., and Jennifer Foote is* Newsweek*'s reporter in London.*

The abortion took only seven minutes, punctuated by the tinkle of stainless-steel instruments, then the gurgle of the suction as it carried the embryo and placenta down a tube snaking through a hole in the wall. On the other side a nurse carrying a small plastic dish collected the remains of the six-week embryo, all two ounces' worth. But this one wasn't going to the incinerator. A technician raced the tissue to a sterile table, whittled out a few grams of neural cells and put them on ice. Other scientists performed rapid-fire tests: No genetic defects. No AIDS. No bacterial contamination. Six hours later the tissue was rushed upstairs to the hospital operating theater, where surgeons drilled a hole the size of a thimble into the skull of a Parkinson's patient. The surgeon pulled the fetal cells into a tiny needle and, using an MRI scan to pinpoint the area crippled by the incurable disease, shot them into the brain of the awake and alert patient.

What happened in that hospital? A life was ended and a life was saved. Or, an unborn child was killed, and a desperate, dying man underwent an experimental operation unlikely to help him.

Freeing Science

It is the Rashomon of science. There are as many ways to describe the use of tissues from aborted fetuses as there are individual values through which the practice is refracted. On his third day in office, President Bill Clinton rescinded the Reagan-era ban on spending federal funds for the transplantation of tissue from aborted fetuses into humans. His goal, Clinton said, was to "free science and medicine from the grasp of [abortion] politics." Maybe he succeeded: the right-to-life movement didn't offer any irate denunciations. But scientists, long frustrated at being held hostage to political debate, were ecstatic. "For years this field has practically stood still," says Dr. Gary Hodgen, a fetal researcher at East-ern Virginia Medical College who left the National Institutes of Health (NIH) because of government restrictions on research. "It's the greatest day for science since the Scopes monkey trial," [a 1925 trial that ultimately affirmed the teaching of evolution in the classroom, although teacher John Scopes was convicted in this Tennessee trial for teaching it].

"There are as many ways to describe the use of tissues from aborted fetuses as there are individual values through which the practice is refracted."

Scopes, of course, was convicted. Rather than ending the debate, Clinton may have only brought it to a boil. In early February 1993 Congress held hearings addressing the regulation of fetal-tissue research. The questions did not lend themselves to sound bites. May a child be conceived with the express purpose of aborting it in order to donate its cells to an ailing relative? Should a woman weighing an abortion be told that her fetus might save another child? Can doctors change their abortion procedures in order to get more usable fetal tissue?

Donna Shalala, secretary of health and human services, promised Congress quick regulations on all these issues. She said HHS would make sure that the new frontier of fetal research and therapy did not become an excuse to encourage more abortions or cheapen fetal life. But HHS was playing catch-up. The ban, which President Reagan decreed in 1988 as part of his anti-abortion policies, affected only the use of federal money for the transplantation of tissues obtained by elective abortion, of which there were 1.6 million in 1992. Fetuses aborted spontaneously, or from ectopic pregnancies (in which the fetus grows in a fallopian tube rather than the uterus and can kill the mother), were fair game. So was pure research, using fetal tissue to study fundamental scientific puzzles. Thanks to such exceptions, a handful of researchers have been performing both clinical and basic experiments throughout the ban. Using private money for transplants and close to $45 million from NIH for scientific work, they have been trying to treat Parkinson's disease and diabetes, fathom the mystery of how embryonic cells decide whether to turn into heart or skin, and untangle the secrets of the nascent brain. The removal of the stigma that the ban caused means fetal-tissue research will multiply. And the prospect of more experiments has only sharpened the ethics debate over this brave new field.

"Plastic" Tissue

In theory, fetal cells are perfect for a host of scientific and medical uses. The cells grow quickly and divide rapidly, and so are more likely to insinuate themselves into a patient's existing tissue. They lack the surface markers that a recipient's immune system recognizes as foreign, and so are unlikely to be rejected. Perhaps most important, they are "plastic": a very young fetal cell has the potential to be a kidney, a liver cell or just about anything else. Studying the genetic switches that determine the road not taken can yield insights into why some fetuses do not develop properly. And under the right circumstances (which researchers haven't figured out yet), science might one day grow a full, functioning kidney from a few fetal kidney cells.

In 1928, surgeons in Italy became the first to exploit these properties. They transplanted pancreatic tissue from three fetuses into a patient with diabetes. The patient did not get better. In 1939, physicians in the United States tried the operation, twice, also without success. In 1959 another American researcher tried to cure a leukemia patient with transplanted fetal cells; there was no lasting improvement. Scientists had better luck with vaccines: immunizations for polio, rubella and Rh disease were all developed using fetal kidney and other cells. The first glimpse of success with transplants came in 1968, when fetal liver cells were grafted into patients suffering DiGeorge syndrome, a rare and usually fatal genetic disorder marked by multiple abnormalities of glands and organs, including the heart. DiGeorge's, which strikes 1 in 10,000 newborns, became the only condition for which fetal-tissue transplants were accepted treatment.

> *"The removal of the stigma that the ban caused means fetal-tissue research will multiply."*

Today the most tantalizing target for fetal-tissue therapy is Parkinson's disease. More than 500,000 Americans suffer from this disorder, in which the motor-control area of the brain does not receive a steady supply of the neurotransmitter dopamine from a region of the brain stem that the disease somehow has wiped out. Patients cannot control their movements; they suffer tremors, rigidity and eventually paralysis. Drugs that stimulate brain cells to produce dopamine have horrible side effects, including psychosis, and become less and less effective over time. So researchers, after years of animal experiments, hit on the idea of implanting into the brains of Parkinson's patients a permanent source of dopamine. That source was neural cells from fetuses.

From the Ambiguous to the Miraculous

In 1988, Dr. Curt Freed of the University of Colorado Health Sciences Center performed America's first fetal-cell transplant into a Parkinson's patient. Don Nelson, 52, was so far gone he could barely walk. Today he has returned to his beloved woodworking and is taking less medication—mainly the dopamine-boosting drug, L-dopa—than before the transplant.

Other cases range from the ambiguous to the miraculous. Freed has reported on 6 more patients: none is completely cured, but they're all taking less medication and one, who could neither speak nor drive, now does both. At the Yale

School of Medicine, Dr. Eugene Redmond has done 13 similar operations; in the first group, 3 of the 4 patients improved somewhat. A Swedish team led by Anders Bjorklund and Olle Lindvall of the University of Lund, who in 1987 first reported that fetal cells remain alive and pump out dopamine in the recipient's brain, announced in December 1992 that brain-stem tissue from 6- to 8-week-old fetuses blossoms into fully functioning cells that substitute for the missing dopamine cells. "It brings patients back [to where they were] five to seven years" earlier, says Bjorklund.

For all the promise, though, the verdict is still out on the success of fetal transplants for Parkinson's. In a sort of "why throw good cells after bad" logic, opponents of fetal transplants claim that the less than clear-cut results argue against more widespread testing of the procedure. But as Bjorklund points out, "What is needed [to determine the efficacy of the surgery] is very controlled clinical trials in a well-designed scientific framework. This is what is vitally important about the lifting of the moratorium in the U.S."

Renewed Hope

Clinton's action has also renewed hope among other patients whose otherwise incurable diseases might one day be treated with fetal transplants. Among them:

• *Juvenile-onset diabetes.* There are 14 million diabetics in the United States; this year 200,000 will die from complications of the disease, in which the pancreas does not produce the vital hormone insulin. Since 1987 a University of Colorado team led by immunologist Kevin Lafferty has transplanted fetal pancreatic tissue into 16 diabetics. In all of them, the tissue insinuated itself into the patient's tissues, differentiated into the islet cells that churn out insulin and survived. None of the patients has been able to stop insulin shots completely, but all require less than before. Some 38 diabetics in the United States and 600 worldwide have received fetal transplants, says bioethicist Arthur Caplan of the University of Minnesota. The results have been good enough that Clinton's lifting of the ban will likely lead researchers who avoided the experiments back into the field. "The government's put its stamp of approval on this research, and you'd be surprised what that means," says Sara King, research director of the Juvenile Diabetes Foundation.

> *"Science might one day grow a full, functioning kidney from a few fetal kidney cells."*

• *Huntington's disease.* Like Parkinson's, it destroys a specific part of the brain; it culminates in dementia and death. Medicine has no treatment to offer the 25,000 U.S. victims. But in one promising approach, Paul Sanberg of the University of South Florida implants tissue from the brains of fetal rats into rats with symptoms mimicking Huntington's; the results are good enough to consider human experiments.

Other neurological disorders are also candidates for fetal grafts. In Alzheimer's disease, for instance, the nerve cells in the brain begin churning out the neural equivalent of arterial plaque: the substance cripples neurons' ability to communicate, eventually killing nerve cells outright and robbing patients of their memories, their abilities, their very lives. Alzheimer's will be a challenge for transplant surgeons, however, because neuronal death is so widespread it's hard to see where cells could be im- planted. It's more obvious that trans- plants might one day repair spinal- cord damage, which 180,000 Ameri- cans suffer from every year: neural cells grafted into animals make the damaged neural fibers grow back.

> *"Immunizations for polio, rubella and Rh disease were all developed using fetal kidney and other cells."*

Neural transplants might also cure victims of myelin diseases, such as ALD, made famous by the film *Lorenzo's Oil*. Lorenzo's father, Augusto Odone, has set up a foundation to research myelin diseases; he says the first transplants of human fetal cells into an ALD victim may be carried out [soon]. . . .

Converting Abortion Foes

• *Hurler's syndrome.* The Rev. Guy Walden and his wife, Terri, vocal abor- tion foes, had lost one son and were losing their second child, a daughter, to this inherited enzymatic disorder, which strikes 50 to 80 babies a year and causes massively overgrown organs, deformities, blindness and death. When the fetus Terri was carrying was diagnosed with Hurler's, they refused to con- sider an abortion. They agreed instead to the first fetus-to-fetus transplant. In May 1990, Dr. R. Nathan Slotnick, then at the University of California, Davis, took liver cells from a 13-week-old fetus in an ectopic pregnancy and injected them into the abdomen of the Waldens' 15-week-old fetus. Liver cells have many more talents than might be apparent to anyone who knows this organ only as the brownish thing under a pile of bacon: liver cells are the body's plenipo- tentiaries, able to give rise to the cells of the immune and blood systems. The liver cells migrated to the bone marrow, and six months after the little boy was born they were producing the missing enzyme. "If we could offer parents [preg- nant with incurably ill children] some hope," says Walden, a Baptist minister, "we felt we could materially decrease abortion [of these fetuses]."

There are at least 155 other genetic disorders, including sickle cell anemia, thalassemia, metabolic disorders and immune deficiencies, that could be cor- rected before birth with fetal tissue. "The potential is quite fabulous," says Dr. Michael Harrison of UC, San Francisco. "Fetuses have a whole variety of prob- lems that can be cured for their lifetime with in utero transplants."

• *Female sterility.* The ovaries of a 2-month-old fetus contain a few million eggs. Dr. Roger Gosden of the University of Edinburgh has shown, in animal tests, that the transplanted fetal ovary goes through normal estrus cycles and confers "full fertility" on a sterilized animal. If such a transplant can give a woman born without ovaries a chance to conceive, the abortion of one fetus could give life to a whole family of babies. None, of course, would bear the genes of the woman who bore them .

Basic Research

Although using fetal tissue to treat disease is the splashiest application, the cells are also being used for more basic research. And for a lot of it: for three decades a program at the University of Washington has collected more than 10,000 fetuses through private clinics and distributed them to some 60 research labs nationwide. Reagan's ban did not affect these scientific experiments, but they, too, have nevertheless been engulfed by abortion politics. Some scientists contacted by *Newsweek* did not want to discuss their work for a story that also described previously banned fetal-tissue work, for fear of being targeted by anti-abortion protesters.

A pioneer in fetal transplants for basic science is J. Michael McCune, research director of a Palo Alto company called Systemix. In 1990 he transplanted tiny pieces of thymus, liver and lymph from human fetuses into mice born with no immune system. Within two months the transplants had grown to the size of a peanut and were producing human immune cells. Now the mouse has become a unique animal model for AIDS (the AIDS virus does not infect nonhuman tissue) and is used to screen possible AIDS treatments. [In 1992] the mouse also helped Systemix isolate the crucial precursor cell that differentiates into all the varied cells of the human blood system. That may help scientists understand how the blood and immune systems develop, and how they go awry.

> *"Transplants might one day repair spinal-cord damage, which 180,000 Americans suffer from every year."*

The brain, too, begins life with cells that aren't sure what they want to be when they grow up. In the intricate choreography that is an embryo's development, there is no more complex, or baffling, dance than the one that turns a few wisps of neurons into a brain that can see, think, love and ponder its own existence. The only way to find out how this happens is by studying embryonic neural cells before they have cast their lot with, say, the motor-control center or the visual cortex. At the Massachusetts Institute of Technology, Ron McKay has found a gene that keeps neural cells from differentiating: as long as the gene is working, the cells retain their limitless potential. He's interested in finding "what all these genes do in the brain." If he can understand how a neural cell in a fetus finds its destiny, "it will provide a deeper understanding of the biochemistry that underlies diseases" such as schizophrenia.

Cells of the brain differ from those of the skin in not being able to repair themselves. That's why strokes are forever, but scraped knees aren't. At UC, San Diego, Fred Gage is studying fetal neural cells to understand how they mature into discrete types and, even more wondrous, migrate to precisely the right spot in the brain where all the other language neurons, for instance, are gathering. By growing fetal cells to identify what makes them differentiate and migrate, Gage and others have identified brain chemicals that affect neural survival and growth. "It's a revolution," he says. "Now molecules are available to attempt real brain repair and surgery." That's been tried in animals; people may get their turn in a few years.

Science has a way of defusing incendiary issues through breakthroughs that make the controversial anachronistic. In 1991 it looked as if endangered Pacific yew trees would have to be harvested in order to extract a compound, Taxol, that shows promise against ovarian and breast cancer. But now there's another source of Taxol. A similar fate may await fetal-tissue research. "If we can use cells [grown in the lab] to accomplish the same goals," says bioethicist Dorothy Vawter of the University of Minnesota, fetal tissue may turn out to be just a "temporary solution." In fact, at least two researchers are perfecting ways to grow dozens of cell types for unlimited generations. If they succeed, it will be no more necessary to obtain fast-growing, rejection-resistant tissue from fetuses than it is to get sponges from the ocean. And the value of fetal-tissue research and therapy can finally be assessed on its merits, free at last from the distorting cloud of abortion politics.

Research Using Aborted Fetuses Is Morally Justified

by Bonnie Steinbock

About the author: *Bonnie Steinbock is professor of philosophy at the State University of New York, Albany. She has written extensively on the subjects of medical ethics, euthanasia, and abortion; her books include* Killing and Letting Die *and* Life Before Birth: The Moral and Legal Status of Embryos and Fetuses, *from which this viewpoint is excerpted.*

There is on the part of many people a gut reaction against experimentation using living fetuses, stemming from the assumption, perhaps unconscious, that such experimentation inflicts suffering on a tiny, innocent, living human being. It is bad enough, they may feel, that the fetus must be aborted and not permitted to live. To experiment on live abortuses goes too far, regardless of the scientific and medical value that may be thereby obtained.

This objection has validity only on the assumption that the aborted fetuses used in these experiments can feel pain. Some experts have objected that no one knows whether a fetus feels pain. John P. Wilson, a lawyer who submitted a report to the National Commission [established under the Department of Health in 1974 to look into fetal tissue research], noted that fetuses react to stimuli at a gestational age of only a few weeks.

> This may be a reflex action not indicative of pain, but there is no clear evidence proving the validity of this assumption, nor is it apparent that conclusive evidence can be obtained in the near future. As many capacities which serve no functional purpose until after viability and birth are acquired and develop during the previable stage, there is no reason to believe that the ability to experience pain does not also begin to develop early in gestation.

However, there is good reason to think that the ability to experience pain does not develop until well into the second trimester. Pain perception requires more than brain waves. It involves the development of neural pathways and particular cortical and subcortical centers, as well as neurochemical systems associated with pain transmission. In light of this, it seems extremely unlikely that a first-trimester fetus could be sentient. Surely, more than a remote possibility of sentience at this stage of fetal development is required to justify banning research that could save lives and prevent a good deal of suffering.

It is ironic that even the barest possibility that a procedure might cause pain to a fetus is considered sufficient reason to prohibit it, when millions of clearly sentient animals are routinely subjected to experiments that cause them considerable suffering. For example, in order to determine whether fetal-tissue transplants could alleviate the symptoms of Parkinson's disease, the disease was experimentally induced in monkeys. (Inducing the disease was necessary because Parkinson's disease does not exist in animals.) A major motivation for funding such research is the devastating impact of Parkinson's disease on its sufferers. Yet no one expressed any moral reservations about subjecting healthy monkeys to severe impairment from profound parkinsonism for several months and then killing them. My point is not that such research cannot be justified—I think that it can, based on the special moral status of rational agents. But even if the important interests of rational beings ultimately outweigh the equally important interests of nonrational sentient beings, that does not justify ignoring the interests of animals. In particular, it is puzzling to me why so little attention should be paid to the interests of sentient animals, who can suffer, and so much concern expressed on behalf of beings, who, we have good reason to believe, cannot experience harm or suffering at all.

Fetuses As Human Subjects

Theorists who agree on the moral status of fetuses may nevertheless disagree about the permissibility of using fetuses in research. For example, Paul Ramsey and Richard McCormick both consider fetuses to have the same moral status as children, and so to be entitled to the same protections. However, Ramsey opposes *all* nontherapeutic research [research not benefiting the subject] on children, on the grounds that children are incapable of giving the consent necessary to justify experimental procedures. Similarly, he opposes nontherapeutic research on fetuses. Experimenting on a dying, aborted fetus would be comparable to experimenting on a dying child. Ramsey views fetuses as vulnerable, helpless, and nonconsenting human subjects, precisely those whom regulations on experimentation are intended to protect.

> *"There is good reason to think that the ability to experience pain does not develop until well into the second trimester."*

By contrast, Richard McCormick argues that parents may give proxy consent for a child to participate in nontherapeutic experimentation where there is no discernible risk or undue discomfort. Proxy consent is morally legitimate insofar as it is a reasonable construction of what the child ought to choose. This position is rooted in the premise that all humans have an obligation to contribute to the benefit of the human community. Applying this analysis to the fetus, McCormick concludes that research on the living fetus is justified, so long as it poses no discernible risk or discomfort, appropriate consent from the parents is obtained, and the experiments are genuinely necessary for medical knowledge calculated to be of notable benefit to fetuses or children in general

At the other extreme is the view taken by the ethicist and theologian Joseph Fletcher. In his report to the National Commission, Fletcher says, "The core question at stake in the ethics of fetal research is whether a fetus is a person." Answering that question negatively, Fletcher concludes:

> Only the pregnant patient is a "human subject" to be protected in clinical experimental and research; the fetus is an object, not a subject—a nonpersonal organism.

> A fetus is "precious" or "has value" when its potentiality is wanted. This means when it is wanted by the progenitors, not by somebody else.

The interest view differs from Fletcher's position in two respects. First, on the interest view, an entity need not be a person to have moral status. All that is required is that it have interests [according to the author's theory (based on Joel Feinberg's "interest principle") that only sentient beings with an interest in what is being done to them—for example, an interest in avoiding pain—can have a moral claim on the concerns and actions of others]. Sentient fetuses should not be exposed to painful experiments, regardless of whether they are considered to be persons. It is not their personhood, but their capacity to suffer, that provides us with reasons for protecting them. The core issue is thus not whether the fetus is a person, but whether the fetus has moral status.

"Surely, more than a remote possibility of sentience at this stage of fetal development is required to justify banning research that could save lives."

Second, the interest view acknowledges that entities can have moral value or worth even if they lack interests and thus do not have moral status. Fletcher's treatment of the fetus as object implies that there would be nothing wrong with selling preserved fetuses as lucky charms, or turning aborted fetuses into lipsticks. This would be not only profoundly offensive to most people, but also morally objectionable. A human fetus, even a preconscious one, is a potential person and a powerful symbol of humanity, and, as such, should be treated with respect.

The Equality Principle

The National Commission maintained that all fetuses should be protected from potentially harmful research, regardless of whether they were going to be aborted or going to be born: ". . . the same principles apply whether or not abortion is contemplated; in both cases, only minimal risk is acceptable."

Most of the Commissioners interpreted the principle of equality to mean that no procedures should be applied to a fetus-to-be-aborted that would not be applied to a fetus-going-to-term. On the interest view, such a position is indefensible. The reason for banning potentially harmful nontherapeutic research on fetuses-going-to-term is not to protect the fetus per se, but rather to protect the future child. If there will be no future child, then there is literally no one who can be harmed and no one to be protected. The woman's decision for or against abortion is thus crucial to the justification of experimental procedures on the fetus *in utero*, because her decision determines whether there will be a being with interests, who can be harmed.

> *"It is puzzling to me why so little attention should be paid to the interests of sentient animals . . . and so much . . . [paid to non-sentient fetuses]."*

Some members of the Commission felt that there was a way to acknowledge both the difference between fetuses-going-to-term and fetuses-to-be-aborted, *and* the principle of equality. They agreed with their fellow members that all fetuses, whether or not they were going to be aborted, had equal moral status, and were entitled to equal moral concern. However, they argued that what is likely to *harm* a fetus depends on whether or not it will be aborted. "For example, the injection of a drug which crosses the placenta may not injure the fetus which is aborted within two weeks of injection, where it might injure the fetus two months after injection." After noting this disagreement, the Commission summarized its views by saying that its members were in "basic agreement" as to the validity of the equality principle, although they disagreed as to its "application." It recommended review at the national level to resolve such disagreements of application.

A Disingenuous Distinction

This attempt at reaching consensus obscured a real moral disagreement among the Commissioners. It is disingenuous to proclaim that all fetuses deserve equal moral concern while at the same time maintaining that some fetuses cannot be harmed. Beings who cannot be harmed cannot have claims to our moral attention and concern. It would have been more honest for those Commissioners who agree that early-gestation fetuses cannot be harmed to have rejected the principle of equality, maintaining that it is permissible to use fetuses who are going to be aborted in ways that would be impermissible if the fetus is going to be born. The difference between the Commissioners on this issue was a substantive moral one, and not simply a matter of "application."

I must stress that the rejection of the equality principle does not imply that there are *no* reasons for restricting research on fetuses-to-be-aborted, only that these reasons do not refer to the interests of the fetus. Some restrictions might protect the interests of pregnant women. For example, in the rubella-vaccine tests, women who requested abortion were asked to accept vaccination and to postpone abortion for *three to four weeks!* Since any delay in having an abortion is likely to increase the medical risks to the woman, as well as create psychological stress, this strikes me as an outrageous request. Certainly, current guidelines prohibit any research that exposes pregnant women to such risks.

Other reasons for restricting scientific research on living, preconscious fetuses may refer to our own sensibilities. Experiments most likely to offend public sensibilities are not those performed on the fetus *in utero* in anticipation of abortion. Rather, they are experiments performed on the living fetus *ex utero*.

Research on Living Fetuses Ex Utero

Consider the following experiments:

> Using movie films, the reflexes of previable fetuses outside of the uterus have been documented along with the response of the fetus to touch. These studies have shown a response to touch in a 7-week fetus, swallowing movements in a 12-week fetus, and crying expressions at 23 weeks; the fetuses were studied after hysterotomy [cesarean section] while they were immersed in a salt solution.

> To learn whether the human fetal brain could metabolize ketone bodies [normal byproducts of lipid metabolism, or breakdown], brain metabolism was isolated in eight human fetuses (12 to 17 weeks gestation) after hysterotomy abortion [cesarean section] by perfusing [forcing liquid through the arteries of] the isolated head (the head was separated from the rest of the body). The study demonstrated that, similar to other species, brain metabolism could be supported by ketone bodies during fetal life, suggesting avenues of therapy in some fetal disease states.

> In a 1963 study done in the United States, scientists immersed fifteen fetuses in salt solution to learn if they could absorb oxygen through their skin. One fetus survived for twenty-two hours. The knowledge gained by the experiment contributed to the design of artificial life-support systems for premature infants.

Experiments like these provoked public concern and outrage, and led to a moratorium on all research with living fetuses. Are such experiments morally objectionable, and if so, on what grounds?

As we have seen, ethicists differ on whether *any* nontherapeutic research on nonconsenting subjects is permissible. However, if it is permissible to

> *"Current federal regulations impose a* **more** *restrictive risk standard on research using . . . fetuses than on research using children."*

use *children* in nontherapeutic research that poses minimal risk to them, it should be equally justifiable to use viable fetuses *ex utero* in such research. Oddly enough, current federal regulations impose a *more* restrictive risk standard on research using embryos and fetuses than on research using children. The reason for this is probably general opposition to abortion and therefore opposition to any research that makes use of aborted fetuses. However, for those who are not opposed to fetal research in principle, there are three possible grounds for objecting to research on living fetuses after abortion: viability, sentience, and the potential for brutalization.

Reasons for Limiting Research

Viability is important because the viable fetus *ex utero* has the same legal standing as any other premature infant, and is entitled to the same protection. As Alexander Capron explains, "The viable fetus *ex utero* is a person in the eyes of the law, and its interest in life and well-being are clearly recognized by the civil and criminal law. In fact, even *nonviable* living fetuses have the same status in law as full-term live-born infants. Separation from the mother and the existence of some signs of life are, Capron says, "the customary indicia of birth, and hence of the creation of a new human being with full claim on society's concern and protection through the laws." Nevertheless, viability makes a difference in the treatment of abortuses. For example, it is reasonable both to require that life-sustaining measures be used on viable fetuses who survive abortion (whereas this would be pointless in the case of fetuses who cannot survive) and to prohibit research that interferes with a viable fetus's chance of survival.

"There is virtually no chance that fetuses become sentient before the end of the first trimester."

The limit of fetal viability at present and for the foreseeable future remains at 23 to 24 weeks. However, fetal viability cannot be determined directly, but only estimated, based on measurement of head size using ultrasound. In the best hands, this technique is accurate within ±1 week at 20 to 26 weeks. [According to the National Commission,] "Relating gestational age to fetal weight, and taking into account the range of error and normal variation, an estimated gestational age of 22 weeks or less by ultrasound would virtually eliminate the possibility of fetal weight above 600 grams and actual gestational age greater than 24 weeks." To avoid the risk of using a possibly viable fetus in research involving more than minimal risk, the National Commission recommended that, should research during abortion be approved by national review, the estimated gestational age [g.a.] should be below 20 weeks.

An earlier cutoff for using living fetuses after abortion in research might be defended on grounds of sentience. It is possible, though unlikely, that a fetus of 20 weeks g.a. is sentient; but there is virtually no chance that fetuses become sentient before the end of the first trimester. Thus, a first-trimester cutoff on all but the most innocuous research on living fetuses *ex utero* would provide adequate protection against the possibility of inflicting pain on a sentient fetus.

Another reason for limiting research on living abortuses to the first trimester has nothing to do with the interests of the fetus, but rather with public sensibilities. By 12 to 14 weeks of gestation, a fetus *looks* human. It evokes in most people the same instinctive responses of protection that newborn babies do. It is thus not surprising that many people should be deeply distressed to learn of experiments involving the decapitation or immersion in salt solution of living second-trimester fetuses. In addition, performing such experiments is likely to take a toll on researchers, who may have to suppress their own protective responses to carry out the research. Given the social and evolutionary value of these responses, suppressing them seems a dangerous path. Such considerations argue for a ban on research using living fetuses *ex utero*. However, symbolic concerns or a speculative risk of brutalization should not be allowed to ban research using nonviable and nonsentient fetuses, if such research is likely to have important scientific and medical benefits. While societal feelings of protectiveness toward fetuses should not be ignored, neither should they be emphasized at the expense of the interests of actual interested persons. A reasonable compromise would be to require that invasive research on living fetuses have the potential for significant human benefit, and to limit such research to the first trimester.

Fetal Tissue Research Will Not Increase Abortions

by Glenn C. Graber

About the author: Glenn C. Graber is a professor of philosophy and the director of the Center for Applied and Professional Ethics at the University of Tennessee, Knoxville.

Medical research using human fetal tissue offers considerable promise. Fetal liver, thymus, pancreatic and neural tissues have been transplanted in an attempt to combat Parkinson's, diabetes and twenty or so other diseases. Initial results of these experiments are encouraging, but far from definitive. Human fetal tissue is especially suited for such transplants because it grows rapidly and adapts readily (as it would have done in the womb). Also, the fetal immune system is relatively undeveloped, so fetal tissue is less likely than mature tissue to trigger an immunological response in the recipient that leads to rejection. Transplantation is not the only promising avenue of research. Cell lines derived from fetal tissue are valuable in the laboratory for studying species-specific viruses such as cytomegalovirus and human immunodeficiency virus-type 1 (HIV-1).

A Tainted Association

In any other circumstances, research directions as hopeful as these would be endorsed enthusiastically by the scientific community, politicians, medical ethicists and other policy analysts, as well as by the media and the general public. However, the issue of fetal tissue research is tainted by its association with abortion.

In 1988, the Reagan administration imposed a moratorium on federal funding of fetal tissue research. Despite proposals by several distinguished advisory groups that the complete ban be removed, the Bush administration maintained it until May 1992, when President Bush relaxed it just far enough to permit research on tissue from spontaneous abortions or miscarriages. Both houses of

Glenn C. Graber, "Should Fetal Tissue from Induced Abortions Be Used for Medical Research?" *Priorities*, Summer 1992. Reprinted by permission of the American Council for Science and Health.

Congress passed legislation that would reverse the ban (with some safeguards), but President Bush vetoed the bill. Furthermore, twenty-five states have passed laws either restricting fetal tissue research or prohibiting it altogether. [The federal ban was lifted by President Clinton in 1993.]

Inconsistent Guidelines

A total prohibition is blatantly indefensible. Surely there can be no serious objection in the case of a spontaneous abortion or miscarriage to allowing the parents to donate fetal tissue for either experimental transplantation or basic research. The family of a person who has died without expressing personal wishes about organ or tissue donation is permitted by law and accepted ethical standards to make such a decision, so why shouldn't the same guidelines apply to the fetus who dies spontaneously?

> *"Is it not paradoxical that abortion based on a financial judgment is permitted, but abortion motivated by an altruistic interest in promoting medical research would not be?"*

If sufficient and appropriate tissues could be obtained from spontaneous abortions, perhaps the controversy could be stilled. Unfortunately, however, there are problems with both the amount and kind of tissues obtained in this way. The principal causes of spontaneous abortion are diseases or genetic anomalies that render the fetal tissues less than ideal as a transplant or research material. Furthermore, the ideal stage of development of tissues for transplantation is further along in gestation than miscarriages typically occur. Another problem is that the quantity of tissue obtainable from spontaneous abortions may well be insufficient to meet the demand for research purposes, not to mention for therapeutic transplantation if and when this is proven to be effective in treating Parkinson's, diabetes and other diseases.

An Ironic Argument

The concern of fetal tissue research opponents is that the option of tissue donation might serve as an enticement for elective abortions. The first thing to note about this argument is that it is ironic, to say the least, that a woman is legally permitted to have an abortion for any reason whatsoever *except* the possibly altruistic motive of providing for medical research that will benefit humankind. I am quite sure, for example, that there have been cases in which a prospective mother had an abortion because she judged that she could not afford to continue the pregnancy, much less care for the child. There may not be documentation of such a case—but that is only because no justification needs to be given by a woman seeking an early abortion. The *Roe v. Wade* decision ruled that a woman's right to privacy gives her the right to an abortion without having to explain or justify herself. Is it not paradoxical that abortion based on a financial judgment is permitted, but abortion motivated by an altruistic interest in promoting medical research would not be?

The claim that the option to donate fetal tissue for research would persuade some women who are ambivalent about the matter to have an abortion has some interesting implications. First, it needs to be empirically tested before it can serve as the basis for serious argument. How many women would be persuaded by such an option who would not have the abortion for other reasons? I suspect that, rather than talking about a significant increase in the abortion rate, we are more likely to be talking about a shift in the pattern of reasoning and motivation by people who are already strongly inclined towards abortion. And, if we look at the issue of motivation from the perspective of moral development or evaluation of character traits, it might be maintained that this shift is a positive thing. Surely, it is better to do the same act from the motive of altruism than from self-interest or financial incentive; and if we have prompted women who are contemplating abortion to think the matter through from an altruistic perspective, we have improved the quality of their decision from an ethical perspective.

If there is concern that financial considerations will enter the arena of fetal tissue therapy, we can enact safeguards against that. Just as U.S. law does not permit the sale of organs, we could prohibit the sale of fetal tissues. If a woman is to provide tissues from an aborted fetus, we could mandate that it be a donation rather than a sale.

> *"If there is concern that financial considerations will enter the arena of fetal tissue therapy, we can enact safeguards against that."*

The most compelling ethical principle that applies to our situation is a principle of respectful treatment. But a mandate for respectful treatment of the fetus says more about the kind of research that would be permitted and the manner in which it is to be conducted than the issue of allowing it at all. It would be disrespectful to make use of fetal tissue for frivolous research or to use callous harvesting techniques or handling procedures in the laboratory. However, sensitively conducted research on human diseases would be respectful, just as similar research is which employs cadaver tissues, tissues removed in surgery or excess tissues from biopsies and other diagnostic tests.

Research *Is* Therapeutic

Some state laws permit use of at least some fetal tissues for "therapeutic" research but ban "non-therapeutic" experimentation. The problem here is that the distinction between therapeutic and non-therapeutic fetal tissue research is very fuzzy. Transplant of fetal pancreatic cells into the pancreas of a diabetic is clearly intended to have a directly therapeutic result. However, laboratory research using fetal brain cells to study cytomegalovirus has a longterm therapeutic goal. The only use that has been proposed for fetal tissues is research on human diseases and their therapies, and all of this is therapeutic in overall intent.

In short, the use of fetal tissues for medical research ought to follow the same guidelines as the donation of cadaver organs and tissues. Since the fetus cannot speak for itself, the next of kin should be called upon to make the decisions.

It is unjustified to infect the discussion about the use of fetal tissues in medical research with the polarized and strident debate about abortion. In any situation in which we consider that abortion is justified, it will be justified for the mother to allow the tissues to be used for medical research.

Women Support Fetal Tissue Research

by Fionn Anderson, Anna Glasier, Jonathan Ross, and David T. Baird

About the authors: *Fionn Anderson is a registrar at the Dean Terrace Centre's Family Planning Clinic in Edinburgh, Scotland. Anna Glasier is a consultant gynecologist who lectures at the University of Edinburgh's Department of Obstetrics and Gynaecology. Jonathan Ross was a medical registrar in the Department of Genito-Urinary Medicine at the Royal Infirmary of Edinburgh. David T. Baird is the Medical Research Council Clinical Research Professor of Reproductive Endocrinology at the University of Edinburgh's Department of Obstetrics and Gynaecology.*

The use of human fetal tissue for research purposes is a subject which arouses strong feelings. Although there is no doubt that scientific research using fetal tissue has enormous potential, different governments impose very different restrictions on its use. In the United Kingdom an advisory group was asked in 1970 'to consider the ethical, medical, social and legal implications of using fetuses and fetal material for research'. The resulting *Peel Report*, published in 1972, recommended that research should be allowed on fetuses weighing less than 300g, provided there was no objection on the part of the mother and the research had been approved by an ethical committee.

In the late 1980s, concerned principally about experiments in which human fetal tissue was being grafted into the brains of patients suffering from Parkinsonism, the British government invited a second committee, led by the Reverend Dr John Polkinghorne, to review *Peel*'s guidelines. The Polkinghorne Committee took advice from organisations involved in medical research and in the provision of abortion services and also from a significant number of religious organisations and groups campaigning against abortion. The recommendations of the committee were published in 1989 and accepted by the Department of Health in 1990.

Fionn Anderson, Anna Glasier, Jonathan Ross, and David T. Baird, "Attitudes of Women to Fetal Tissue Research," *Journal of Medical Ethics* 20:36-39 (1994). Reprinted by permission of the BMJ Publishing Group, London.

One of the principal concerns of the committee and of opponents of fetal tissue research was that women might be pressurised into terminating a pregnancy in order to provide fetal material. To safeguard women from exploitation the new recommendations included a recommendation that doctors involved in obtaining fetal tissue, ie those who agreed to a woman's request for abortion or who performed the termination—called in the report 'the source'—should be totally separate from doctors and scientists carrying out research—'the user'. Indeed the two parties were specifically prohibited from discussing the proposed research. Women from whom tissue was obtained should give a general informed consent to the research but should not be told what the research was about or even whether the tissue was used.

Although the committee sought the views of many relevant bodies, no attempt was made to seek the opinions of women of reproductive age and in particular of women about to have a termination of pregnancy.

In this study we have sought to investigate the attitudes of women to fetal tissue research by a questionnaire based on the points brought out in the *Polkinghorne Report*.

Subjects and Methods

Thirty questions were devised to investigate the attitudes of women to a variety of aspects of fetal tissue research and to the main recommendations of the *Polkinghorne Report*. The questionnaire was designed to be completed by women while waiting at clinics. Effort was made to simplify the questionnaire by providing explanatory paragraphs where appropriate, giving examples of relevant research areas. A pilot version of the questionnaire was given to 30 women attending a family planning clinic, minor modifications were made and a final version prepared.

Two groups of women were selected in an attempt to identify differences of opinion that might relate to different reproductive experience. Five hundred twenty-seven consecutive women attending a large family-planning clinic in the centre of Edinburgh, Scotland (The Dean Terrace Centre) were given the questionnaire; 108 of these women had a history of termination of pregnancy while 419 women had never had an abortion. A second group of 167 women attending the Royal Infirmary of Edinburgh who were pregnant and requesting termination of pregnancy were also asked to complete the

> *"Few women felt that the doctor agreeing to and carrying out the abortion (the source) should be separate from the researcher (the user)."*

questionnaire. One hundred and fifty-eight women did so; 2 women were short of time; 2 said they found the subject too upsetting, while 5 refused to participate as they felt that they held no strong views. None of the women were given the questionnaire until after the gynaecologist had agreed to the request for abortion and the woman had left the consulting room. The person who asked the patient to complete the questionnaire was not involved with the consultation. It was made clear that women were not being asked to participate in the sort of research being discussed nor was any part of their treatment dependent upon their responses to the questionnaire. The study and the questionnaire both received the approval of the Paediatric/Reproductive Medicine Ethics of Medical Research Sub-committee of the Lothian [Scotland] Health Board.

The data were entered onto a computerised database and initial analysis performed by summing the answers for each question and subdividing by group. . . .

Results

Demographic Details. The demographic details of the women completing the questionnaire are shown in Table 1. Women attending for termination of pregnancy were younger and more likely to be unmarried while women who had never had a termination of pregnancy were less likely to have had children than women in the other two groups. Forty-two per cent of women attending for an abortion had had a previous termination of pregnancy, while only 13 per cent of women at the family planning clinic who had had an abortion at some time in the past had had more than one.

Table 1

Demographic details of respondents

	Hospital outpatient clinic Attending for abortion	Family planning clinic History of abortion	No abortion
Number	158	108	419
% younger than 20 years	20	2	13
% 20–39 years	74	90	82
% older than 39 years	6	8	5
% with children	29	28	15
% married/cohabiting	28	50	47
% higher education	58	66	68

Fewer women attending with a request for abortion were aware of the existence of research using fetal tissue (28 per cent v 53 per cent).

Attitudes Towards Fetal Research. Only 6 per cent of women said they thought it was unjustifiable to use fetal tissue for research. Of the 94 per cent of women who felt that research was justifiable, 88 per cent thought it appropriate to undertake research aimed at improving our understanding of the basic physiology of the developing fetus and 84 per cent said they would allow this sort of research to be done on their own fetus. All women who approved of research agreed with the idea of undertaking research into clinical problems affecting the fetus and neonate, such as investigating the effect of giving drugs to accelerate lung maturation in the event of premature labour. Only 2 per cent of the women felt reluctant to allow their own fetus to be used for this kind of research. Eighty-seven per cent of the total sample approved of research which aimed to improve methods of abortion although significantly fewer of the women who had never had an abortion approved of this kind of research (84 per cent v 92 per cent). Eighty-seven per cent of women felt

"For each type of research no more than 2 per cent of the women felt unable to offer their own fetus for research which they had approved in principle."

that research aimed towards using fetal tissue for transplantation was in principle right and 86 per cent of them would allow their own fetus to be used. Overall fewer women felt that research on a live fetus was justifiable but significantly more of the women about to undergo termination of pregnancy found this idea acceptable (68 per cent) and more than half of them would have permitted research to be carried out on their own live fetus. Significantly fewer women not currently pregnant would permit research on a live fetus (44 per cent) and even fewer would allow research on their own fetus (32 per cent).

Considering both groups together, women who had had at least one child (regardless of whether they were seeking, or had ever had, an abortion) were significantly less likely to agree, in principle, with research using fetal tissue (89 per cent v 95 per cent). However, no differences between parous and nulliparous women [respectively, women who have and have not produced offspring] could be distinguished with regard to their feelings about the different types of fetal research.

Consent to Fetal Research. Overall 63 per cent of women said they would wish their permission to be sought before their fetus was used for research purposes; significantly more women who had never had a termination felt this to be important (71 per cent v 53 per cent). Less than half the women in each group would wish to know the exact details of the research but again women who had never had an abortion felt they would want more information (38 per cent v 23 per cent) and these women were more likely to want to ask questions of the researcher (54 per cent v 33 per cent). Over 75 per cent of all the women would be happy to give general consent to research using fetal tissue.

No Need for Separation

Few women felt that the doctor agreeing to and carrying out the abortion (the source) should be separate from the researcher (the user). Only 8 per cent of women about to undergo an abortion said they felt the doctor should have nothing to do with research being undertaken. Of the women not currently pregnant, less than 25 per cent thought the source and the user should be separated and less than 15 per cent felt that gynaecologists who were performing abortions should not undertake any research using fetal tissue. Thus women about to undergo abortion felt even less strongly about the issue of separation than other women and 85 per cent of them compared with 72 per cent of the women not currently pregnant said their decision to consent to fetal research would be unaffected by the knowledge that the doctor advising them about abortion was personally involved with the research.

Practicalities of Research

Less than half of the women felt that abortions should be especially timed to allow research to take place. However, once again women about to undergo an abortion were more likely to feel this would be acceptable (41 per cent v 27 per cent). Few of the women felt their decision to allow research on their fetus would be affected if either they (8 per cent) or their fetus (7 per cent) had to be tested for HIV infection. Only 45 per cent of women felt they would be more likely to take part in research were it likely to produce information which might be of direct relevance to them as individuals (for example, the discovery of an inherited disease).

Discussion

In the introduction to the *Polkinghorne Report* the authors stated that 'it is evident to us that there is much concern over any use of fetal tissue, whether it is described as research or therapy'. The women who took part in this study did not appear to show much concern—94 per cent of them believe there is nothing wrong with research using fetal tissue. They made little if any distinction between pure research and that which had obvious clinical relevance, including the use of fetal tissue for treating adult diseases. It must be remembered that the bulk of research uses tissue obtained after the abortion when the fetus is already dead. The women—particularly those not pregnant at the time—were less likely to approve of research involving a fetus which was still alive, perhaps out of some concern for the moral status of the unborn child, albeit a child destined to die.

> *"The separation of source and user imposes constraints on ... research which could be directly beneficial to women of reproductive age and their babies."*

Although it is possible that the women may have responded differently had they been asked to donate fetal tissue, we did try to approach this question by distinguishing between approving of research in principle and allowing tissue from their own fetus to be used. For each type of research no more than 2 per cent of the women felt unable to offer their own fetus for research which they had approved in principle. Moreover, the women who were about to have an abortion were more likely to approve of all types of fetal research and to offer their own fetus for use—at least in theory. The women about to undergo an abortion were younger and less likely to have had children than the women in the other group and 42 per cent of them had had an abortion before. It is possible therefore that they had less regard for the unborn child; alternatively they may have agreed with the idea of research using fetal tissue because they felt relieved of some of the anxiety associated with an unwanted pregnancy and received some comfort from the idea that a fetus which they did not want might be put to good use. Whatever the reasons for their overwhelming approval these are the very women that *Polkinghorne* thought might be pressurised into participating in research of which they did not approve.

In an attempt to reduce any possibility of pregnant women's being exploited, *Polkinghorne* recommended that the source of fetal tissue and the user should be separated and suggested that the best way to achieve this separation was to involve an intermediary. However, the separation of source and user imposes constraints on the design of certain types of research which could be directly beneficial to women of reproductive age and their babies. For example, research on the effects of corticosteroids on the maturation of the fetal lung would require careful timing of the abortion procedure and would therefore involve the source. Most of the women in our study did not feel it was necessary to separate the doctor who was counselling or treating them from the person who was doing the research. The decision to have a pregnancy terminated is almost always made before a woman reaches a gynaecologist (the potential 'source'), whose role in the counselling process is to make certain she understands the procedure involved and its attendant risks and that she is absolutely certain of her decision. It seems unlikely to us that a woman would deliberately embark upon a pregnancy in order to have it terminated solely to provide tissue for research purposes, since for the vast majority the decision to have an abortion is painful and difficult and not undertaken lightly. . . .

> *"It seems unlikely to us that a woman would deliberately embark upon a pregnancy in order to have it terminated solely to provide tissue for research purposes."*

Positive Explicit Consent

The report recommends that 'positive explicit consent' should be obtained from the mothers to the use of the fetus or fetal tissues. However, the information on which she is to base her informed consent has to be general (not 'explicit') because it has to embrace all the potential research. It would not be permissible to give the mother any indication of the exact use, indeed it would be impossible because the doctor who gained her consent to research (the source) is prohibited from communicating in any way with the user. While many of the women we asked agreed to giving general consent, a significant minority (32 per cent) felt they would want some detail about the proposed research and would like the opportunity to ask questions. There seems no reason to deny more specific information to those women who want it. With both the woman and the doctor ignorant of the precise use of the tissue it is hard to imagine circumstances in which consent would be either sought or given.

Notable Differences

There are some notable differences between the membership and emphasis of the Peel Committee and the Polkinghorne Committee. The members of the Peel Committee specifically stated that they had tried to maintain a balance between ethical concerns and the important contributions which could be made to medical science and 'to the health and welfare of the entire population' by the use of fetal tissue. In contrast the Polkinghorne Committee did not consider any 'particular contemporary developments' taking place either in society or in science but couched the report purely in terms of ethical principles. The Peel Committee was chaired by a gynaecologist and included, among others, two other doctors, two nurses and a social worker. The membership of the Polkinghorne Committee comprised the president of a Cambridge college, the president of an Oxford college (the only medical practitioner—a general physician approaching retirement), a professor of medical law and ethics and a sociologist. In the letter to three secretaries of state which introduces his report, the Rev Dr Polkinghorne wrote that the members of the committee 'brought with them a variety of experience relevant to this inquiry'. While we do not intend to argue the rights or wrongs of the use of fetal tissue for research it seems clear to us that the women whom Polkinghorne was trying to protect feel very differently about the subject than the members of his committee would appear to. It seems odd to us that it was not considered relevant to include on the committee more people who came into direct contact with women faced with an unwanted pregnancy. . . . One could even argue that it might have been even more relevant to seek the opinions of women in general and in particular of those women considering having an abortion.

Fetal Tissue Transplants Are Ethically Wrong and Medically Unnecessary

by Paul Ranalli

About the author: *Paul Ranalli is a neurologist and lecturer at the University of Toronto's Neurology Division. He has written several articles on the ethical and medical problems associated with fetal tissue research and transplantation.*

National Right to Life News editor's note: On January 22, 1993—on his third day in office—President Bill Clinton issued five pro-abortion executive orders. One lifted the Bush Administration ban on tax funding of fetal tissue transplantation using body parts taken from induced abortions. In so doing, the new President furthered the agenda of pro-abortion extremists.

Pro-lifers have sharply attacked abortion-dependent fetal tissue research on a host of grounds: it is flat-out morally wrong; it encourages medicine to become dependent on a steady stream of fetal body parts; it will increase the number of abortions; it will make women even more hostage to pressure by boyfriends, husbands, and parents; and it tries to put an ethical sheen on an abominable practice.

But there are two other major considerations: (1) there is no credible research suggesting such transplants work, and (2) there are many alternative approaches which have demonstrated more promise of curing or ameliorating such diseases as Parkinson's and diabetes. . . .

The Nature of Parkinson's Disease

Parkinson's disease (PD) is a progressive, degenerative brain disorder characterized chiefly by a loss of motor control, tremor, muscular rigidity, slowness of movement, and problems with balance and walking. The disease develops in middle to late life, and will strike 1 in 100 above age 60, which currently repre-

From Paul Ranalli, "Exciting, Viable Alternatives to Fetal Tissue," *National Right to Life News*, June 4, 1993. Reprinted with permission.

sents upwards of half a million Americans.

No cure is yet available for Parkinson's disease. All of the treatments described below represent attempts to "manage" the disease, by minimizing troublesome symptoms enough to permit the patient to live as normal a life as possible. In the earliest stage of the dis-
ease, no treatment is required, because symptoms are minimal.

Indeed, symptoms of many people
in the early stages of Parkinson's disease are unrecognized and undiag-

> *"Abortion-dependent fetal
> tissue research . . . is
> flat-out morally wrong."*

nosed, until symptoms eventually declare themselves at a later time. When
treatment is required, the initial response is usually rewarding, but the later
stages of the disease are fraught with many complications.

The fundamental problem in Parkinson's disease begins with the decline in
the production of the brain chemical dopamine, and leads to subsequent effects
that trigger overactivity in nearby cell groups. Treatment strategies can be cate-
gorized in five ways: (1) drugs to replace the loss of dopamine; (2) drugs which
interact directly with dopamine receptors in the brain; (3) drugs to stabilize diseased brain cells and limit further deterioration; (4) drugs to encourage brain
tissue regeneration; and (5) surgical lesions (cuts) into deep brain structures
which are abnormally overactive in Parkinson's disease.

Medical Treatments

L-Dopa Therapy. One popular therapy is to replace the dopamine, which itself cannot be given in pill form, because it will not cross the blood-brain barrier. Its antecedent molecule, L-dopa, however, does pass through, to be later
transformed into dopamine by enzymes in the brain. This "trojan horse" approach has been the cornerstone of PD treatment since the mid-1960s.

Problems crop up, however, after several years. Fortunately, technical improvements in the administration of the L-dopa drug *Sinemet* show considerable
promise in delaying the onset of treatment complications.

Dopamine Receptor Agonists. Such drugs do not replace the brain's
dopamine, but rather enter the brain and interact with dopamine receptors directly—in essence, imitating the dopamine molecule. This therapy is generally
added onto L-dopa medication, in an effort to boost performance which may be
flagging after several years of treatment.

Until recently, only one drug was available. Now a more powerful dopamine
receptor drug has passed clinical trials—*Permax.*

Other Drugs. Drugs which reset the balance between the depleted dopamine
and acetylcholine, another brain chemical, have been useful for years at reducing tremor in PD.

A recently published large trial in the *New England Journal of Medicine* has
shown benefit of the drug *deprenyl*, which, when given as initial therapy, can

delay the need for more conventional drugs by several months.

Whether this action occurs because *deprenyl* has a *protective* effect on the brain or whether the drug boosts performance (as in conventional therapy) is not clear.

However, recent experimental work by Dr. William Tatton at the University of Toronto has shown a possible role for *deprenyl* to "rescue" dying neurons. If this is proved in clinical trials, *deprenyl* could be given to patients in the earliest stages of PD (and, possibly, other degenerative disorders) to *slow down* the progress of the disease.

GM1 Ganglioside. In early 1992, Dr. Jay Schneider, of Philadelphia's Hahnemann University, discovered that this substance may go further at stabilizing damaged neurons in animal models of Parkinson's disease. GM1 ganglioside is a natural substance believed to enter the brain and interact with the cell membrane in a protective, stabilizing role not yet fully understood. A full clinical trial with PD patients has begun, and results might be expected by the late 1990s.

Nerve Growth Factor (NGF). Another natural body chemical may prove to be the key to "regeneration" of brain tissue, something thought impossible until recently. NGF was recently isolated by a team at the University of Southern California and a wide variety of clinical applications may soon begin.

In addition to NGF, over half a dozen new agents have been discovered which are believed to "nurture" neurons of one form or another. The

> *"[Fetal tissue research] tries to put an ethical sheen on an abominable practice."*

most exciting development for patients suffering from Parkinson's disease is that a newly isolated protein called GDNF has shown specific benefit in promoting the survival of the dopamine-secreting neurons that typically degenerate in the disease. This natural substance, which derives from the supportive "glial" cells in the brain, is powerful, and exquisitely sensitive at promoting the survival of the dopamine neuron.

Although the drug must pass through the various animal and human experimental hoops, experienced researchers believe that, ultimately, such drugs will provide much more workable therapy than brain transplantation with fetal tissue. In the May 21, 1993 issue of *Science*, neuroscientist Lou Reichardt of the University of California at San Francisco (UCSF) states that these neurotropic factors "will be an improvement over these difficult and dicey surgeries and transplantations."

Surgical Treatments: Real and Imagined

As most pro-lifers know, uncritical media attention has fostered the illusion that fetal tissue transplants "work." A recent, thorough review by St. Louis neurology professor Dr. William Landau may help to dispel this ignorance, if not in the popular press, perhaps in the medical journals.

Landau recently wrote in the journal *Neurology* that, without control groups, fetal tissue transplant results are worthless. (A "control" group would be a set of patients who enter the clinical trial and receive the same treatment except for the fact that they do not receive the transplants.) Without this—and, in fact, virtually every study conducted using fetal tissue has lacked such a control group—there is no scientifically valid way to attribute any alleged improvement to the tissue. Other factors may cause improvement, such as damage to deep structures caused by the needle bearing the fetal tissue.

Fetal tissue researchers believe that the fetal tissue replaces the lost chemical dopamine, which then causes the "improvement." But recent work in animals disproves this theory. A variety of different tissues, none of which secrete dopamine, were transplanted into animals with experimentally induced Parkinson's disease. Remarkably, all of these parkinsonian animals improved *just as much* as those transplanted with tissue that contained dopamine-secreting cells.

A Once-Forgotten Treatment

In fact, Landau's article points out clearly that behavioral improvement correlates, more than any other factor, with the degree of damage done to clusters of cells deep in the brain which are known to be overactive in Parkinson's disease. This calls attention to a once-forgotten method of PD treatment, that of "lesion" surgery. That is, the neurosurgeon can improve a patient's function by making a small cut (or "lesion," in neurology parlance) in one of the deep nuclei responsible for movement.

There is a rationale for this seemingly paradoxical treatment method. Although the slow death of dopamine-secreting neurons in the substantia nigra nuclei of the midbrain is the primary event in PD, a subsequent chain of events leads to overactivity of another nearby nucleus, an almond-sized cell group known as the globus pallidus (GP). There is one on each side of the brain.

Overactivity of the GP interferes with movement since it is intimately wired to a group of nearby nuclei which fine-tune our motor control. Thus, the selective destruction of a part of the GP can release the patient from much of the rigidity, poverty of movement, and slowness of movement which make up the cardinal features of the disease. Tremors can be improved by a lesion in another related nucleus in the circuit, the thalamus.

The first attempts at lesioning the globus pallidus (or "pallidotomy") took place in the early 1950s. After some initial success, results were disappointing and the operation fell out of favor. A review of these pioneering procedures has now revealed that in many cases the needle had made cuts in the *wrong* part of the GP! It is now recognized that only lesions made in the "nosteroventral" GP will be fully successful.

> *"There is no credible research suggesting such [fetal tissue] transplants work."*

Recent studies have shown remarkable improvements in humans, results which dwarf the claims for improvements using fetal tissue. The work of Dr. Enrico Fazzini and others seem to be on the threshold of eliminating the one significant drawback—partial loss of the visual field on one side. Dr. Fazzini revealed some of his recent results at the April 1992 meeting of the American Academy of Neurology in New York.

He reported "significant improvement" with *"no side effects"* in all ten patients. Moreover, "dyskinesias"—troublesome involuntary movements typical in late-stage parkinsonians—were "totally alleviated in all patients."

Unpublished information indicates that Dr. Fazzini's successful patient list has now grown to 23, and that these updated results have been submitted in the form of a complete article to be published in the near future.

These encouraging results will soon offer Parkinson's disease patients hope for treatment beyond drug therapy, treatment which is not only ethically solid, but is emerging as far more successful than the heavily promoted surgical adventures involving fetal transplant tissue.

Fetal Tissue Transplants Violate Moral and Legal Codes

by *Commonweal*

About the author: Commonweal *is a biweekly Roman Catholic review of public affairs, religion, literature and the arts.*

Editor's Note: Federal funding of some medical research using aborted fetal tissues was banned in 1988. A congressional attempt to repeal the ban was vetoed by President George Bush in 1992. Although the prohibition was lifted by President Bill Clinton in 1993, the following article—which predates Clinton's action—is still a relevant argument against the use of aborted fetal tissue in medical research and treatment.

Abortions may save lives. That paradoxical claim lies behind congressional support for lifting a ban on medical research using fetal tissue derived from abortions. Although the vote on a National Institutes of Health [NIH] reappropriation bill, which includes funding for such research, was not sufficient to override a presidential veto, the measure is likely to come up again. The ban has been in place since 1988 [it was repealed by President Clinton in 1993]. It is tough to argue in favor of maintaining the ban, as the votes of normally pro-life advocates in Congress show. In fact, anti-abortion Senator Mark Hatfield (R-Oreg.) said he found the use of fetal tissue to save lives "prolife."

Little Resistance

If the ban is ultimately lifted, cures are predicted for Parkinson's disease, Alzheimer's, diabetes, genetic disorders, and radiation injuries. Congress seems to have little resistance to the pleas of the sick and their advocates, especially when they are dramatic and especially when they show up on the congressional doorstep or are related to a member of Congress (Senator Strom Thurmond

"Saving Lives?" *Commonweal*, June 19, 1992. Reprinted by permission of Commonweal Foundation, ©1992.

[R-S.C.] sees a potential cure for his diabetic daughter). But dramatic appeals and promises of medical breakthroughs always need to be scrutinized with a skeptical eye, especially in circumstances where the claims for cure far exceed the data, and even more so when the promise of a cure rests upon the availability of aborted fetal tissue.

> *"Taking innocent human lives in order to save other human lives undermines a basic principle of the moral code that sustains our society."*

For dramatic appeal before Congress, consider the example of the man suffering from kidney failure who, in the 1970s, was dialyzed before a congressional committee in a compelling plea for federal funds to make the treatment more widely available. Congress obliged. As a result, the prior system of rationing dialysis, especially for those who might eventually find a compatible kidney for transplant, has disappeared. Many people now survive because of the federal program that pays the cost of dialysis. Who could object?

Unfortunately, for large numbers of patients, no compatible transplants are available. So dialysis has become a necessary, and costly, treatment for kidney failure, and, of course, its use has been extended far beyond the otherwise relatively healthy people for whom it was first devised as a bridge between kidney failure and a kidney transplant. The case is relevant to the current debate over fetal tissue research.

To begin with, the promise of a dramatic cure or a treatment that will save lives is an effective tool in prizing federal support and funds for research. In the debate over use of fetal tissue, men and women with Parkinson's testified to the remission of their symptoms after being given fetal-cell implants. The Reverend Guy Walden, a Southern Baptist minister, told a congressional hearing of the implant's potential in extending the life of his son who has Hurler's syndrome, a fatal genetic condition that killed two other sons. Proponents argue that the fetal tissues, organs, and cells now abundantly available are simply being wasted. They should be made available to researchers along with federal money to test the potential for alleviating symptoms of crippling disease or curing fatal ones. Among the supporters there are those who, though opposed to abortion, would further argue that this research is one way to see good come from the deaths caused by abortion.

Institutionalizing a Need

And then, there are the unforeseen consequences of beginning and funding research and treatment programs that it will be impossible to end, indeed even to control, after thousands or hundreds of thousands become dependent on their availability—in this case, dependent as well on the availability of abortion. In 1992, research with fetal tissues is being conducted on a very small scale with private funds and, at least in this country, only with tissues from ectopic pregnancies. miscarriages, and stillbirths (in fact, federal funding is available for this form of fetal tissue research). But because these kinds of tissue may have become infected or may be genetically defective, researchers say they would prefer tissues and organs from "healthy" fetuses, ones that have been aborted.

And it is here that the argument becomes very difficult, as illustrated by the testimony of Guy Walden. For Walden is opposed to abortion, and according to news reports, his son was treated with fetal cells that came not from an abortion but from an ectopic pregnancy. Yet in testimony before Congress, Walden argued, "Right now this tissue [from aborted fetuses] is being thrown in the trash cans. If we can save a life [by using it], shouldn't we?" If prolifers like Walden can make the moral jump that separates the use of fetal tissues from the means by which they are made available, then the argument against approval is very tough indeed.

Taking Life

Yet the argument must be made. And it is clear enough: the ends are contradicted by the means. Taking innocent human lives in order to save other human lives undermines a basic principle of the moral code that sustains our society and the legal code that regulates our common life. Of course, one assumes that in most cases there would be no direct relationship between the abortion decision—it was not made "in order to" save a life—and the use of the fetal remains for medical life-saving. But lifting the ban would allow an indirect link to be forged, and not simply for this or that exceptional case. Abortion would become that much more an institutionalized part of the health-care system, factored into research plans, providing returns to the pharmaceutical industry, and sharing in the moral legitimacy of the lifesaving enterprise.

> *"To refer to fetal tissue as if it were mere tissue disembedded from its human provenance . . . evades the morally obvious."*

Mr. Walden's very language shows how easy it is to become insensitive to the morally problematic character of this enterprise. To refer to fetal tissue as if it were mere tissue disembedded from its human provenance, or to speak of finding it in a trash can as if magically transported from we-know-not-where, evades the morally obvious. Of course, fetal tissue is human tissue—not even *Roe v. Wade* denies that. This tissue was once part of a developing life that has been destroyed and dispatched. Harvesting that tissue in order to save or sustain another, wanted human life cannot redeem the taking of life in the first place (drawing good out of evil). For that reason after World War II the scientific community chose to forego whatever knowledge might derive from Nazi medical experiments.

Among those who do not see abortion as the taking of a human life, there are certainly some who, nonetheless, might agree that there is no reason to capitalize on what may be a tragic necessity for some women. For others who support abortion and have no problem using the tissue, more pragmatic arguments have been mounted against using aborted fetal tissue: that it might encourage women to have abortions, even late abortions, especially if a fetal organ might be transplanted into a relative, for example, another child; that it might lead to the selling and buying of fetal body parts: that by encouraging, rewarding, or pressuring women to serve as reproducers of surplus parts and tissues, it would demean them as persons, as women, and as mothers (an argument some feminists have raised against surrogate motherhood).

Legislative efforts, embodied in the NIH bill, to create a wall between abortion and the subsequent use of fetal tissue [by prohibiting (1) medical personnel from discussing the use of fetal tissue with women considering abortion, (2) the pregnant woman from designating the recipient of the fetal tissue and, (3) anyone from selling fetal tissue] suggest one way to meet some of these objections. Yet we find it improbable that these strictures would stand if researchers did devise treatments or find cures. Once again, Congress would find itself listening to stories of human suffering that they do not have the heart—or the moral resources—to resist.

Fetal Tissue Research Will Lead to More Abortions

by Stephen G. Post

About the author: *Stephen G. Post, chairman of the American Academy of Religion's Medical Ethics Group and associate editor of the* Encyclopedia of Bioethics, *teaches in the School of Medicine at Case Western Reserve University, Cleveland, Ohio.*

Human fetal tissue transplanted into adults is a potential treatment for Parkinson's Disease, diabetes, radiation-induced anemia and other ailments. Because fetal tissue grows rapidly, is adaptable and evokes little or no immune response from the host, many researchers are optimistic about its therapeutic possibilities. The curative potential of fetal tissue transplant, for at least some diseases, is very probably considerable.

The Objections

However, there are three commonly stated moral objections to the use of *elective* aborted fetuses for transplant research and/or therapy. First, the successful use of fetal tissue could encourage abortions, and requests for government research funding are therefore ensnared in the acrimonious abortion debate. Assistant Secretary of Health James O. Mason has stated that the use of fetal tissue would prove to be a "powerful inducement" for women to have abortions, since the knowledge that the tissue might help a disease sufferer could "tip the scale toward an abortion." Second, if the medical research establishment becomes dependent on elective aborted fetuses, an irreversible institutional and economic bond between abortion centers and biomedical science will have been established. Medical science could have a great deal at stake in the continued flow of elective aborted fetuses. Third, the use of elective aborted fetuses might create political turmoil in a nation already deeply divided over elective abortion.

This viewpoint contends that opponents of fetal tissue transplant have the right to make an argument. Theologian Gilbert Meilaender writes that over 10

Stephen G. Post, "Fetal Tissue Transplant: The Right to Question Progress," *America*, January 12, 1991. Reprinted by permission of the author.

years ago, he used an essay entitled "Can the Fetus Be an Organ Farm?" in his course at Oberlin College in Ohio. "It didn't really generate much discussion," he recalls. "No one was willing to answer 'yes' to the question—and this among students almost all of whom would have called themselves pro-choice." There may be considerable ambivalence about benefiting from the death of a fetus, perhaps because on some level of conscience there is a sense of compunction about the wanton destruction of life potential that is a means toward the proposed benefit. There is, at a minimum, integrity to the claim that abortion (other than in the cases of rape, incest or threat to the bodily health of the mother) is such a grave affront to the potentialities of the entity within the womb that all benefit is categorically out of the question, regardless of consequences.

A Grave Affront

It is this sense of grave affront that underlies resistance to fetal tissue transplant and may inform the . . . [federal] ban on research-grant support for fetal tissue transplant involving elective aborted fetuses [a ban that was lifted by President Bill Clinton in 1993]. Kathleen Nolan, a pediatrician-ethicist formerly of the Hastings Center, has argued that sufficient fetal tissue could be harvested from the removal of ectopic pregnancies, 75,000 of which occur in this country annually. Nor did the ban affect research using fetuses from miscarriages and stillbirths, although these are not considered good sources for tissue because of possible chromosomal abnormalities.

I will not present the arguments on behalf of fetal tissue transplant in any systematic way, since these boil down to the obvious claim, grounded in beneficence: Such transplants could help many persons regain their health to varying degrees. Indeed, this is such a compelling line of argument that any reluctance to abide by it is met with considerable shock by researchers and by the usual cast of biomedical ethicists. But I do not think that the argument against using elective aborted fetuses in fetal tissue transplant should be quickly dismissed or repressed, nor do I think that the wider public has reached anything like a consensus on this matter.

The public has a right to question medical progress that may be moral regress. The field of biomedical ethics, which is rather young and sometimes too desperately seeking legitimation from the medical establishment, knows that it is on weak ground if it relies on the public's am-

> *"The public has a right to question medical progress that may be moral regress."*

bivalence regarding progress. It is safer to side with medical progress, that admixture of genuine moral idealism and hard economic self-interest, especially if one depends on the good graces of the medical establishment for grant support and salary. I believe that this explains, in part, why the field of biomedical ethics focuses on procedural questions about informed consent, confidentiality, treatment refusals and the like, rather than on questions about the actual ends of medicine and the relation of medical science to images of human fulfillment.

I concentrate here on the arguments against the use of elective aborted fetuses not only because these arguments have been too quickly dismissed, but also because, with Jeffrey Stout, I hold that "secular moral philosophy has often repressed diversity, rendering it invisible and unchallenging, rather than taking its full measure and working through a relation to significantly different moral traditions."

Because the field of biomedical ethics has become increasingly the domain of secular moral philosophers, many of them committed to the same empirical utilitarian strain of thinking that characterizes medical science itself, those who would question so-called progress from the viewpoint of other traditions of moral thought need all the more to be heard.

The Incidence of Elective Abortion

There is fear that with the use of elective aborted fetuses, terms of the abortion debate will change. Dr. Nolan worries about "harmful shifts in our attitudes toward fetuses and elective abortion while permitting pursuit of medical benefits for those desperately in need." Could this happen?

Fortunately, neither side in the debate wants to encourage abortions. Those who favor the use of elective abortuses argue that a woman should decide whether to permit use of tissue from her aborted fetus only after

> *"Instead of thinking about how to make use of fetal tissue, we really should be considering ways to encourage contraception."*

she has elected to have an abortion. This would prevent her from having an abortion for the purpose of donating tissue. They also argue that a woman should be prohibited from selecting the recipient of fetal tissue and that no commercialization should be permitted. In this way, transplantation specialists would be unable to exert direct pressure on a woman who is in the throes of a decision on abortion; a woman could not conceive in order to provide tissue for a particular person in need, such as a parent or spouse; and there would be no market in fetal tissue to encourage poor women to supply fetuses for a fee.

Currently, we simply do not know what the ultimate impact of fetal tissue transplant on the incidence of elective abortions would be. The question requires more study. Presumably, if those who support research with elective abortuses see that it is leading to more abortions, they would be ready to reconsider the issue. Biomedical ethicist Mary Mahowald, who favors the research, argues that "retrospective scrutiny" would be required, for perhaps fears about "possible exploitation of women, encouragement of elective abortion and disregard for immature human life" might be confirmed.

It might be that those outside the clinical setting who pressure a woman into

257

abortion (boyfriends, family and others), who marshal all the practical considerations on its behalf, will tie the ethics of abortion to the ethics of helping the needy victims of disease. These persuaders will not be subject to any regulations specific to the clinical context. They can bring into conversation the benefits of fetal tissue transplant before a woman makes her choice for or against abortion. In this way, fetal tissue transplant would be one of several arguments made in the harangue that often results in abortions that are not authentically desired. Abortion decisions are often very difficult, and the appeal to beneficence, to "harvesting" good tissue, might be highly manipulative of women.

"Groups that would benefit from fetal tissue transplant could make wide and emotionally powerful appeals for more tissue."

Even in the absence of direct interpersonal pressure, the beneficence of giving up a fetus for the sake of a disease victim will be widely discussed. This opportunity for idealism may become a part of the cultural milieu in a way not entirely unlike blood or organ donation. Currently, the last thing a woman would consider in making an abortion decision is fetal tissue transplant. But attitudes and frameworks for decision-making can shift. Groups that would benefit from fetal tissue transplant could make wide and emotionally powerful appeals for more tissue, especially if the successes of this technology turn out to be great. To cite Dr. Nolan: "Life-saving cures resulting from the use of cadaveric material might indeed make abortion, and fetal death, seem less tragic. Enhancing abortion's image could thus be expected to undermine efforts to make it as little needed and little used a procedure as possible."

The obligations to preserve the unborn from a "harvest," and to protect women from additional pressures to abort, create morally significant concerns about the use of electively aborted fetuses.

Those who worry about this potential slippery slope do have a right to an argument. Already, millions of abortions take place annually in the United States, and abortion is, relatively speaking, much more common here than in European countries. Perhaps, instead of thinking about how to make use of fetal tissue, we really should be considering ways to encourage contraception, sexual morality and adoption. Possibly we need a movement to provide homes and job training for the many unwed mothers who would not choose abortion if they thought their child could have a decent life.

Medical Dependence on Elective Abortion

This is the strongest argument against the use of elective abortuses in fetal tissue transplant because it does not rely on predictions about future cultural trends. Absolutely no one can reasonably doubt that the medical-industrial complex would be set in motion were elective aborted fetuses found to be of therapeutic use. (It is true that science is already dependent on fetal tissue research, e.g., in the development of cell lines grown in fetal tissue. This does not mean that such dependency is morally acceptable.)

With the advent of widespread fetal tissue transplant, elective abortion would no longer be a political issue that biomedical researchers, as scientists, could ignore. Rather, livelihoods and institutional grants would demand that elective abortion be continued. I wince at the idea of biomedical science entering the abortion policy fray.

How likely would the medical-industrial complex be to slow its own growth on the basis of "retrospective scrutiny" over the effects of fetal tissue transplant on decisions for abortion? If this area of high medical technology develops through the use of tissues from elective abortuses, there might be no turning back. Abortion would be firmly tied to medicine, deeply ensconced in "scientific progress." With large government grants tied to elective abortion, opposition to it might be viewed negatively by the biomedical establishment. Biomedical science will depend on a steady supply of elective abortuses. Research interests could become a powerful voice in the abortion debate.

Politics and Civility

One proper moral goal of the state is civic peace. The Preamble to the United States Constitution notes that one purpose of government is to ensure tranquility. Abortion is already an extremely divisive issue, one that creates considerable civil disobedience and tension. Government, with tax dollars that come from those who fervently oppose elective abortions, may have a moral-political interest in mitigating a deepening societal cleavage that would only be worsened by Federal support of research with elective abortuses.

Many who view elective abortions as murder of the innocent akin to the Holocaust have already invoked the Nazi analogy in the context of the fetal tissue debate, thereby placing transplants in the category of absolute evil. I am deeply suspicious of this use of the Nazi analogy and reject it. But its use indicates how seriously opponents feel. Analogies aside, biomedical science, they contend, should not stoop so low as to desecrate further the electively aborted. To use these tissues, it is argued, would be to sin doubly, i.e., not only in the abortion process itself, but in its aftermath. These victims of abortion, if brought back to life and enabled to look back in time after experiencing the fullness of years, would surely reel in resentment against having had their potential interrupted and might well resent the idea of anyone benefiting from their tragic demise.

> *"With large government grants tied to elective abortion, opposition to it might be viewed negatively by the biomedical establishment."*

Should government ask those for whom the use of tissue taken from elective aborted fetuses is morally repulsive to participate in funding research? This is a difficult question that allows no easy response. . . .

I have not reached final conclusions about the use of fetal tissue transplant. The medical utilitarians no doubt have a strong case for progress and healing. There is something to be said for the argument that the tissue might be used without in any way condoning elective abortions. It can equally well be argued, however, that instead of inventing new ways to become medically dependent on this tissue, everything morally possible should be done to discourage the elective abortions of which such tissue is the fruit. Ultimately, it is the specter of a society whose medical institutions are inextricably bound up with elective abortions and whose people come to believe that for their own health they have every right to feed off the unborn, that gives pause.

Arguably, the use of elective aborted fetuses will have no impact on abortion levels, and will not result in widespread civil disobedience. Nevertheless, the high art of medicine will have a vested interest in the flow of dead fetuses, and we as a people will extend our lifespans and improve our quality of life at the expense of the unborn. This is why, even though my friends in research and in ethics find it puzzling, I do not see any quick answers to this debate. It is not easy to make the case that medicine, in the name of progress, *should* do everything that it *can* do.

Fetal Tissue Research Leads to the Exploitation of Women

by Janice G. Raymond

About the author: *Janice G. Raymond is a professor of women's studies and medical ethics at the University of Massachusetts, Amherst, and associate director of the Institute on Women and Technology at MIT, a research group studying the effects of new technology on women. Raymond's most recent book is* RU 486: Misconceptions, Myths and Morals, *which she cowrote with Renate Klein and Lynette Dumble.*

The crisis over a woman's right to abortion and reproductive self-determination in the United States has produced a situation in which many women's health supporters have leaped to advocate problematic and potentially dangerous technologies for women. With this advocacy, they are abandoning the kind of critical thinking and independent judgment that has, for the last 20 years, characterized the women's health movement. Why is it that to be prochoice has come to mean that we must accept a problematic chemical abortion method called RU 486, as well as a host of experimental new reproductive technologies—in-vitro fertilization (IVF), embryo transfer, and now the new, much-touted field of tissue research and transplantation?

What About Women?

Why is it, for example, that the consequences *to women* of fetal tissue research have all but been ignored in the fetal tissue debate now being waged by opponents and proponents of abortion? Medical research involving fetal tissue has been going on for decades, but only since 1988 has it been used to treat people; there is a particular hope for its efficacy in treating devastating illnesses such as Parkinson's and Alzheimer's.

The altering of abortion techniques is one of the more immediate conse-

Janice G. Raymond, "Taking Issue with Fetal Tissue," *On the Issues*, Spring 1993. Reprinted with permission.

quences for those women undergoing the procedure who consent to donate their fetuses for research and transplantation. In the suction or curette methods, for instance, fetuses are macerated before they are removed from the uterus; this causes the woman as little discomfort and danger as possible. However, it makes it difficult to identify specific sorts of tissue and to retrieve, intact, fetuses with the fully developed cells and tissues necessary for fetal tissue transplants. Doctors who need good tissue samples must therefore modify the suction method and extend the time it takes to perform an abortion, something which could put women at additional risk of complications. To obtain usable tissue in the first trimester of pregnancy, the Institute for the Advancement of Medicine, the largest U.S. supplier of fetal tissue, encourages doctors to employ ultrasound to find the fetus in the woman's uterus and then to vary the amount of suction so as to trap the whole fetus in the catheter. This method, however, is not very successful. Other doctors use a method by which a suction abortion takes 15–25 minutes instead of the usual 5–7 minutes. For Australian doctors, the preferred method of obtaining intact fetal tissue is to dilate the woman's cervix to the point where the fetus can be extracted whole and alive. Disagreement in the medical community over whether older or younger fetuses are more useful for fetal tissue transplants raises the possibility that women will be induced to have abortions after the first trimester to thus insure that the fetuses will be intact.

> *"Why is it . . . that the consequences to women of fetal tissue research have all but been ignored in the fetal tissue debate?"*

Since salvaging intact fetal tissue requires that a fetus be delivered as whole as possible, yet it is generally better for the woman if a fetus is fragmented in the womb, the question must be asked: Who is the primary patient in abortions involving fetal tissue procurement—the aborting woman or the possible recipient of the tissue? Will doctors determine the timing and methods of abortions to conform to the need for a certain kind of intact and/or usable fetal material?

One primary effect of fetal tissue research and transplants has been to turn women into fetal tissue containers; mere maternal environments for the fetus. (In many of the new reproductive technologies—egg extraction and donation, for instance—women can all too easily be objectified as "natural resources" whose bodies are mined for medical and scientific "gold.") The role of women in fetal tissue research is, after all, to provide the raw material.

Seeking "Redemption"

Ironically, a justification for fetal tissue transplants cited by medical researchers is that all this tissue is "going to waste." And with the increased assault on abortion in the United States, even some prochoice advocates have come to feel they must justify abortion by citing a general benefit from it. Unfortunately, women themselves are made to feel that their abortions should have a redeeming virtue. Fetal tissue donation can provide "redemption" for what is often a difficult and painful decision. But to have an abortion is a hard enough decision for women without their having to be burdened with worry over whether or not to donate fetal tissue.

Is it possible that one day abortions could become the handmaidens to fetal tissue procedures? A majority of respondents in a 1989 survey conducted by *Glamour* magazine argued that donating fetal tissue to medical research will give women the chance to be altruistic by putting the tissue to good use instead of wasting it.

More and more, it is women who are expected to be altruistic with what issues from their bodies. Donor systems, especially in the reproductive realms, mainly depend on women. In surrogacy arrangements women contribute gestating capacities; women undergoing hysterectomies are being asked to donate their eggs for IVF research. Comparatively, where men donate sperm, the procedure is quite different: It is simple, short lived and procured from a pleasurable act. Eggs, however, are procured from an uncomfortable and unpleasurable medical procedure—laparoscopy. Prior to laparoscopy, a woman must submit herself to risky hormonal injections for five to seven days to increase the production of eggs, have her blood drawn three times, and undergo ultrasound and 30 minutes of anesthesia. Women undergoing tubal ligation, too, are being asked in increasing numbers to donate their eggs for IVF research. In 1988, *U.S. News and World Report* estimated that about 125 medical centers in the U.S. offer to purchase eggs and advertise quite widely for donors. Whether or not women donating eggs are compensated, the egg donation is pitched by the clinics as aiding the infertile. The pervasiveness in our society of appealing to women's personal and social obligation to nurture and give is clearly being exploited in these medical contexts.

> *"One primary effect of fetal tissue research and transplants has been to turn women into fetal tissue containers."*

It is with the advent of fetal tissue transplants however—still a questionable field—that we see just how readily the pervasive notion of women as givers and donors comes to the fore. There has been a lot of miracle talk about the promise of fetal transplants, but it is, so far, only a promise.

A Cause for Caution

The first operations using fetal tissue took place in Mexico City in 1987, and then in Stockholm, Sweden, and Birmingham, England. The first U.S. fetal tissue transplant was performed at the University of Colorado in 1988. Initially, the Mexican team reported that the condition of one of the Parkinson's patients receiving a fetal tissue brain graft was markedly improved, yet three of the eight

Mexican transplant patients had died within two years of the operation. In 1988, the Swedish team reported that their implantations had not had any clinical significance. In the same year, the American Academy of Neurology issued a statement urging great caution in expanding the use of fetal tissue transplants in the treatment of Parkinson's disease. Two weeks before their position was publicized, the American Association of Neurological Surgeons had issued warnings to their membership about performing fetal tissue surgery.

> *"To have an abortion is a hard enough decision for women without their having to . . . [consider donating] . . . fetal tissue."*

Both groups took the position that what little we know about the actual results of fetal tissue surgeries, especially with Parkinson's patients, is more a cause for caution than a case for cure.

A UNESCO [United Nations Educational, Scientific, and Cultural Organization] report also found that despite great initial enthusiasm, the promise of fetal tissue transplants has not been fulfilled. In the wake of largely discouraging results researchers continue to perform experimental transplants of fetal tissue into the brains of Parkinson's patients. People with no other hope of cure are lining up for fetal tissue grafts.

Although newspaper headlines in November 1992 reported success using fetal tissue to repair the brains of a small group of Parkinson's patients, the text told a different story. The *Boston Globe*, for example, reported that the techniques "did not alleviate all symptoms or achieve consistent results." Three patients gained "modest improvement," and one patient died four months after the implant surgery. The results of eight other patients "could not be discussed." Success, it seems, was limited to two people who, after injecting themselves with synthetic heroin, had become literally frozen in place. The study reported they regained the ability to walk, dress and feed themselves. Researchers also admitted that to improve the survival rate of transplanted tissue, multiple abortions would have to be scheduled within hours of the fetal implant operation, as only 10 percent of the implanted fetal cells survive. Clearly this raises a question about the even larger amounts of fetal tissue needed, and where it will come from.

Legislative History

The only restraint on fetal tissue research and surgery has been the Bush administration's ban on federally funded fetal tissue transplants into humans. The administration's ban was based on its position that "permitting the human fetal research at issue will increase the incidence of abortion across the country." It was this decision that linked the fetal tissue debate with the controversy over abortion. Ever since then, liberals and feminists have been supporting fetal tissue research and transplantations in what appears to be a line of defense against the erosion of abortion rights.

Several Congressional hearings have been held, and legislation has been proposed to overturn the ban on federally funded fetal tissue research and transplantation. In 1991, the House of Representatives Subcommittee on Health and Environment held public hearings on a bill to overturn the ban, and I appeared before this subcommittee as the only witness to testify against this bill. All of the witnesses in favor of lifting the ban testified on the presumption that the research was progressive, proven to be therapeutic, and lifesaving. No one questioned its claims or seemed aware of the skepticism in the scientific community. None of those in favor of lifting the ban, including all the Congressmen on the subcommittee, addressed the consequences for women of fetal tissue procurement. All those supporting the research appeared to acquiesce in the widely expressed sentiment that abortions were a waste if fetal tissue was not put to medical use. These supporters were willing to give the legal go-ahead to a *system* of routinely harvesting fetal tissue *before* its success has been proven. [The fetal tissue ban was repealed by President Clinton in 1993.]

Some have argued that fetal tissue donation and procurement should be legally regulated to insure the aborting woman's informed consent. In 1988, the Institute for the Advancement of Medicine did insist that its clinic and hospital suppliers obtain a woman's consent before giving fetal tissue. But about half the suppliers refused, and they no longer provide the Institute with tissue. In England, where hospitals must get a woman's consent before distributing her fetal tissue for research, only 50 percent of women undergoing abortion give it. But even if all the women undergoing elective abortions consented, there would still not be enough fetal tissue to meet the demand.

> *"The pervasiveness in our society of appealing to women's . . . obligation to nurture and give is clearly being exploited."*

Dubious Safeguards

Regulations that would ban the sale of fetal tissue have also been proposed. They would: Insure that fetal dissection cannot take place while fetuses are still alive; dissociate doctors performing abortions from those using fetal tissue; prevent women from designating beneficiaries of fetal tissue; and confine research and treatment with fetal tissue to quality controlled medical centers. Aside from the fact that none of these regulations addresses the changes in abortion methods and the consequences for women, a system of regulation that would allow fetuses to be used for medical research and treatment will begin a process that is likely to end with the widespread use of fetal remains for a host of purposes—experimental, therapeutic and commercial. And, as we have seen with attempts to regulate surrogacy, those who have the most to gain—surrogate brokers and lawyers—are those who are at the forefront of influencing and crafting the direction of the legislation. The incentive for legal regulation of fetal tissue is coming from the medical researchers and fetal tissue processors, not from the women directly involved. True, the proposed regulation of fetal tissue would close some of the loopholes now present in the unregulated world of fetal tissue procurement but, if enacted, would give the procurers and researchers a stable marketing and experimental environment. Finally, regulation doesn't address the political reality that has cast women in the role of human incubators.

Fetal tissue legislation is discussed as if there are only two sides to the issue: Those who are prochoice are in favor of fetal tissue research, those who are antiabortion are opposed. Public debate over the use of fetal tissue has already been stereotyped as a controversy between the forces of medical progress and the retrogressive right wing. Within this camp of only two recognized positions, there has been no room for others. It is a tragedy and a travesty of feminist thinking and politics that feminist critics of fetal tissue procurement and research are accused of being in league with the right wing, and genuine feminist dissent is suppressed.

Bibliography

Books

Randy Alcorn	*Pro Life Answers to Pro Choice Arguments.* Sisters, OR: Multnomah Books, 1992.
Robert M. Baird and Stuart E. Rosenbaum, eds.	*The Ethics of Abortion: Pro-Life vs. Pro-Choice.* Rev. ed. Buffalo: Prometheus Books, 1993.
Dallas A. Blanchard and Terry J. Prewitt	*Religious Violence and Abortion: The Gideon Project.* Gainesville: University Press of Florida, 1993.
Eugene B. Brody	*Biomedical Technology and Human Rights.* Paris and Brookfield, VT: UNESCO and Dartmouth Publishing Co., 1993.
Ruth Colker	*Abortion and Dialogue: Pro-Choice, Pro-Life, and American Law.* Bloomington: Indiana University Press, 1992.
Barbara Hinkson Craig and David M. O'Brien	*Abortion and American Politics.* Chatham, NJ: Chatham House, 1993.
Gary Crum and Thelma McCormack	*Abortion: Pro-Choice or Pro-Life?* Washington: American University Press, 1992.
Ronald M. Dworkin	*Life's Dominion: An Argument About Abortion, Euthanasia, and Individual Freedom.* New York: Alfred A. Knopf, 1993.
Joseph Lapsley Foreman	*Shattering the Darkness: The Crisis of the Cross in the Church Today.* Montreat, NC: Cooling Spring Press, 1992.
David J. Garrow	*Liberty and Sexuality: The Right to Privacy and the Making of Roe v. Wade.* New York: Macmillan, 1994.
Sue Hertz	*Caught in the Crossfire: A Year on Abortion's Front Line.* Englewood Cliffs, NJ: Prentice Hall, 1991.
Sumi Hoshiko	*Our Choices: Women's Personal Decisions About Abortion.* Binghamton, NY: Harrington Park Press, 1993.
Frances Myrna Kamm	*Creation and Abortion: A Study in Moral and Legal Philosophy.* New York: Oxford University Press, 1992.
Andrew Kimbrell	*The Human Body Shop: The Engineering and Marketing of Life.* San Francisco: Harper, 1993.
Philip Lawler	*Operation Rescue: A Challenge to the Nation's Conscience.* Huntington, IN: Our Sunday Visitor Press, 1992.

Bibliography

Patricia W. Lunneborg — *Abortion: A Positive Decision.* New York: Bergin & Garvey, 1992.

Kate Maloy and Maggie Jones Patterson — *Birth or Abortion? Private Struggles in a Political World.* New York: Plenum Press, 1992.

Michelle McKeegan — *Abortion Politics: Mutiny in the Ranks of the Right.* New York: Free Press, 1992.

Elizabeth Mensch and Alan Freeman — *The Politics of Virtue: Is Abortion Debatable?* Durham, NC: Duke University Press, 1993.

Patricia G. Miller — *The Worst of Times.* New York: HarperCollins, 1993.

Harold J. Morowitz and James S. Trefil — *The Facts of Life: Science and the Abortion Controversy.* New York: Oxford University Press, 1992.

Marvin Olasky — *A Social History of Abortion in America.* Wheaton, IL: Crossway Books, 1993.

Eric Pastuszek — *Is the Fetus Human?* Rockford, IL: Tan Publishers, 1993.

Suzanne Rini — *Beyond Abortion: A Chronicle of Fetal Experimentation.* Rockford, IL: Tan Publishers, 1993.

Roger Rosenblatt — *Life Itself: Abortion in the American Mind.* New York: Random House, 1992.

Eva R. Rubin, ed. — *The Abortion Controversy: A Documentary History.* Westport, CT: Greenwood Press, 1994.

Don Sloan with Paula Hartz — *Abortion: A Doctor's Perspective/A Woman's Dilemma.* New York: Donald I. Fine, 1992.

Bonnie Steinbock — *Life Before Birth: The Moral and Legal Status of Embryos and Fetuses.* New York: Oxford University Press, 1992.

Randall A. Terry — *Operation Rescue.* Springdale, PA: Whitaker House, 1988.

Randall A. Terry — *Why Does a Nice Guy Like Me Keep Getting Thrown in Jail,* Lafayette, LA: Resistance Press, 1993.

Oliver Trager, ed. — *Abortion: Choice and Conflict.* New York: Facts On File, 1993.

Laurence H. Tribe — *Abortion: The Clash of Absolutes.* Rev. ed. New York: W.W. Norton, 1992.

U.S. Senate Committee on Labor and Human Resources — *Finding Medical Cures: The Promise of Fetal Tissue Transplantation Research.* Washington: U.S. Government Printing Office, 1992.

U.S. Senate Committee on Labor and Human Resources — *The Freedom of Access to Clinic Entrances Act of 1993.* Washington: U.S. Government Printing Office, 1993.

Sara Ragle Weddington — *A Question of Choice.* New York: Penguin Books, 1993.

Peter S. Wenz — *Abortion Rights as Religious Freedom.* Philadelphia: Temple University Press, 1992.

Periodicals

Meg Abbey — "Inconvenient Human," *America*, March 12, 1994.

Bruce Agnew	"Fetal-Tissue Ban: Now for the Money," *The Journal of NIH Research*, March 1993.
American Medical Association Council on Ethical and Judicial Affairs	"Mandatory Parental Consent to Abortion," *JAMA*, January 6, 1993. Available from Subscriber Services Center, American Medical Association, 515 N. State St., Chicago, IL 60610.
Dave Andrusko	"'Spare' Embryos and 'Symbolic' Life," *National Right to Life News*, February 28, 1994. Available from 419 Seventh St. NW, Suite 500, Washington, DC 20004.
Hadley Arkes	"The Eight-Week Solution," *Crisis*, March 1994. Available from the Brownson Institute, PO Box 1006, Notre Dame, IN 46556.
Janet Benshoof	*"Planned Parenthood v. Casey," JAMA*, May 5, 1993.
Joan Biskupic	"Freedom of Speech Is Put to the Test," *The Washington Post National Weekly Edition*, May 2-8, 1995.
Robert J. Blendon, John M. Benson, and Karen Donelan	"The Public and the Controversy over Abortion," *JAMA*, December 15, 1993.
Melanie Bush	"The Doctor Is Out," *The Village Voice*, June 2, 1993.
Lisa Sowle Cahill	"Abortion, Sex, and Gender: The Church's Public Voice," *America*, May 22, 1993.
Byron C. Carrier	"Moral and Civil Issues of Abortion," *The Human Quest*, September/October 1993. Available from Churchman Co., 1074 23rd Ave., St. Petersburg, FL 33704.
Mona Charen	"A New Moral View on Abortion?" *Conservative Chronicle*, January 19, 1994. Available from PO Box 11297, Des Moines, IA 50340-1297.
Mary Carrington Coutts	"Fetal Tissue Research," *Kennedy Institute of Ethics Journal*, March 1993. Available from Journals Publishing Division, 2715 N. Charles St., Baltimore, MD 21218-4319.
Diane Curtis	"Doctored Rights: Menstrual Extraction, Self-Help Gynecological Care, and the Law," *New York University Review of Law and Social Change*, vol. 20, no. 3, 1993-94.
Neil de Mause	"Counterfeit Clinics, Genuine Pain," *On the Issues*, Winter 1994.
Sara Diamond	"No Place to Hide," *The Humanist*, September/October 1993.
Ronald M. Dworkin	"Life Is Sacred. That's the Easy Part," *The New York Times Magazine*, May 16, 1993.
Wanda Franz	"The Shameful Legacy of *Roe v. Wade:* Twenty Years of Death and Destruction," *National Right to Life News*, January 1993.
Michael Fumento	"Fetal Attraction," *The American Spectator*, July 1992.

Glamour	"What Is an 'Undue Burden' in Seeking an Abortion?" Readers' responses to a questionnaire. September 1993.
Richard D. Glasow	"The Most Commonly Asked Questions About RU 486," *National Right to Life News*, April 28, 1993.
Katharine Greider	"The Un-Pregnancy Pill," *In These Times*, April 18, 1994.
William Norman Grigg	"'Epidemic' of Clinic Violence?" *The New American*, February 7, 1994. Available from 770 Westhill Blvd., Appleton, WI 54915.
William Norman Grigg	"A New FACE to Oppression," *The New American*, June 27, 1994.
Byron C. Hall Jr.	"Ranking the Rights of Life, Liberty, and Property," *Lincoln Review*, Fall/Winter 1993-94. Available from the Lincoln Institute for Research and Education, 1001 Connecticut Ave. NW, Washington, DC 20036.
Gayle M. B. Hanson	"'Morning After' Pill Has Political Side Effects," *Insight*, July 4, 1994.
Stanley K. Henshaw and Jennifer van Vort	"Abortion Services in the United States, 1991 and 1992," *Family Planning Perspectives*, May/June 1994. Available from the Alan Guttmacher Institute, 111 Fifth Ave., New York, NY 10003.
Warren M. Hern	"Life on the Front Lines," *Women's Health Issues*, Spring 1994.
Merle Hoffman	"Praise the Lord and Kill the Doctor," *On the Issues*, Summer 1994.
Karen Houppert	"John Burt's Holy War: One Minister's Dangerous Battle to Save the Unborn," *The Village Voice*, April 6, 1993.
Jeffrey Kaplan	"America's Last Prophetic Witness: The Literature of the Abortion Movement," *Terrorism and Political Violence*, Autumn 1993.
Michael Kinsley	"Bad Choice," *The New Republic*, June 13, 1994.
Lawrence Lader	"RU-486, Made in America," *The New York Times*, March 17, 1994.
Marianne Engelman Lado	"*Planned Parenthood v. Casey*: Eroding Access to Reproductive Services," *Health/PAC Bulletin*, Summer 1992. Available from 853 Broadway, Suite 1607, New York, NY 10003.
Kim A. Lawton	"Curing or Killing?" *Christianity Today*, May 18, 1992.
John Leo	"Not the Way to Stop Abortions," *U.S. News & World Report*, March 29, 1993.
Tamar Lewin	"Abortions in the U.S. Hit Thirteen-Year Low, a Study Reports," *The New York Times*, June 16, 1994.
Jo McGowan	"Fetal Research: The Ethical Dimension," *The Human Life Review*, Fall 1993.

J. Jennings Moss and Joyce Price	"Pro-Choice Wins Battle in Congress," *Insight*, June 20, 1994. Available from 3600 New York Ave. NE, Washington, DC 20002.
Nancy Myers and Kim Gandy	"Abortion: The War That Won't Go Away," *The World & I*, September 1992.
National Right to Life News	Special issue on abortion and the national health plan, January 1994.
The New England Journal of Medicine	Original article section on fetal tissue transplantation, November 26, 1992.
Kathleen Quinn	"Defend the Moral High Ground," *Mother Jones*, November/December 1993.
Loretta J. Ross	"A Simple Human Right: The History of Black Women and Abortion," *On the Issues*, Spring 1994.
Richard Sherlock, Richard G. Wilkins, and Camille S. Williams	"A Fair Abortion Policy? The Approach of the American Law Institute's Model Penal Code," *The World & I*, August 1994.
Carson Strong	"Fetal Tissue Transplantation: Can It Be Morally Insulated from Abortion?" *Journal of Medical Ethics*, June 1991.
Laura L. Sydell	"The Right-to-Life Rampage," *The Progressive*, August 1993.
David Van Biema	"Your Activist, My Mobster," *Time*, February 7, 1994.
James Q. Wilson	"On Abortion," *Commentary*, January 1994.
Bronwyn Winter	"Why We Need *Roe*," *Off Our Backs*, October 1992.
Charmaine Crouse Yoest	"RU-486—Sunny Rhetoric vs. Bloody Reality," *The Wall Street Journal*, May 25, 1994.

Organizations to Contact

The editors have compiled the following list of organizations concerned with the issues debated in this book. The descriptions are derived from materials provided by the organizations. All have publications or information available for interested readers. The list was compiled on the date of publication of the present volume; names, addresses, and phone numbers may change. Be aware that many organizations take several weeks or longer to respond to inquiries, so allow as much time as possible.

ACLU Reproductive Freedom Project
132 W. 43rd St.
New York, NY 10036
(212) 944-9800
fax: (212) 869-4314

A branch of the American Civil Liberties Union, the project coordinates efforts in litigation, advocacy, and public education to guarantee the constitutional right to reproductive choice. Its mission is to ensure that reproductive decisions will be informed, meaningful, and without hindrance or coercion from the government. The project disseminates fact sheets, pamphlets, and editorial articles and publishes the quarterly newsletter *Reproductive Rights Update*.

Advocates for Youth
1025 Vermont Ave. NW, Suite 200
Washington, DC 20005
(202) 347-5700
fax: (202) 347-2263

Advocates for Youth is an educational organization dedicated to improving the quality of life for adolescents by reducing the incidence of sexually transmitted diseases and unwanted teenage pregnancies and by advocating minors' access to legal abortion. It opposes laws mandating parental consent or notification for a minor's abortion. The organization publishes educational guides and curricula, fact sheets, reports, and the quarterly newsletter *Transitions*.

American Life League (ALL)
PO Box 1350
Stafford, VA 22555
(703) 659-4171
fax: (703) 659-2586

ALL is an organization of individuals opposed to abortion. Its primary goal is the passage of an amendment to the U.S. Constitution that would recognize the personhood of the unborn fetus and secure constitutional protection from the moment of fertilization.

ALL monitors congressional activities dealing with pro-life issues and provides information on the physical and psychological risks of abortion. The league produces and publishes books, booklets, fact sheets, pamphlets, the biweekly newsletter *Communiqué*, the bimonthly magazine *Celebrate Life*, and the educational video series *Celebrate Life!*

Center for Bio-Ethical Reform (CBR)

3855 E. La Palma, Suite 126
Anaheim, CA 92807-1700
(714) 632-7520
fax: (714) 632-8231

CBR opposes legal abortion and focuses its arguments on abortion's moral aspects. Its members frequently address conservative and Christian groups throughout the United States. The center also offers training seminars on fundraising to pro-life volunteers. CBR publishes the monthly newsletter *In-Perspective*, produces audiotapes such as "Is the Bible Silent on Abortion?" and "No More Excuses," and distributes a videotaped debate with the American Civil Liberties Union and California Abortion Rights Action League.

Center for Reproductive Law and Policy (CRLP)

120 Wall St.
New York, NY 10005
(212) 514-5534
fax: (212) 514-5538

The center is an organization of reproductive rights attorneys and activists united to secure women's reproductive freedoms in the United States and around the world. It works as lead counsel in challenging restrictive abortion laws in several U.S. states and territories. CRLP publishes fact sheets, analyses, and the biweekly *Reproductive Freedom News*.

Human Life International (HLI)

7845 Airpark Rd., Suite E
Gaithersburg, MD 20879
(301) 670-7884
fax: (301) 869-7363

HLI is a pro-life family education and research organization that believes that the fetus is human from the moment of conception. It conducts an annual conference entitled "Love, Life, and the Family" and distributes books, fact sheets, and the monthly newsletters *HLI Reports* and *Special Report*.

National Abortion Federation (NAF)

1436 U St. NW, Suite 103
Washington, DC 20009
(202) 667-5881
fax: (202) 667-5890

The federation is a forum for providers of abortion services and others committed to making safe, legal abortions accessible to all women. It upgrades abortion services by providing them with standards and guidelines, and it serves as a clearinghouse of information on abortion services. NAF publishes fact sheets and bulletins, the booklet *Empowering Clinics: A User's Guide to Victim Impact Statutes*, the semiannual *National Abortion Federation* newsletter, and the *Consumer's Guide to Abortion Services* (in English and Spanish).

National Abortion and Reproductive Rights Action League (NARAL)
1156 15th St. NW, Suite 700
Washington, DC 20005
(202) 973-3000
fax: (202) 408-4698

The goal of NARAL, which has groups in more than forty states, is to develop and sustain a pro-choice political constituency in order to maintain the right of all women to legal abortion. The league briefs members of Congress and testifies at hearings on abortion and related issues. It publishes the quarterly *NARAL Newsletter*.

National Conference of Catholic Bishops (NCCB)
3211 Fourth St. NE
Washington, DC 20017-1194
(202) 541-3000

The NCCB, which adheres to the Vatican's opposition to abortion, is a coalition of American Roman Catholic bishops and is their organ for unified action. While pursuing its ultimate goal of a legal ban on abortion, the conference suggests that states restrict abortion by passing parental consent/notification laws and strict licensing laws for abortion clinics. Its publications include the annual magazine *Respect Life* and the monthly newsletter *Life Insight*.

National Right to Life Committee (NRLC)
419 Seventh St. NW, Suite 500
Washington, DC 20004
(202) 626-8800

NRLC, with its affiliate state right-to-life groups, is one of the largest organizations that oppose abortion. The committee is active in advertising and campaigning against legislation that favors legalized abortion. It encourages ratification of a constitutional amendment granting embryos and fetuses the same right to life as living persons, and it advocates alternatives to abortion, such as adoption. NRLC publishes the book *School-Based Clinics—The Abortion Connection* and the biweekly tabloid *National Right to Life News*.

Operation Rescue (OR)
PO Box 740066
Dallas, TX 75374
(214) 739-4620
fax: (214) 739-4618

OR has been one of the most prominent organizations conducting abortion clinic demonstrations in attempts at reducing the incidence of abortion. Targeting clinics in large cities, Operation Rescue's tactics were threatened in 1994 when the U.S. Supreme Court ruled that abortion clinics could sue demonstrators. A law passed later that year also made obstructing access to clinics a federal crime. OR publishes the quarterly *Operation Rescue National Newsletter*.

Planned Parenthood Federation of America (PPFA)
810 Seventh Ave.
New York, NY 10019
(212) 541-7800
fax: (212) 245-1845

PPFA is a national organization that supports people's right to make their own reproductive decisions without governmental interference. It provides contraceptive counseling and services at clinics located throughout the United States. Among its extensive publications are the pamphlets *Abortions: Questions and Answers*, *Five Ways to Prevent Abortion*, and *Nine Reasons Why Abortions Are Legal*.

Pro-Life Action League
6160 N. Cicero Ave., Suite 600
Chicago, IL 60646
(312) 777-2900
fax: (312) 777-3061

The league consists of doctors, lawyers, business leaders, and other individuals who oppose abortion. It conducts demonstrations against abortion clinics and other agencies involved with abortion. It produces and publishes videotapes and brochures, the book *Closed: 99 Ways to Stop Abortion*, and the *Pro-Life Action News*, a quarterly newsletter.

Religious Coalition for Reproductive Choice (RCRC)
1025 Vermont Ave. NW, Suite 1130
Washington, DC 20005
(202) 628-7700
fax: (202) 628-7716

RCRC is an organization of more than thirty Christian, Jewish, and other religious groups committed to enabling individuals to make decisions concerning abortion in accordance with their conscience. It educates policy makers and the public about the diversity of religious perspectives on abortion. RCRC publishes booklets, an educational essay series, and the quarterly *Religious Coalition for Reproductive Choice Newsletter*.

Index